A Life Shared

Margaret Cornell

BALBOA.
PRESS
A DIVISION OF HAY HOUSE

John Paul Jackson. Needless Casualties of War. Copyright 1999 Library of Congress Catalog. Card number 99-61076. ISBN 9780985863807 Poem sourced from the internet by Roy Lessin. Dayspring. Used by permission Cover art work . . . Virginia Mull Art and Portraits Cover design and layout . . . by www.freestyledesign.co.uk All scriptures from the King James Bible unless otherwise stated

Balboa Press books may be ordered through booksellers or by contacting:

Balboa Press
A Division of Hay House
1663 Liberty Drive
Bloomington, IN 47403
www.balboapress.com
1 (877) 407-4847

Printed in the United States of America.

ISBN: 978-1-4525-8399-0 (sc)
ISBN: 978-1-4525-8401-0 (hc)
ISBN: 978-1-4525-8400-3 (e)

Library of Congress Control Number: 2013918185

Balboa Press rev. date: 02/03/2014

The Impact of One Life

When a stone is dropped into a lake,
It quickly disappears from sight—
But its impact leaves behind a series of ripples
    that broaden and reach across the water.
In the same way,
The impact of one life lived for Christ
Will leave behind an influence for good
That will reach the lives of many others.[1]

—Roy Lessin

Dedication

This book is dedicated with thanksgiving to my dear husband Tony who has supported and loved me through thick and thin, and my children who graciously shared their parents with many others who feature in this story and the hundreds of people who have made my life such an amazing experience

Contents

Preface

I wrote this book primarily because I want to encourage people to walk with God in an intimate way, hearing His voice and doing what He says. It is a wonderful way to live. All we did was hear God and obey Him, which enabled Him to lead us on an exciting and unexpected spiritual journey. The road was full of experiences that are common to millions of ordinary Christians through the ages but not nearly enough people yet to change our world.

The second reason I wrote this book was because I saw the power of Christian storybooks to inspire people to believe Bible truth can be lived today. These were the four books that inspired me:

- *Realities* by Basilea Schlink tells of a German evangelical sisterhood that lived a life of faith and repentance, trusting God for everything from bricks to paper clips.
- *Nine O'clock in the Morning* by Dennis Bennett is the story of the renewal of an Episcopal church in the United States because of the baptism of the Holy Spirit.
- *When the Spirit Comes* by Colin Urquhart is the story of charismatic renewal in Luton, England.
- Finally, *Chasing the Dragon* by Jackie Pullinger is about a young missionary to Hong Kong who inspired us to pray in tongues.

I hope you will be moved to discover that God is real and He gladly shows Himself to ordinary people like you and me and can make us all world changers!

CHAPTER 1

Small Beginnings with God

During World War II, London was bombed heavily. As my mum gave birth to me, the Germans celebrated by dropping what was known as the flying bomb a few yards from where it was all happening. Yes, my parents declared that I, too, dropped into their lives like a bomb! What an entrance!

I was an only child. My parents and I lived in one room of a small flat in London which we shared with my grandmother Daisy and my Aunty Mary. It was above a noisy pet shop on a busy high street called Watling Avenue, almost opposite Burnt Oak underground station. Because of the street fights and knifings, people used to call it the Chicago of northwest London

We did everything in our one room. We ate, slept, and sat together there in the evenings. When I went to bed they put a large clothes horse around my bed. Ostensibly it was to help me get to sleep but I guess that it also gave them some privacy too. My mother cooked lovely meals using a tiny Baby Belling cooker which was in the hearth, mostly using a pressure cooker as she only had two rings and a small grill. How she turned out such lovely meals is a source of amazement to me. I don't remember being exactly unhappy because my parents did their best to enhance my life with ballet and piano lessons, but I do remember there being quite a lot of tension and stress around.

The person I spent most time with in my early life was my grandmother Daisy, whom I adored. She cared for me when my mother and father were at work. My mother worked part time in a restaurant. When I was old enough I was allowed to go with her sometimes in my school holidays and help lay the tables but was banished to sit with a warm and friendly lady called Griff behind the cash register when customers came in. I thought that it was great fun, because I think everyone made rather a fuss of me. My father often worked long hours and attended night school to study for a higher national diploma in mechanical engineering so he was absent a lot of the time.

I was comfortable with adults and with myself, but I wasn't very comfortable around other children, who were a mystery to me. Because of our cramped living conditions, it was impossible to invite children in to play and unlikely that I would be allowed out alone to play with a friend although when I was nearly ten I was allowed to go to Girls Brigade and walked the short distance to school by myself. Before I went to school, my experience with other children was limited to holidays with my cousins in Eastbourne. My lack of contact with other children meant that when I first went to school, at playtime I clutched the dinner lady's hand because I was absolutely terrified of the other children. It took me quite a while to make friends.

As a child I do not remember feeling lonely. I amused myself with reading, painting, and listening to the radio. My grandmother took me to the park and we sometimes played ball together. However it was nothing boisterous as in photos that I have, I am wearing little white socks, white gloves and white shoes looking very ladylike and prim! We sometimes went as a treat to the pub at the top of the road called The Bald Faced Stag and sat in the garden there. I had lemonade and grandmother had a mysterious looking dark beer called a Guinness. My happiest times were the moments I spent sitting in the sun on our rooftop balcony where there were many interesting things to watch. I often felt God's presence there.

When I was about ten years old, a woman my mother worked with drew my parents into spiritualism. My grandmother did not approve and said if my parents ever practiced it in the house, they would have to leave. Sadly, this was not the only bone of contention between them and there were definitely two opposing camps in my home. I sometimes played one against the other to get my own way.

As I grew up, I felt ambivalence toward my parents' séances, even though I went along to them willingly right into my late teenage years. I read lots of books about spiritualism and visited the Spiritualists Association in London. However, it never felt like the complete truth. When I visited a famous medium and waited in a dark room for messages from disembodied voices with my parents and their friends, it was interesting but I found that it had little lasting satisfaction for me. The spiritualists we knew were sweet and loving and many of them quoted the Bible and talked about Jesus or 'The Christ' but they usually prayed to dead spirits rather than God. They called it "sending out thoughts." which were directed towards spirit guides. I could never bring myself to do that because I felt strongly we should only be praying to God.

Although I realise what happens in these séances is a lie and not to be trusted, there was an odd moment in a séance once that puzzled me. My family asked, "Is Margaret of our group?"

After a pause, the spirit person said, "No, Margaret is of a different group."

I think this was evident to me from an early age because I am told that one day when I was about four years old, we were passing a big church near my home, and I asked my dad to take me there to Sunday school. I loved it: the Carey Bonner songs, Bible stories about Jesus, kneeling at a chair, colouring pictures, and collecting the little Scripture stamps they gave us to stick into a little book. It was there, I suppose, that I first turned toward Jesus.

Because of the war, housing was in very short supply, so we did not have a home of our own until I was ten years old. It was then also that we had our first television so that we could watch the coronation of Queen Elizabeth. The council offered us a maisonette adjacent to green belt land in Mill Hill that backed onto a large cemetery. At least the neighbours were no trouble!

I began to attend a free church there and threw myself into various activities. I helped with Sunday school and joined the dramatic society, the youth club, the Girl Guides, and later the Brownies as a pack leader. I loved it all.

At the youth club, I met a boy who was a guitarist in a rock group. I regularly traveled with the group on Saturday nights to dance halls and seedy nightclubs. I suppose it was risky, but I don't think I ever *felt* in danger. I suppose you would have called me a groupie! What amazes me now is how much my parents must have trusted I would not do anything silly and get into trouble.

As it happens with many young people, during my teenage years, my simple faith wobbled. I was confused because although the church people were lovely, nobody seemed to actually believe the Bible. Nobody expected anything supernatural to happen or believed Jesus changed lives as He did in Bible days. In contrast, spiritualists believed in spiritual gifts and practised healing. I really had no idea who had the real truth.

I attended Copthall a nice girls' grammar school, but I was not very happy at school. I did not have much interest in schoolwork and did as little as possible. Drama was my true passion. I wanted to apply for drama school when I left school. My family, on the other hand, seemed to believe I was destined for a life of quiet domesticity. They encouraged me to get a sensible job and then get married. When we discussed my options I can remember the exact words they said: "Well, it's not like you are a career girl, is it?"

Hmm . . . maybe they are right, I thought. I left school with five O levels and took a job working long hours as a dental nurse. Hard work has never bothered me, and I really loved tending the patients and keeping a rather demanding Scots dentist happy.

At that point, when I was still intent on applying for drama school, there were two main questions that eventually held me back from a career in acting: What if I was not good enough? What if I did not get enough work? At least as an amateur I consistently got challenging and interesting lead parts, along with rave notices in the local paper. I knew I must be reasonably good because I had been headhunted by at least one group. By the time I was in my late twenties, I had taken at least thirty leading roles in plays, musicals, and pantomimes. I had also produced a couple of large cast pantomimes and many plays. At least on the stage, I had broken out of shyness and found great success! But my intense busyness had also crowded God out of my life. I decided I could manage life myself.

At eighteen, I found my third reason for not going to drama school. I met Julian, a gentle, handsome young man. Romantically, our eyes met across a crowded room, and we were drawn instantly to each other like magnets. He was all I thought I ever wanted—cultured, well educated, fun to be with, and interested in many of the things that interested me. I fell deeply in love.

At that time I was still partially involved with Spiritualism. He was interested in it too and when Julian and I went to a séance a spirit guide told us that we were ideally suited.

However, just before we were married, Julian's father and I had a serious conversation. He asked me, "Do you know Julian has previously been very involved with a young man?"

I did know because I had seen the two of them together many times in the library, where I had a Saturday job, but I was completely blind to the implications. Julian seemed attracted to me and affectionate, so I dismissed any doubts. I naively believed love would overcome all. Even when Julian wanted to call it off a few weeks before the wedding, I would not hear of it. I felt sure it was just pre-wedding nerves. When Julian's father had a heart attack and died just a few days before the wedding, we had an ideal opportunity to a call it off or at least postpone it, but we still went ahead. Deep in my heart, as we were standing side by side in the registry office, I heard a voice inside me saying, *don't do it. don't do it.* But it was too late.

We had an agonizing marital relationship for two years. One day I could see Julian was heading for a breakdown, and I did not feel far behind. Our relationship was physically and emotionally difficult. Julian accused me of being a different person from the one he had married and said that maybe I had just pretended to be someone else. Of course that was untrue but I did not realise how much I had changed

What had actually happened was that when we had been married about a year, a friend who was a lecturer at a teachers' training college encouraged me to apply to his college as a mature student. He told me I was ideal material for teaching because I was a good communicator. I applied just because he said so and was amazed to be accepted. The other attraction was that drama could be my main subject.

Julian had seemed to be fully in agreement with me having a real career, but as time went on, he began to resent me rising from the lowly status of a relatively ignorant young woman to someone who actually had opinions. I was blossoming as a person because I was being stretched in every way. Nobody was more surprised than I, having left school thinking I was a dunce to find that I was now getting A marks for essays and projects.

Despite the joy of the success I was having, I was increasingly distressed at Julian's coldness toward me. His rejection made me feel unattractive and as if I had an abnormal sexual appetite. I never thought of divorce for one minute. I believed we would just go on working for a breakthrough in our relationship. However, feeling absolutely desperate on one very bleak day, I plucked up courage to ask him, "Julian, what can I do to make you happy?"

His terse, shocking, and unexpected reply was, "Leave me."

What a bombshell! It was definitely not what I wanted or expected to hear. In that instant, the world seemed to stand still, and my heart froze. I felt completely devastated because I was now facing the worst decision ever. Because I loved Julian and wanted to make him happy, feeling dazed and numb, I silently packed my bags, hoping beyond hope he would say, "No, please don't go."

He drove me to my unsuspecting parents' home. They were terribly shocked, because I suppose we had always looked so happy. They had no idea of the strained situation between us. Initially they insisted that I was being ridiculous and that I must go back, but after my father had spoken to Julian, they understood that it was more than a little tiff and that the marriage, through no choice of mine, was actually over.

I cried and cried for about three weeks. I sat on the bus and cried; I sat in college lectures and cried; I cried myself to sleep. I could hardly eat anything and lost lots of weight. I grieved deeply, feeling cruelly rejected. My heart was utterly broken.

I also felt like a complete idiot. How could I have been so foolish as to ignore good advice from wise people or even to ignore the truth in my own heart?

Chapter 2

A New Beginning

One Sunday afternoon, I was in the bedroom at my parents' flat, staring aimlessly out of the window. Without consciously thinking about it, I found myself asking God what to do. Suddenly a voice from somewhere behind me clearly said, "Go to JK [which I knew was John Keble Church] and find Richard Buck." The voice was so real, but when I turned around, there was nobody to be seen.

Richard Buck was a curate at the church and was in the church dramatic society, to which I also belonged. Richard was a very likeable and warm-hearted Australian. Instantly when I heard the voice I recognized I had received a divine instruction, so I jumped onto my Lambretta and went to church for evensong. I was surprised to find the church empty because in the morning service there were usually three hundred people. On the dot of 6:30, who should walk in to lead the service but Richard Buck! Later I realised what a miracle it was that the four or five clergy serving at the church took it in turns to take the evensong and I had come on just the right day. Could that possibly have been a coincidence?

Afterwards I asked Richard if I could talk to him, but when he got out his diary to make an appointment, my heart sank.

"No," I said desperately. "Please can I see you now?"

In his flat, I tearfully spilled the beans. Before I left, he laid hands on my head and prayed for me. Anglicans in those days did not expect experiences, but as he prayed, I felt instantly engulfed in tremendous warmth and peace, and my aching heart felt comfort. A grain of hope crept into my heart that perhaps there was a way out of even this humiliating mess. As I left his flat, a thank you seemed inadequate.

"God bless you," he said.

"Thank you," I said. "I think He has."

As I mounted my Lambretta, these words settled into my heart: "Don't be afraid. This is not the end; it's a new beginning."

It was, of course, not the end of shame and unhappiness, but it was a pivotal moment that started me back on the path to Jesus. I began to attend this lively, surprisingly full high Anglican church regularly. When they discovered what had happened, people there took me to their heart. This was not what I had expected. I had feared disapproval and rejection.

One Sunday after the service, I was talking to a couple, and the wife asked me if I was happy being back at home with my parents. Really I was far from happy to be back there. Every time I went home, it emphasized my shame and failure.

Then she said, "We have a spare room. Would you like to come and live with us?"

I was so amazed and thrilled, and I gladly moved into the spare room in their pleasant flat. I tried to fit in with their very ordered way of life, which contrasted dramatically with mine , pulling my weight by helping wherever I could and contributing to the household expenses. Their simple act of kindness gave me back some self-esteem and sowed a seed in my life that bore much fruit. It was also during this time that, totally unbidden by anyone, I decided wholeheartedly to turn away from spiritualism and only seek Jesus.

I knew that I needed to be changed because I knew I could once again head for disaster if I wasn't. I was a strong personality, which some people found hard to handle. I was gifted in many ways, which unfortunately often stirred up jealousy. Conflicting emotions sometimes threatened to overwhelm me and erupt over others. Actually I was not a very happy person because I did not really like myself. This self-hatred had been increased by the rejection I had experienced in my marriage. There were some difficulties that had seemed insurmountable in our relationship, but I never saw myself as a completely innocent party in the relationship breakdown; I had certainly played my part in making it a disaster.

It was my hope that as I attended church, God would help me to change. I certainly felt comforted by the church members. I was becoming happier, and I felt glad to be part of a vibrant community of faith. I loved the drama of the highly structured services and the beauty of the words spoken, but how much I changed is doubtful.

I threw myself enthusiastically into drama productions at the church and into my college work, intending to develop my career as a teacher and be self-supporting. The college staff had been immensely supportive and wonderful to me as I went through the trauma of the marriage breakup. I also knew I was marked down for a distinction in education practice as well as a distinction in my drama studies. I simply loved the children and found teaching to be challenging and stimulating.

The last thing I wanted was another relationship; I was so afraid of being deceived and hurt again, so I completely avoided getting involved with men. My college work became much more important to me because I saw that it was a path to a wonderful career and financial independence.

CHAPTER 3

An Unwelcome Intrusion?

Just as I was finishing my teachers' training course, a fellow thespian named Harry invited me to attend a carol concert at his school in Edgware, where he taught French. I only went because he was lonely and I felt sorry for him. Previously he had taken me to a posh French restaurant called Chez Solange for a wonderful meal, but I had eaten so little for months that my stomach could not tolerate such rich food, and I was violently sick in the ladies' cloakroom.

As soon as we arrived at the school, Harry introduced me to a blond, handsome young man named Tony who was front of house manager for the concert. He took great delight in showing us to our seats. He was very polite, but he definitely gave me the eye, which I was careful not to respond to. Afterwards when I discovered this was his last day at the school because he had a new job as head of physics in Soham, Cambridgeshire, I was relieved I would never see him again. When he invited me to his leaving party, I was delighted to be able to tell him that I could not come because I was playing the part of an angel in a nativity play. I felt with any luck this might put him off me for good! I heard no more from him and totally forgot about him.

Tony had decided wisely to make no further pursuit at that time because he knew I was in a delicate state, but one Sunday afternoon six months later, he invited me to the cinema, cheekily suggesting I invite him for tea first! We had a good time together and began to see each other fairly regularly. Tony had been badly hurt by two broken engagements, so both of us were wary of involvement and commitment. Our relationship was very on and off for a while until one fateful day.

One afternoon he arrived at my flat in his open-topped car, looking suave, cardigan casually slung over his shoulder. He announced he was not going to see me that night because he would be taking someone else out.

"That's fine by me," I said happily. "See you sometime."

After I had shut the door, the enormity of what had happened hit me, and I was utterly furious. I found myself muttering, "What nerve, taking someone else out when he had said he was going to see me!"

I would have been even more furious if I had realised at the time that the girl he was taking out was one I had introduced him to at a recent college party! When I found myself pacing furiously up and down my sitting room, I was stopped in my tracks by the thought, *Oh dear! Oh no, I am upset . . . That means it really matters to me. Oh no! How awful—I have grown fond of him!* In an instant, I knew he had captured my heart and I really wanted more from our relationship than I had previously thought.

I sat down and wrote a letter, saying I now realised I cared about him more than I had ever thought it possible to care for another man. I said if he was serious about a relationship with me, he could contact me again, but if he wasn't serious about me, he could stay away. Amazingly, a couple of days later, I received a letter from him expressing similar sentiments. Our letters had crossed in the post. How romantic!

A phone call confirmed that we were both serious about each other, and we agreed that despite being scared of commitment, we wanted to get married. We waited eagerly for my divorce to come through and spent the next year or so speeding up and down from Soham to London. He was busy teaching in Soham, and I was still teaching in a primary school in Queens Park, enjoying my probationary year. We became involved with each other's friends, and sometimes Tony helped me with school work. We both took my class of thirty children to a museum one Saturday, and they delighted in loudly calling us mummy and daddy as we walked them in a crocodile along the streets of London.

When I introduced Tony to Richard Buck and he heard we were getting married, he asked me if I was sure I should be marrying a man who was not a Christian. Unknown to me, he had questioned Tony on my behalf and discovered that he was what Australians call a blue domer—someone who believes creation is wonderful and there is probably somebody behind it, but he could not say quite what or who.

I thought about what Richard said carefully because I respected him. I was also aware that I had previously ignored wise counsel, but I felt reassured as I listened to the still, small voice in my heart that said, "This is okay." When I had married the first time, the still, small voice within me was definitely saying, "No! No! No!" even though my heart and emotions were saying, "Yes! Yes! Yes!" I reasoned that since the still, small voice had it right the first time, I could not go far wrong by following it this time, though at the time, I had no idea quite what that voice was! I also believed with all my heart that Tony would eventually become a believer. I think if I had known how long that would take I might have been a lot less confident!

We were married at a register office in Acton Town Hall. On the way there, I was so nervous that if I could have stopped for a stiff brandy, I would have! I shook all the way through the ceremony. I was so nervous that my large pink hat trembled violently in sympathy. But afterwards, having done the deed, I felt enormous relief and relaxed. I enjoyed the rest of the day, and I knew deep inside I had done the right thing. After the wedding ceremony and the reception, we drove to a hotel, where we were to spend just one night, returning to our flat the next day after some friends in Isleham had given us a lovely meal.

Because it was not yet the end of the school term we only had a weekend together, and then we both had to return to work, seventy miles from each other for two weeks. Our time had been further blighted because on the way to the hotel, I began to feel very sick and ill, as if I had flu, and I very unsociably went to bed and slept for hours. Tony was remarkably patient with me. He was only concerned for my welfare and comfort, but as a honeymoon, the weekend was not a success! The next two weeks seemed interminable, and Tony only lasted until the Wednesday; at lunchtime he parked his car outside the school facing London so he could make a quick getaway. He drove to London at top speed and got there before I got home from my day at school. He sped back again at six o'clock the next morning for his school day.

Worse still, immediately after the term ended, Tony had a long-term commitment which he had made before we had set the wedding date to take a Party of Venture Scouts camping in Wales for two weeks. To avoid further separation, our plan was simple. I would pass my driving test by then and would drive to Wales to join them all for a rather different kind of honeymoon. Camping was not a particular love of mine, but anything seemed better than being apart for another two weeks. Unfortunately, I did not pass my test, so I moved into our flat in Soham and spent another week alone! But I felt quite philosophical about it all because I expected us to spend the next fifty or sixty years together, so in the scale of things what was a few weeks.

I had found a job teaching English and history at the Soham Village College just by knocking on the principal's door one Sunday afternoon just before the start of term. I had not taught in a secondary school before, and it took some adjustment but I really enjoyed it, although I found the teenagers much more challenging than the young ones I had taught in London. I ran a little toddler group with the fourth year leavers even helped with the college youth club, where Tony and I delighted and impressed them by our ability to jive and enjoy their music. All was going really well. We were both settled and happy in our careers. We loved Soham, and we loved our flat. I loved Tony as much as my bruised heart dared to, but I was not in love with him as I had been with Julian. I think I was sometimes a little difficult because I was testing him to make sure that he was genuine and really loved me for who I was before I gave him my whole heart.

Since we didn't plan to have children anytime soon, we invited Mr. Bilbo Baggins, an adorable, bouncy, black Labrador puppy, into our lives. We shared a love of animals and already had two kittens, which Tony had bought me for my birthday, called Tabs and Ina, whom we had named after the deputy heads of our respective schools.

We were happy together, and our life was good, if somewhat stormy from time to time as we were both strong characters, each with a temper and strong ideas about things. We had the typical arguments many married couples have about which end of the toothpaste tube should be pressed and how the frying pan should be used or cleaned. Tony boasts that he taught me how to make omelets and perfect chips, and I have to admit that he certainly did!

I was a vegetarian and he was not but I cooked him meat and something else for myself. I felt a bit embarrassed going to the butchers for two ounces of mince and two sausages. I did wonder what he thought! However after a while Tony liked my food so much that he said he would not bother with meat any more. I began to enjoy cooking and with Tony's continual compliments I began to improve!

We each had our own hobbies and interests. Tony continued as a Venture Scout leader, and I was in a drama group in Soham and Ely. Tony was not into drama. He was much too shy. I once persuaded him to take a small part of the warder in *Witness for the Prosecution* by Agatha Christie. He was so nervous that when he was supposed to say, "There's a nasty crowd out there, madam," instead he said, "There's a crowd of nasties out there, madam."

Sometimes Tony attended the Anglican Church with me just to be kind, but he regarded religion as a crutch, and concluded—somewhat contemptuously—that I obviously needed it but he did not. He saw no point in it. As far as he was concerned, we were just like a tribe of Hottentots dancing round a fire. I was sad that he thought this, but at this point, it was not a crisis.

I was surprised when I unexpectedly became pregnant, but just when we were beginning to feel pleased about it, I miscarried. We were both so upset, and we decided to have a baby on purpose. Our beautiful baby boy Philip was born in the following January. To begin with I struggled with motherhood, feeling the strain of the dependence of this new person in my life. I was also devastated I was unable to feed him myself, and I felt I had been cheated out of it by the nursing home where he was born. They offered no help to me with getting the feeding started and could not wait to give the baby a bottle. I cried a lot in those early weeks. People said I was lovely mother, but that was not the reality of how I felt. Inside I felt like a failure and utterly inadequate for the task. I felt Tony was more attached to Philip than I was and much better at mothering!

When Philip was nine months old, we bought The Old Dairy an old clunch-stone house in a nearby village that belonged to a fellow teacher. We had already fallen in love with this beautiful old cottage when we visited our friends. On the day we heard they were selling it, I was overjoyed. As I walked home from school I spotted Jo driving past me and literally waved at him to stop his car and speak to me. I shouted, "Do I hear you are selling?"

"Yes," he said.

"We'll buy it . . . How much do you want for it?"

"Four thousand pounds."

"Done!"

And it was. Fortunately, his word was his bond, and he refused many bigger offers. We soon found ourselves in the tiny village of Isleham, where our life was to take many strange turns.

We led busy lives. I continued with as many drama commitments as I could squeeze into my life and was very involved with church life. Playgroups were becoming popular around that time and because there was no playgroup in Isleham a friend and I started one. It was great fun! It met in our home, so we had over twenty children coming twice week to play, and with an army of willing mothers did all the fund raising necessary to keep it afloat. Somehow, I also got involved in being a speaker and coordinator for the Children's Country Holiday Fund. I spoke at women's meetings and persuaded people that they would like to give a London child a holiday in the country. We loved having the children, who came mostly from deprived backgrounds in Hackney, and so did most of the other families who embraced the children. I could usually find successful holiday homes for about twenty children in the area. Only once did someone who took two boys become desperate and ask me to come and take them away. Fortunately we had decided not to take any children ourselves that year so we were able to look after them. I could not bear to think of sending them home. They certainly were a couple of scallywags, but by showing them lots of love and firmness, we managed to have a great time with them.

By 1972, we had two children. Philip was joined by Benjamin. After he was born, I was determined, come hell or high water, to feed him myself, and I found that because I had got a lot more information about it, I was able to feed him easily myself. I was convinced I had been unable to breast-feed Philip because of ignorance, so I got involved with the National Childbirth Trust and learned how to be a breast-feeding counselor. I knew that armed with the right information and support, almost any woman could feed her baby and not suffer the disappointment I had. Later I trained to be an antenatal teacher and was part of the National committee. I wrote a leaflet on starting solid foods. I found it most rewarding because it helped women when they were feeling very vulnerable. Tony got so used to hearing me give advice on the telephone that he was as good at the counseling as I was!

When I was pregnant with our third boy, something happened that would change everything.

My parents-in-law were staying with us, and I was feeling particularly stressed. During dinner, one of the children knocked over a glass of water, and I scolded him impatiently. My father-in-law leaned back in his chair and said sarcastically, "The trouble with you Christians is that you spend half your life at church, but it doesn't make a bit of difference to the way you behave."

I was stung and ashamed; he had spoken the unpalatable truth. I stomped upstairs to talk to Tony, who had disappeared earlier to do some GCE exam marking. Through gritted teeth I said, "Would you please ask your father to stop being so rude to me?"

"Why?" he said. "What has he said?"

I repeated the stinging remark that had convicted me so badly.

"Well," he said, quite calmly, and not unkindly, "but it's true, isn't it?"

At that moment, I lost all control. I took off my high-heeled shoe and hit him over the head. As the blood ran down his temple, I froze in horror before running as fast as I could down the length of our upstairs corridor in fear of retribution. Tony followed hotfoot and caught me at the top of the stairs. He put his arms round me and held me in a secure embrace.

As we sank down together and sat on the top step, I had the horrifying realization that murder was in my heart and I could have killed him. I could only say meekly, "I am so sorry. I am so, so sorry."

I was indeed *so* sorry. *Is this how a Christian behaves?* I thought. I was so confused. Two very unpalatable thoughts came to me. The first was that Christianity was not the truth at all, and the second, even more unthinkable, was that maybe I was not really a Christian.

Since the day I had spoken to Richard Buck in such distress, I had faithfully attended church. I had been baptised and confirmed. I was secretary of the parochial church council (PCC). I sang in the choir, cleaned the church, did the flowers, and made the rolls for the parish breakfast, and we helped people whenever we could—all good Christian stuff!

My many good works ought to have given assurance that I was a real Christian, but I knew in the very core of my being that despite all I did, my heart had remained hard and unchanged. I was a pillar of the church, but where were the love, joy, and peace in my life? I was unhappy and dissatisfied on the inside, reactive and defensive—not usually in public, of course, but in my home. Soberly I realised that I was actually no different from the people I had criticized in church as a teenager; in fact, I was probably a lot worse!

I was desperate to know the truth. I knew Tony was totally committed to me and really loved me, but maybe, if I continued to treat him badly, I would be on my way to a second divorce.

Unexpected help came when the vicar announced we were going to have a parish mission the following year. It all sounded very scary indeed. It sounded even worse when I discovered they expected us to go from house to house in pairs, telling people about Jesus. At the time I thought, *Hmmm . . . I know a few Bible stories, but that is my limit!* I could not imagine what I could tell people about Jesus.

Later when Tom Rees came to meet the PCC to explain about the mission, I was absolutely flummoxed when he announced, "A Christian is not someone who prays. A Christian is not someone who reads the Bible. A Christian is not someone who does good works. A Christian is not someone who goes to church. A Christian is not someone who believes in God."

At this point, I thought, *Come on, man! What on earth are you are talking about?* Bit by bit, he was whittling away all the things I had assumed qualified me to be a Christian.

Then he dropped what to me was a bombshell! He said, "A Christian is someone who has a personal relationship with Jesus Christ."

A personal relationship with Jesus? Crumbs, I thought, *I don't have one of those, and I have no idea how to get one.* I quickly scanned the faces of everyone in the room, hoping nobody had noticed my reaction, but mercifully, everyone was looking into the mid-distance with stony faces. We were not a very responsive bunch of people! I went home reeling. Was there any hope for me at all?

Shocked by this revelation, I decided that I had to find out once and for all if Christianity was true or false. If it was the absolute truth, it obviously deserved a lot more of my time and attention than I had given it. If it were false, I would find something more productive to do with my Sundays. This stunning new revelation made me even more determined than ever to discover the truth, and what I really believed, especially now that I knew what a Christian was supposed to be!

CHAPTER 4

An Awesome Meeting

I had a plan of action. Life had slowed down because I was very pregnant. I would go to my bedroom at nine o'clock every night, read the Bible, pray, and ask God to show me the truth. However, when I was faced with the silence of my bedroom, it did not seem quite so simple. My mind went blank, and I did not have a clue what to do. Just presenting God with a list of requests seemed utterly futile. Then I hit on the idea of getting a book of prayers out of the library, and it worked a bit. It increased my prayer life from two minutes to at least ten!

For some weeks reading the Bible seemed a complete dead end, but I was desperate enough to persist. Sometimes I would finish and just close the book with a sigh, but after a while, I began to enjoy it. I felt drawn into the stories and found my heart strangely warmed toward Jesus. He seemed like a real person who was supernatural and remarkable but also human. I had so many questions. Could all of these things about Him possibly be true? Was the Bible true?

One night in my room, I recalled visiting Athens on a student holiday. As we stood on Mars Hill overlooking the Acropolis, the tour guide had said, "This is where St. Paul stood and preached the gospel."

I remember thinking that day, *Oh? Maybe this means that the Bible is true.* This was a completely new thought for me because most of the people I knew said the Bible was just man-made stories that could not possibly be true. Even some Christians weren't sure it was all true.

During my search for the truth, the entire New English Bible was published, and when I bought a copy, I was puzzled that Tony picked it up and read it quite purposefully. My unbeliever wanted to do this?

As weeks went by, I treasured many moments in my room. I sensed growing intimacy with God and felt His presence with me there. I had a growing expectancy that I was about to discover something wonderful.

One night I had read the Bible and knelt and prayed from my heart. I was simply enjoying His presence when suddenly I was startled by a bright shaft of light that came streaming across the room, filling the whole room with the most glorious, amazing presence. In the midst of the dazzling light was a wonderful being. Slowly it dawned on me that this amazing person was . . . Jesus. It was Jesus in all His resurrection glory.

I cannot tell you how I knew it was Jesus, but with my whole being, I knew it was He. Revelation tumbled into my heart. At that second, I knew Jesus really was who the Bible said He was. I knew He was truly the Son of God and that I was, at that very moment, in the presence of the very Son of God. This was actually the Jesus of the Bible who, at that very moment, was choosing to make Himself real to me and was showing me He was actually a living being who is absolutely alive today, truly risen from the dead, and an awesome person.

The effect on me was electric. I was awestruck, transfixed, and very overwhelmed by the sheer holiness of His presence. His presence was so real, so beautiful, great, and awesome, that I wanted to melt into the carpet. A holy reverence filled my heart, and even my breathing seemed too noisy. In an instant, I saw so clearly that He and He alone was the only one worthy of my life and my worship. The famous old hymn by Isaac Watts says it all: "Love so amazing, so divine, demands my soul, my life, my all."

I was acutely aware of my own uncleanness, yet I did not feel condemned. I just felt His love. I managed to blurt out His name, "Jesus," and continued drinking in the glory of His presence. Speaking was difficult and even felt irreverent and unnecessary somehow, and He was communicating loudly without words.

How long I was there in His wonderful and wholesome healing presence I do not know. I hardly moved; I hardly dared to breathe because I did not want that moment to ever end. Without being conscious of the words forming in my mind, I said, "Jesus, I love You. I am so sorry I have tried to live my own life without You. I have made such a mess of it. I do not want to do that anymore. I just want to serve You and obey You. I want to do anything You want me to do. Take my life; I give it all to You. From now on, I don't want to live my own life. I want You to live Your life through me."

I buried my face in the bed and drank and drank of a great river of life that flowed out of Him to me. No words were adequate to express my thanks. The struggle was over. Every question that had been a problem was immediately settled with finality in just one brief moment.

Long after the glorious light had gone from my room and His presence had left, I was trembling with excitement and holy fear. I had had a thrilling, life-transforming encounter with the living God. However, the experience did not end that night; something utterly amazing and wonderful had happened in my heart. A small glow of love, joy, and peace had settled there, and I felt so different—so light, clean, and new on the inside! I was afraid that when I awoke in the morning it would have evaporated and that it would turn out to be a great experience with passing feelings.

When I awoke the next day, to my delight I found that the warm feeling was still there. Somehow I knew I would never be the same. This feeling began to influence my life and my behavior; it did what no information, doctrine, or philosophy had done. I was changed and at the start of an amazing journey of transformation. Today I know that only Jesus can change a heart in this way.

For the first time ever, I felt an inner warmth and security. Daily I felt a tremendous lightness and a new love for everyone. *What do I do now?* I was bursting with joy, but who on earth could I tell about this amazing experience? I could not tell Tony because I was afraid he would squash it with a sarcastic remark.

What a secret I carried! It was so big inside of me! I could barely think of anything else, and I longed to tell the whole world. I did eventually tell a fellow churchgoer, but she looked at me blankly in a way that suggested I might have gone completely off my head. It silenced me for a long time. But of course I could not contain the results of my new relationship with Jesus; it spilled over into everyday life.

I eagerly continued my times with God every evening, which were no longer dry and difficult but became the greatest joy of my life. I would daily watch the time, waiting for nine o'clock, when I would run upstairs; open the door, and say, "Here I am, Jesus!"

Lively conversation and sweet worship between my God and me became the norm. The Bible was no longer black ink on white paper. God began to speak to me clearly, and daily, Jesus came alive from the pages of it. I was amazed. How could I have missed the truth in a lifetime of church-going that was now so obvious?

I had always enjoyed even the staid traditional Anglican service, but now it became a truly glorious experience. I sang the creed: "I believe in one God, the Father Almighty, Maker of heaven and earth and of all things visible and invisible. I believe in one Lord Jesus Christ, the only Son of God . . . Who, for us men and for our salvation, came down from Heaven." As I sang those words, because I truly believed with all of my heart, joy and faith burst in my heart like fireworks. After communion, we sang the Gloria: "We worship thee, we bless Thee, we glorify Thee; we give thanks to Thee for Thy great glory." As I sang, it felt as if the angels were singing with me and the glory of heaven was in me and around me.

I found it hard to cope with the reactions of others when they complained that it was all dead and dry. I had tasted and drunk of the Living Water, and nothing in church was ever dry again! I did not realise I had been born-again and had become what 2 Corinthians 5:17 calls "a new creation." It was ages before I understood the doctrine of what had happened to me.

I was so thrilled with the experience that I now not only longed for Tony to come to church but longed for him to have this wonderful experience too. I told the Lord, "I will say nothing to Tony, but I will pray every day until he has made a commitment to You or until You tell me to stop."

I do not know why I prayed like that because I had little experience with prayer and scant knowledge of the Bible. In hindsight, I know it was a Holy Spirit idea. I had never heard anyone at the Anglican Church—except Tom Rees—speak about having a personal relationship with Jesus. They talked impersonally about God and Christ. I had thought that all the talk about relationship with Jesus was just a peculiarity of the overenthusiastic nonconformist with the big black Bible. It was something I had always found slightly embarrassing, and I avoided people like that. *Heavens*, I thought, *I might become one of them!*

As the mission week approached, we were told that Tom Rees could not come, and instead a man called David Payne would be coming.

I felt a strange rising excitement about meeting the new man and had a sense in my heart that destiny was being fulfilled. As I watched David enter the church, I noticed that he had a glow about him. I had seen that same glow in the vicar's wife's face. I had often looked at her and wondered what she had that others did not have. At that moment I also recalled two other people I had known in the past with that glow. One was a Sunday school teacher who had taught me at the Free Church which I attended in London as a teenager and the saintly religious education (RE) teacher at my grammar school. I didn't much like doing RE, but I loved *her*. She exuded such sweetness. I saw that all four of these people possessed something inside them that was enviable.

David spoke like no other vicar I had ever heard. He spoke with faith, and it sounded as if he really knew God personally. He made sense of the old prayer book. He made it come alive. This man talked so intelligently, making things clear that I had never understood before. He spoke about the Holy Spirit in an entirely new way, not just as an add on, as in "Father, Son, and . . . Holy Spirit" at the end of a prayer.

I felt so excited and I hardly knew how to restrain myself from running home to blurt it all out to Tony. I longed to persuade him to come to the meetings, but I knew I could not break my promise to God to say nothing. I knew I had to let go and trust God to bring Tony to Himself without any pressure from me.

One night Tony asked me what the meeting had been like, and as casually as I could, I said, "It was good," nearly laughing aloud at the understatement because I could hardly wait for the next night. However, unable to restrain myself any longer, I said airily, "Do you think *you* might come to one of the meetings?"

"Maybe," was the brief reply.

"Perhaps Wednesday would be a good day. David is going to talk about the marriage service."

I said no more and dared not show how excited I was when Tony actually agreed to come on that Wednesday night. Everyone had been asked to dress up as if they were actually going to a wedding. One of the recently married couples in the church was going to wear their wedding gear, stand at the front of the church, and "get married."

Just for fun, we both dressed up. Tony wore his best suit, and I wore a long elegant blue voile dress. We walked to church arm in arm, feeling grand, never dreaming for a moment what was going to happen next.

When we got to the church door, David met us and said, "Well, folks, this is your night!"

He explained that the couple scheduled to be the bride and groom could not come and asked us to take their place. Tony immediately said he would do it, but I felt awkward. I explained to David, that I could only do it if the vicar, who had been very vocal about the evils of divorce, knew I had been divorced. If he agreed knowing that, I would do it

I was staggered. He agreed.

As we stood together going through the ancient service, we were not *really* being married, but I was experiencing a marriage service in a way I never had been able to before. Ironically, the first time I was married, I did not want to be married in a church. The second time, when I would have liked to have been married in church, by church law I was not permitted to do so. We were only able to have our marriage blessed by the church.

For me this experience was a holy moment. My heart was singing, and as we left, I was walking on air. I thought, *Surely, Tony's heart has been touched by this wonderful evening.* As we passed the pub, Tony said, "Let's go in. We've had the wedding; let's have the reception!"

We sat at the bar. Feeling fairly secure, I ventured a question: "Well, what did you think of that?"

After a pause, he said honestly, "I thought that it was a lot of old rubbish."

It was a heart-stopping moment. I did not feel that he was deliberately being unkind, but I was deeply shocked because I was sure Tony would have been as impacted by the service as I was. However, I bit my lip. I knew that if I argued or made any untoward remark, it could lead us into strife and endanger everything God might have done. I made a split-second decision just to say, "Oh dear, that's a pity." It was a gross understatement of what I felt, and I felt deeply shaken and disappointed. Only God could have enabled me to have such self-control.

The moment passed, and we went home.

CHAPTER 5

The Truth Emerges

In hindsight, what Tony had said about him thinking that it was all rubbish was untrue. It was a defensive remark to stop me from probing into his feelings more deeply. What happened the next night confirmed it because when I got home after the meeting, Tony said, "I would have liked to talk to David, but it's too late to do that now, it's past nine thirty."

Staying calm and cool and trying to sound disinterested, I said, "Well, why don't you ring him and ask?"

I was surprised that Tony agreed to call, and David readily agreed to come. I did not want my presence to be a hindrance to Tony speaking freely, so I popped out for a walk to leave the field clear for honest conversation. I was not too sure where to go, but I thought my friend who had just had a baby might still be up feeding her and might not mind a brief visit. Thankfully she seemed pleased to see me, but after half an hour, it became evident that I must go because she wanted to go to bed.

I wandered out of her house, glad it was a warm night. I prayed as I walked, asking God what to do. I saw my American neighbour's curtains open and her light on. I could see clearly that she was dressed and watching television. Her husband was in the military and away on overseas duty, so despite the late hour, I knocked on her door.

As we sat chatting, I could see our upstairs windows. I kept an eye out for any activity that might tell me Tony had finished his conversation and was on his way to bed. Suddenly the boys' bedroom light went on. Just as David had left, Giles had woken up, and Tony had gone up to see him.

After a long conversation David left Tony with a commitment card to fill in when he had made his commitment to the Lord. He had told him that becoming a Christian was a bit like going to the swimming pool: everyone says, "Come on in; it's lovely." As you hesitate on the edge of the pool, the water seems too cold and remains so until you decide to jump in. Then you understand what everyone else is experiencing.

The commitment card was put away, and life went on with no apparent change in Tony. What he did not let on was that on the night of the wedding service, he too had heard the Holy Spirit mentioned in a new way and had been intrigued when David talked of the difference it made when your marriage was baptised in the Holy Spirit. It had whetted Tony's appetite, and unknown to me, he was now considering God seriously.

I had promised God that I would pray for Tony to find Jesus every single day until it happened, or until He told me to stop, and one night when I was praying, to my surprise I clearly heard God say, "Stop. I have done it."

"What do you mean You have done it?"

"I have done it, only you must say nothing. Just praise Me for it."

I was about to say, "No I can't do that, Lord," when I suddenly saw the incongruity of saying no and Lord in the same sentence. If someone is Lord and He tells you to do something, the answer has to be yes or He isn't really Lord!

That night, after hearing this from the Lord, I ran down the stairs eagerly and peeped into the sitting room. I do not know what I expected, but what I saw was . . . nothing; no change at all. I was puzzled. It was a long time later when I read and understood the Scripture that says we must believe that we receive when we ask, not when we see the result. God was obviously urging me to take my answer in faith long before it was visible, according to His divine principles. From then on, I simply thanked God for Tony's salvation.

At one of the follow-up meetings of the mission I had fallen into conversation with Lillian, a girl I only knew vaguely and mentioned that I had spoken to David about the condition of the church. People did not know God in a living way but were content with comforting rituals. The services were stuck in the liturgy of the Middle Ages, which, although meaningful and beautiful, was not going to draw in the crowds, especially the young. There was little real spiritual fellowship between members—indeed, little friendship of any kind except between some individuals drawn together by a natural kind of relationship. Theologically I knew nothing about what church ought to be like, but instinctively I knew what we had in Isleham was not how it should be.

I shared with her what David had said to me: "If you don't like your church the way it is, why don't you get together with some others and pray about it?"

I was not issuing an invitation, but to my horror, she said enthusiastically, "Yes, why don't we do that?"

I wanted to say, "Oh no! I did not mean I wanted to do anything about it." However, that Someone who was becoming bigger in my life all the time would not let me back down. We agreed to meet at my house after evensong every week, where—gulp!—we would *pray*.

It all sounds so simple now, but at the time this suggestion sent me into a panic. How was I going to pray with someone else when I was only just getting the hang of praying by myself? I was a spiritual baby.

The arranged day arrived, and we went to my home after the service, where, trying to sound completely normal, I said to Tony, "We are just going upstairs to pray."

The remark just hung in the air, and I am sure Tony thought it was rather weird. We both went up to our bedroom, we sat down and I closed my eyes . . . tight. I felt so uncomfortable. Lillian began to talk to God easily, just as if He was a friend who was there with us. *Golly!* I thought. *She is a bit more ahead in this game than I am. I wonder where she learned how to pray like this!* My limited contribution was a prayer from my library book!

I was totally unprepared for what happened next. She prayed, "Lord, fill us with Your Spirit."

And whoosh! Something very amazing and very profound, like a warm blanket of love, joy, comfort, and peace, fell upon me. From that point, I was so overwhelmed by what had happened that I was totally unable to say anything more, and it was not awkwardness that had silenced me!

After a while, she asked, "Are you okay?"

I managed to mutter, "Yes . . . fine . . ."

However, I was not just fine. I had experienced something that was amazing and wonderful and at the same time quite disturbing. What had happened to me? I went over her words in my mind. "Lord, fill us with Your

Spirit." Logically it seemed that God had filled me with His Spirit, and I had yet another life-transforming experience with the living God.

I felt a bit wobbly, but I was fairly okay by the time I saw her out. After she had gone, I went back upstairs and savoured the wonderful feelings. There was now a wonderful power dancing inside my heart, which felt glorious and made me dance on the outside too. Again, I hoped that, like my previous experience, the effect of this moment would not have evaporated in the morning. I was again overjoyed to find that it did not go away, but instead, moment by moment, I knew I had the real living force of the Holy Spirit inside me.

I felt incredibly different. Even more than before, my heart was bursting with love, which I began to lavish on Tony, the boys, and anyone else who came into view! Tony was surprised but gladly received it all!

Soon after that, Lillian took me to St. Matthews, an Anglican church in Cambridge. It was totally unlike the village Anglican church I knew. The worship was being led by a music group, and it was real and free. I had never seen people lifting their hands in adoration or people smiling and obviously enjoying worship. I was transported into a totally new realm of corporate worship. At times the music group just seemed to play, and everyone kept on singing a melodious kind of song. I did not know what it was. I could not hear the words they were singing; I just knew that it was wonderful—heavenly even!

Suddenly a man kneeling in the pew in front lifted his hands and began to pray in a foreign language. It was so beautiful. Then someone spoke in English in a way that sounded just as if it was supposed to be God talking to us. The man kneeling in the pew looked Italian, so I thought he was just speaking to God in his own language. I later discovered that he was a local barber and as English as I was! I now know that he was exercising a genuine spiritual gift—the gift of tongues.

When I was sweeping my kitchen floor a few days later, I Ginnydly recalled this beautiful church service I had attended in Cambridge, and without realizing what was happening, I simply ran out of English and began to sing in a strange language I had never learned.

It felt *so* good that I knew it must be something to do with God! I hoped Tony, with his Bible knowledge, would know about it, and so I went to the room where he was reading and asked, "Is there anywhere in the Bible where people just started to talk in languages they didn't know?"

Without looking up, absentmindedly he said, "Oh yes, Acts chapter two."

Excited, I ran upstairs and quickly read that chapter of the Bible. It said, "They were all filled with the Spirit and began to speak with other tongues, as the Spirit gave them utterance."

Wow! I had had yet another real Bible experience. I had spoken in tongues, and the Holy Spirit had given me the words. I had already discovered that when I met with Jesus that night in my bedroom, I had been born again. I later found out that this new experience of speaking in a different language was what some people referred to as one of the signs of the baptism of the Holy Spirit.

The words had bypassed my mind. They just bubbled up effortlessly from inside me. Jesus said, "Out of your belly will flow rivers of living water." The Bible had once again become alive and true for me. I wondered if many other people had experienced this phenomenon. I had never heard of any. Were there some even in Isleham? If there were, they had certainly kept very quiet about it.

I realised that the baptism of the Holy Spirit must be an important thing for a Christian to experience because now, with no conscious effort at all, a radical change took place. Day by day, *He* was working inside me. Sometimes, out of the corner of my eye, I caught Tony looking at me incredulously when I did not explode or answer sharply. I was not the same hot-tempered woman he had lived with for all those years.

Worship became so natural. I understood the hymn that said we could be "lost in wonder, love, and praise," or what the Amplified Bible's version of 1 Peter 1 means when it says, "You believe in Him and exalt and thrill with inexpressible and glorious triumphant and heavenly joy." The Bible suddenly became understandable, and the book of Acts was true. I also saw why the church was so ineffective and unattractive. It did not know or demonstrate the *power* of the Holy Spirit.

I wanted everyone I knew to receive Him, and have their lives changed as wonderfully as mine had been, but I discovered that people were hard to convince, especially the religious ones. There is a quote from Kenneth Hagin, a well-known preacher that says, "Religious people's minds are like concrete, thoroughly mixed up and well set!"

CHAPTER 6

On the Same Track at Last

T ony began confirmation classes. I was pleased, but he would go to class expectant and come back discouraged. I wondered if it was not doing more harm than good. He would shake his head and say, "You know, they just don't believe it. Why do they want to explain it all away?"

Rescue came in the form of a Christian musical called *Come Together*, which in the US had involved Pat Boone and was now touring England with Jean Darnell. Local Christians learned the songs of this musical production and were drawing large crowds to see them perform, sometimes in large marquees. We heard that a performance of *Come Together* was happening locally in The Barn at Snailwell. Later I discovered the barn was also being used regularly for charismatic Christian meetings.

I really wanted to go and see this musical, and I desperately wanted Tony to come too. However, he declined because he was so discouraged by the confirmation classes. I was disappointed, but I accepted it without any fuss and instead arranged to take a friend named Kate.

Just before the day, I received a phone call from the National Childbirth Trust (NCT) in London asking if I could teach a course that weekend to train a group of women to help other mothers succeed at breast-feeding. Apparently the woman who had committed to teach the class was sick, and they urgently needed a substitute. Because this was a work close to my heart, I did not want to let them down.

I told Tony that I felt torn between the two. It really mattered to me to take Kate to the musical, but I did not want to let the NCT down either.

The only answer I could see was for him to go as the transport for Kate, and it would free me to go to London. He agreed straightaway because we both loved Kate, her husband, Johnny, and their family, and he could clearly see Kate needed a great deal of help.

So I went to London, and Tony took Kate to the meeting—just as the transport, of course! On arrival he was embarrassed to find many of his sixth-form students were also there. These students had probably been praying for him and must have been thrilled to see him.

At the end of the musical, people were asked if they wanted to give their lives to Christ. Tony cannot explain what happened that night, but when that invitation was made, he just felt compelled to put his hand up to signify he wanted to receive Christ! When he had seen the real worship, he had seen the glory of the Holy Spirit upon the choir. Over the years in my drama productions he was familiar with the pantomime chorus smiling obligingly for the audience with plastic smiles; this was a very different phenomenon, and it opened his heart. Despite the presence of his sixth-form students and others who knew him from the village, that night, he made Jesus Christ his Lord and Saviour

On the Sunday evening when I got off the train at Ely Station, right at the end of the platform by the ticket office I saw a familiar figure with his face aglow! Nobody needed to tell me what had happened to him or that he was wonderfully and gloriously saved. It was plain to see. Amazingly, he had even gone to church that morning and even in the formal Anglican church had a great experience! God had orchestrated things so cleverly by getting me out of the way at just the right moment.

Much later it emerged that Tony had actually made a simple commitment to Jesus when he was eight years old at a Baptist Sunday school, but as a teenager, beguiled by science, he had turned away. Like me, he had also been unimpressed with church. It was only a small step to become too clever and intellectual for faith.

A few days after finding Christ, Tony had the joy of his commitment radically affecting someone else. Tony had come to collect me from a play rehearsal, smiling broadly and with a spring in his step. One of the players and her husband, Ron, walked up to us. Ron was a teacher at the college too. He had stayed with us on his return from teaching in Africa while looking for somewhere to live. They had settled in a nearby village, and we had become friends. After the birth of their second child, Tom, she was considerably depressed. I talked to Mary about the Lord, and although she had needs, she seemed singularly uninterested and a little hostile. She saw Tony's glowing face, and said, "Wow, you are looking good."

Tony said bouncily, "Yes, I have just made Jesus Lord of my life; you should try it!"

Promptly bursting into tears, she said, "A week ago I would have slapped your face for being so cheeky, but I now know that is what I need to do," and she did!

It was wonderful for Tony to see his salvation affecting somebody's life. Later we also had the joy of leading her husband to Jesus. They went on to serve the Lord in many ways. Soon, more new revelation came to us; we realised the value of a Christian home surrendered to Jesus, so we stood in our hallway, held hands, and solemnly prayed together, "Lord, if you would like us to share our home, our family, and this wonderful happiness with anyone, please send them to us."

Sharing our home was not a new idea to us by any means, but this was different, our home was now dedicated to the Lord.

It was such a simple and trusting prayer—oh so simple. We did not realise how much that simple, heartfelt prayer would change our lives. A week later, I saw an article in the local paper asking for temporary homes for girls who were pregnant but did not want to have an abortion. Remembering my own strong but unexpected response to an early miscarriage, I wondered if abortion was the best response to an unwanted pregnancy. Any immediate sense of relief must surely be followed by a sense of loss. Tony readily agreed, so we asked for more details. Within two weeks, we had been taken through an in-depth interview with Life for the Unborn Child, a Catholic group in Cambridge. Within two weeks, Cynthia arrived.

Cynthia was a thickset, adorable girl with a broad northern accent, the eldest of ten children, and very down-to-earth. Within moments, she shattered all my suppositions about unmarried mothers! Far from being traumatized about being pregnant and her mother throwing her out, Susan was thrilled to be pregnant and really wanted to keep her baby. She had mothered all of her mother's children and wanted one of her own. With her sunny nature and sense of fun, she was an instant hit with our boys. I could not help looking back to my own very nervous beginnings as a new mother. Unlike me, she was obviously going to take it all in her stride—a complete natural!

In due time, Cynthia produced Adrian, a happy, bouncing baby who, predictably, she handled with great aplomb even when his early life was blighted by a bad bout of croup. We inevitably had our ups and downs together, but overall it was a most satisfactory time for all of us.

Cynthia was only supposed to stay with us for six months, but in the end, she actually stayed for eighteen months and was strengthened by coming to know Jesus.

Cynthia's easy bonding with Adrian touched a raw nerve with me. It had not been that easy for me to bond with our first child, Philip. I felt unhappy about the distance. When I considered how I felt about our other boys, I felt that this problem stuck out like a sore thumb. I did *love* Philip, but there was no depth to it. I envied the joy and closeness Tony had with him. Something was definitely missing between us.

I knew this was partly because when he was born, I had been unable to breast-feed him, and in a strange way I felt, quite irrationally, that he had rejected me. The truth was that I had a long labour; I was exhausted, and he was a sleepy baby due to medication I had been given. On top of that, I was not given the help and encouragement I had expected to breast-feed. Naively, I had also assumed it would just come naturally. Breast-feeding was not at all fashionable at the time. At the nursing home, they made me feel I was a bit of a freak for wanting to do it at all. I cannot describe how utterly miserable I was to be bottle-feeding. I cried many times during those early weeks.

It had been so different when Ben was born. I had a very short and easy labour; he was jet-propelled into the world, and I was not at all tired after the labour. The moment I delivered Ben, he looked around at us, wide-eyed. We both instantly fell in love with this beautiful, blue-eyed little person. Not only that, but this time I also made sure I was armed with solid information and the determination to breast-feed at any cost! I made sure I knew exactly what to do in all eventualities. However, I did not need any information at all because he came down the ward in the nurse's arms for his first feed with his mouth wide open. With no effort at all, he latched on and fed wonderfully. I needed very little help at all! Within a week, he had gained a whole pound! I was so full of joy that the midwife, who came to visit me at home, said she had never seen such a happy mother. This was great, but it had a downside because it highlighted the difference between the way I felt about Philip and the way I felt about Ben. I was agonized and felt so guilty.

When Giles was born, the contrast was there too, but it was not so dramatic. He was a lovely child, born quickly, and with such a calm and sunny temperament. I was absolutely besotted with him and found great pleasure in the night feeds when we were alone, just enjoying each other's company without interruption.

It seemed we had the perfect little trio, but I had a persistent niggle that all was not completely well in my heart. I began to talk to the Lord about the disparity of my feelings toward my children. One night, when I was praying about my relationship with Philip, God broke into my prayers and said, "Pray that the love of God will bubble up in both of your hearts so that you are able to make a new beginning."

What a fresh thought—in both of our hearts. *Hmm . . . not just* my *heart?* I dutifully prayed those words in exactly the way God had suggested and then promptly forgot about it.

Ben was about six months old and had been born with a slightly twisted foot and had to wear special soft leather boots at night, which kept his feet at the correct angle. He was surprisingly accepting of them, and I kept a close ear out for him waking up. As soon as he stirred, I would hurry to his room to get them off.

One morning as I passed the bunk beds where Philip slept, without any warning, Philip enthusiastically leapt off the top bunk, flung his arms around my neck, and said, "Mummy, I love you!"

He had never, ever said that to me before. I just stood there, hugging him tightly, and cried and cried. It was like a dam bursting inside my heart, and I knew the barriers were gone between us. I managed to say, "And I love you too."

I wept then, and I am weeping now just thinking about it. It was a pivotal moment in our relationship and truly a wonderful new beginning. What an amazing answer to prayer, so typical of what happens when we simply listen to the Holy Spirit and pray the will of God. I was amazed that God had made it so easy for me.

From that moment on, we were thoroughly bonded. I felt just the same toward Philip as I did toward the other boys. For the first time, I knew

I loved him with all of my heart. It was a life-changing miracle. What goodness and kindness God demonstrates. I marvel at the way God used Philip to make the first move when I had assumed that somehow it would have to come from me. What a tremendous relief! God answers prayer in such unexpected ways.

I discovered that this was clean-up time in my life! God began speaking to me about a second thing in my life that did not please Him. I had been doing some photographic modeling with the boys for Mike, a professional photographer. He planned an exhibition of a series: me pregnant, me giving birth, me breast-feeding, and me playing with the children. I could have as many photos as I wanted, but I began to feel uncomfortable. The photos were discreet and were certainly not sexy in any way, but I also suspected Mike might be getting too fond of me.

In the end, I said, "I'm sorry Mike, but I can't do this anymore."

"Oh," he said, "is that because you have become religious?"

"Hmm. . . sort of . . ." I trailed off, not really knowing what to say.

I suppose that's what it looked like to him, and in a way it was true, but it wasn't about a rule or a law I had come under. All I knew was that not only I but Jesus in me was not happy. This is so hard to explain to an unbeliever.

The other area I unexpectedly felt uncomfortable about was my deep involvement in drama. I had lived it and breathed it for years! Since the age of about fourteen, I had taken part in about thirty-five major play productions, mostly playing the female lead. I had danced and sung in revues, pantomimes, and musicals; I had produced pantomimes and dramas of every kind. I knew I was good at it. At college our examination production was a Greek comedy called *Lysitrata*. It had many small women's parts but only one large women's part, and I felt so privileged that the students voted for me to take the prized female lead. I gained a distinction for that performance and also for my dissertation about Ibsen's women.

Apart from my family and Jesus, I loved drama more than anything else in my life. God convicted me that it was not just a harmless hobby, but that it was actually an idol that vied with Him for position in my life. Deep down I knew it was true and that He obviously did not want to share first place in my life with drama! As addicts do, I tried my best to turn a deaf ear to these uncomfortable promptings. I really did not *want* to give it up. First

I tried reasoning with the Lord that it gave other people a lot of pleasure. Then I explained to Him that it brought me into contact with many people who needed Him, and I could witness to them. I don't think in this instance He was impressed with either of those arguments.

At the time I was producing a French farce called *Hotel Paradiso* by Georges Feydeau. I had played the female lead in it in my twenties and loved it! All went well until I developed bronchitis, and I was coughing my way through rehearsals, feeling grim, and not enjoying it at all.

As I sat miserably sunken into my producers chair watching the play, a horrible revelation struck. Suddenly the scales fell from my eyes, and I saw the content of the play through His eyes. I was cut to the heart. *Oh no*, I thought. *We are laughing at adultery. We are laughing at sin, and I am encouraging others to make light of sin.*

I did not I hear another word of the rehearsal. All my joy in the production evaporated, and I agonized that I had to endure another month before I could back out. I told the Lord that night, "I promise I will end all of my drama activities the minute this production is over." Immediately the bronchitis began to clear up and in days was completely gone. God did not give me the sickness, but when I was not at peace with myself, those germs had power. When the internal war was over, my body recovered quickly.

Soon after the production ended, I was asked to sing at the Baptist women's meeting I attended on Tuesday afternoons. I was quite reluctant to do so because I did not know any suitable songs, and my singing career had mostly been in pantomime, revue, and musical comedy, crooning things like, "Got no diamonds, got no pearls, still I think I'm a lucky girl. I've got the sun in the mornin' and the moon at night." Anyway, I agreed for friendship's sake and found a book called *Songs of Living Water* and taught myself a couple of songs

I was really nervous, but when I stood up, opened my mouth, and launched into the first song, to my utter amazement, a beautiful voice came out that I truly had no idea that I possessed! When I had finished, somebody even asked me if I had been opera trained. How amazing! God had removed something but had given me something better. It felt as if He was saying, "You gave up something that was precious to you for Me, so I am giving you something precious in return, which will bless you and extend My kingdom."

In the next few years, I sang and ministered and gave my testimony at church meetings all over the area, and I know I really touched people's hearts and drew them toward Jesus. Oddly, once I had made the decision to give up drama, I really did not miss it! Neither did the singing fuel any pride because I knew clearly that it was a gift from God and not just something I was good at doing. I loved the singing, but I also began to find that I longed to preach as well.

CHAPTER 7

Supernatural Experience

C hurch life in the village was beginning to perk up. A whole group of us were praying together. Nothing much seemed to be happening, but faith said, "Keep pressing in and it will." God seemed to confirm this by telling us, "Keep praising *Me*."

At the time, we were friendly with the Baptist church ministers who had been baptised into the Holy Spirit just as we moved into the village. There was such vibrant life at their church. It would have been the easiest thing in the world to have jumped ship and join them, but God never gave us permission.

They invited us to charismatic, interdenominational meetings at The Barn in Snailwell. Initially Tony thought it was an extraordinary idea to give up a whole Saturday for church. People came from all over the county to experience the presence of God, good Bible teaching, worship, and wonderful fellowship.

It was there one Saturday that Giles had a miracle. For six months, he and I had been suffering with a tropical disease in the bowel called Giardia Lamblia for which he had been prescribed some terrible-tasting medication. We christened it the yuck medicine because as we spooned it into him, we would all chorus, "Nice, nice, nice," but immediately after he swallowed it, he would screw up his face and say, "*Yuck!*" My symptoms had stopped after the medication but Giles was still sick after repeated doses.

When Tony took Giles for prayer at The Barn meeting, he immediately vomited all over him. Tony smelled terrible for the rest of the day, but from that moment on, Giles was completely well! No more diarrhea!

After Giles was born, because of a thrombosis in my leg, my doctor advised me not to have any more children. Since our success with birth control had been poor, we decided I would be sterilized. My doctor thought I was too young. "What if anything happened to one of your children and you want another one?"

It was a strange argument from the same man who had suggested I abort Giles, saying brusquely, "Two point four children are quite enough!" Obviously it was all right to kill a potential child, but it was not all right to try and prevent one! How upside down!

I felt peace about being sterilized, but on the morning of the surgery, sudden doubt flooded my heart. I asked Him, "Lord, *is* this Your will?"

Straightaway I heard Him say, "Do not be afraid. I will give you spiritual children."

I did not have a clue what that might mean, but it brought me complete peace.

What a blessing it has always been to me to be able to hear God's voice. Jesus says, "My sheep hear my voice," and all Christians need to be able to hear Him clearly so they can walk with Him. It has been such a blessing and built such intimacy with Him. His promise is *to lead us into all the truth* through the Bible and also through the still, small voice in our hearts.

I remember one day when I was praying, I asked the Lord, "Do I have an angel, Lord?"

"Yes," He said, "and he has the same prayer language as you do."

This was jaw-dropping information, but as I sat quietly, a Scripture came to mind that made sense of that statement. I recalled that it says in 1 Corinthians, "If we speak with the tongues of men *and angels* . . ." So, although my heart began to beat very fast and I was overawed by this information, I dared to press Him further: "What is his name?"

I waited. I could not imagine that God would tell me his name.

"His name is August."

The name did not sound like the month of August but like the beginning of the name Augustus. Wow! My heart was full to bursting that God would trust me with this information. When I looked up the meaning of the name, I was amazed: "Dignified, exalted, glorious, and grand, of noble birth, high-ranking, imposing, impressive, kingly, lofty, magnificent, majestic and regal, worthy of veneration." What a wonderful name, and what a wonderful helper to be given! I can just imagine him standing on guard beside me. Hebrews 1:14 says, "Are not all angels ministering spirits sent forth to minister for those who will inherit salvation?" Also, Psalm 103:20 reads, "Bless the Lord, you His angels, who excel in strength, who do His word, heeding the voice of His word."

Knowing that we have angelic assistance is very comforting. I am sure I met angels in the car park of a motorway café. A friend and I, along with several of our children, were on a long journey. We all tumbled out of the car eager for a break and I flicked the door handle up and locked the car to go into the café. However, when we came to drive away, I could not find the keys. To my chagrin I saw that I had shut them in the car. They were still in the ignition. Feeling helpless, we stood and prayed. When we opened our eyes, two men in very smart uniform suddenly appeared as if from nowhere and asked if we were okay. We told them what had happened. One of them seemed only to touch the car door lightly with his hand, and he opened it and took the keys out of the ignition. He held them up and handed them to me with a smile. Whooping with glee, we all piled into the car. Seconds later I turned to thank them, but they had disappeared. We looked in all the nearby cars and all around, but they were nowhere to be seen. Concluding they were angels, we went on our way rejoicing. It was a quick and amazing answer to a prayer

One night, when a particularly violent storm was raging, I was awakened by the sound of tiles falling—*crash, tinkle-tinkle, crash*! I prayed hard, "Lord, please send Your angels to sit on the roof and stop the tiles from being blown away."

Feeling assured that God was looking after the roof, I went back to sleep. The next day, all was quiet. I ran to the window and was shocked to see a vast number of slates missing from the roof of the house across the road. I ran downstairs and went out into the garden to see what the damage had been to our roof. One tile was lying by the front door and another in the flowerbed. Otherwise, not one was missing. I was sorry I had not asked God to send the angels to my neighbour too.

We also had some trouble from different kinds of spiritual beings. We had not lived at one of our houses for very long when I began to be woken at night by what sounded like footsteps in the room above. I quickly dismissed it as my imagination, but one night I heard footsteps coming down the stairs. My bedroom door opened, and a presence entered and stood at the bottom of my bed. I would love to be able to tell you that I rebuked it fearlessly, but actually when it was at the bottom of my bed, I screamed at the top of my voice, waking Tony and giving him a terrible fright. After that we did rebuke it and tell it to leave and never come back!

Spiritual warfare was completely new to us. We had not fully grasped that evil forces could affect our lives. For instance, on another occasion we felt something very strange was happening. Usually our home was a hub of activity and friends dropped in every day, but for a few weeks, we felt puzzled because people simply stopped coming. Nobody dropped in. One day while having coffee with some friends Joan and David, whom we had invited, we shared what was happening. David fell quiet and seemed preoccupied. Then he said, "I can see two ancient warriors standing outside your front door with spears crossed, barring the way to anyone coming in; let's pray." We told the warriors to leave and never come back, and the next day everything returned to normal. When we questioned them nobody could think of any logical reason why they had not called on us. Weird!

CHAPTER 8

We Discover the Christian Camp

Someone suggested something very strange—that we should go to a Christian camp. A camp? It seemed a very daunting prospect to go to the middle of nowhere and attend meetings three times a day while grappling with the rigors of camping with three children, but because Tony was an expert Venture Scout camper, I thought we might just manage it.

Someone kindly lent us an old tent, and we set off for our first experience at Post Green, Dorset, the grounds of Lord and Lady Lees Estate. Our car was not really up to such a long journey, but we were undeterred. The old car seemed to groan under the weight of us and all the equipment. The journey seemed endless, and we all arrived hot, tired, and bad-tempered. As soon as we arrived, people showed us to our designated part of the site, and immediately several people came and offered to help us put up the tent. *So far so good*, I thought

The camp certainly was a test of our relationship. Each of us had strong ideas about how to do things in the kitchen, and this field kitchen was no different! We thought we had done well until we returned the following year and people said to us, "Wow! What's happened to you both? You have changed so much."

Oh dear! Was it that obvious? Did we really seem so bad? Looking at us soberly, yes, we were pretty awful. God had a lot of work to do.

However, despite all the negatives, we all enjoyed the camp tremendously. The children found many new friends and had a great time playing when they were not in their meetings.

The main speaker, John Bedford, called the teaching "Sons, Servants, and Soldiers"—the various roles we have in Christ. I am amazed that I can still remember anything about it after over thirty years! It shows what an impact it made. We loved the teaching and the fellowship with those of like mind. We were hooked!

A very severe test, however, came on the journey home after that first camp. In Salisbury our old car ground to a halt. We had no food and no money. We were unlikely to get any because the bank was closed, and in those days there were no ATM machines and credit cards. We were stranded. We did the only thing we had learned to do; we prayed.

After praying, we felt inspired to call at the vicarage of a big church we could see in the centre of the town and ask for help. The vicar was very helpful and arranged for us to go to the home of a single woman called Primrose. Without batting an eyelid, this complete stranger received us gladly and fed all five of us. She rapidly made arrangements for all of us to stay in her lovely cottage for a few days because we would not be able to get the car mended until the Monday. We felt utterly loved and cared for, and she did not seem at all put out for one minute. What a lovely, godly woman she was! On Tuesday morning as soon as the garage had mended the car, we continued on our journey home. We were sad to leave Salisbury and a very good friend. It seemed miraculous that we left Salisbury having had an adventure rather than a disaster.

In Salisbury and at the camp, we had found members of God's family with inclusive hearts like our own, and one of the most precious things I remember about the camp was the love, kindness, and graciousness we experienced from Lord and Lady Lees. They were delightful Christian people. We forged friendships there that continued year after year.

Tom and Faith Lees had a Christian community in their large mansion at Post Green. They had been influenced by the Pulkinghams from Houston in America. The Dorset community supported the Fisher folk, a worship group that influenced Christian music a great deal in the sixties and seventies. They certainly influenced us. It seemed that they had been changed for the better by sharing their daily life together.

When we read Dennis Bennett's book *Nine O'clock in the Morning* about the community that lived together at his church in Houston, Texas, we were very touched.

Dennis had experienced the baptism of the Holy Spirit and speaking in tongues. He took over an empty church, and a small community formed there that changed the whole area. This community was a mixture of mature Christians and needy people, who then formed the core of the church. Their community life had a radical effect, and the church grew and prospered beyond anything expected at that time.

Many years later, in Cambridge, we met an erudite and highly qualified young man who, as a newly trained Anglican priest, had gone to Houston eager for the Lord to use him. He was rather shocked because the first thing they did was put a broom in his hand. It was not quite the exalted ministry he had envisaged doing when he volunteered to go there, but it was good training for servant hood!

It seemed that the baptism of the Holy Spirit was the key to the growth of this church and the success of the ministry. The Holy Spirit appeared to have released the love of God into people's lives in a way that enabled them to live together in true Christian love, holiness, and righteousness, acting in an opposite spirit to the selfish spirit of the world in which we live. They were recreating the closeness and the radical generosity of the church of the book of Acts where everyone had all things in common.

I read this book avidly from cover to cover and encouraged Tony to do the same. I was so inspired by this wonderful story. As I read it, I heard God saying, "This is the way I will lead you."

However, I thought, *Hmmm . . . well, maybe.*

This was a story from America. Anything could happen in America! I simply could not imagine it happening in our locality.

One year we went to The Dales Camp. It was the year when people heard angels singing over the camp. Both our boys made a commitment to the Lord while attending children's meetings at this camp. We had a great time but were a bit puzzled to see women were wearing headscarves and somewhat wary when we heard rumours about their attitude toward women in the church. It was an interpretation of Scripture we were not familiar with. People also called their church methods heavy shepherding. We were aware of the influence of the Brethren roots of many of those who were in this renewal movement.

Our main camp experiences were at Colin Urquhart's Faith Camp. We went to the first one at Newark and continued to attend this camp for years after at Peterborough. Here we heard the message of faith and such a straightforward gospel message that it strengthened us a great deal. All of these camps were an oasis in our lives. I remember feeling a bit depressed each time we drove back home to Isleham to face the battle with unbelief, lukewarmness, and opposition. The contrast was sometimes almost too much to bear.

Camping brings us all to the same basic level of living. We would all like to think that every day at camp would be idyllic sunshine, with water fights to cool us all down and shared meals under the canopies of our tents. However, in reality, we have also experienced the years when wellingtons, umbrellas, raincoats, and floods were the norm and the tent did not stand up to the weather! Even when camping in a field had lost its dread for me and our relationship had moved on a great deal, the ultimate test came at an Ashburnham Camp when we returned to the campsite after the morning meeting. The wind had blown our tent upside down. There it was looking very ungainly waving its legs in the air! At that moment, I knew beyond all doubt that God had changed me because I just said cheerfully, "Come on, boys, let's cook lunch. Everything will be all right."

And it was! Many people helped Tony to set it to rights, and all was well.

Tony and I became part of the pastoral team at Colin's camps for some years. Most of the time, it was great fun. There was a lot of prayer with the team. There was then a daily tour of our designated units to hear many wonderful testimonies from the campers. Sometimes the unit leader had problems with people, and we spent time with them, praying and offering whatever wisdom we had. Sometimes the leaders themselves had problems! We seemed to rush from leaders meeting to prayer meeting to pastoral care, squeezing in as much of the teaching and worship in between as possible.

One year at Faith Camp, when the offering basket came around, God showed us that we should empty our bank account into it! We did so, knowing that if we hear God and obey, He always blesses us. When we got home and opened the post, all the money we had put in the offering had come back to us through one means or another—every penny!

CHAPTER 9

It's Here Too!

Could what we had read about in *Nine O'clock in the Morning* happen in England?

Yes it could! I bought a book called *When the Spirit Comes* by the Anglican vicar Colin Urquhart. When I got it home, Tony and I went to bed early and stayed awake until we had read it from cover to cover. It was incredible—the Holy Spirit! Here He was, touching a church in England, and what was more, it was an Anglican church! More exciting still, it was happening in *Luton*! Luton? We could hardly believe it! Luton did not seem a very important, nor did it seem a very salubrious place, and it was only about an hour and a half away from where we lived. . . Astounding news! The move of the Holy Spirit was not just happening in America. Here it was on our own doorstep.

In this book, the model of community was popping up again. It seemed God was underlining something in the script of our lives and maybe not just underlining it but writing it in large capital letters!

We bought loads of copies of the book and gave them away or lent them to anyone vaguely interested. We were eager to spread the good news that the Holy Spirit was alive and well in England. It puzzled us that not everyone was as excited as we were. Some people dismissed it as simply impossible for our sleepy village.

Our home was already a mini-community or at least an extended family, and despite building an extension over the garage, we sometimes felt quite crowded.

After our unmarried mum, Cynthia, had left us to visit her family, we gave a home to a teenage boy from Tony's school that was homeless because the school boardinghouse was closing. We agreed to have him for a term. John was unhappy and difficult at home and wet the bed at night. Through remarriage, his family had become large and disjointed. That and the divorce had obviously caused difficulties. During the time that he stayed with us, he was no trouble at all.

Several nights a week, we also had a family of four children sleep over while their mother, a recently separated, single parent, did the night shift as a nurse. On top of this, there were frequent visits from grandparents and other relations. All of this turned my thoughts toward a bigger house. We had only been talking vaguely about the possibility of moving, feeling the need to create more space for the children and to take people into our home, but I knew Tony would definitely not be keen to move.

One day I was passing a large house on Sun Street, and a For Sale sign caught my eye. I heard God say clearly, "I want you to buy that house."

As I anticipated, Tony was not impressed when I told him about the house. He had only just finished seven years of work, refurbishing and extending The Old Dairy, and he was not keen to start again. So I told the Lord, "If this *is* Your will, You need to convince Tony about it. I can't and won't go without him, and I will not press him, so he will have to hear clearly from You."

I was wise to say no more, but when Tony heard that it had a large garden, a paddock, sheds, and a large barn with plenty of space to keep chickens and goats, enabling us to be more self-sufficient, he began to think that maybe this was the opportunity he had looked for, but the house was way beyond our budget. However, God enjoys the impossible because it gives Him space to show His miracle-working power.

One day Tony suggested that perhaps we should just go to see the house. There could be no harm in just looking! He was really impressed with the property but daunted because the house needed so much work. What tipped the balance in its favor, though, were those tantalizing outside features.

It was a splendid lath and plaster construction Queen Anne house built in 1720. It had six large bedrooms, a cellar, beautiful oak beams, a wonderful oak staircase, picturesque fireplaces, and other excellent period features. I loved it, especially its colourful history. It had once been a dame school and at one time a pub. Ellie, the woman who cleaned my house, had been in service in that house when she was a young girl. She told me how the mistress used to hide a sixpence under different pieces of furniture each day so she would know if Ellie had cleaned properly.

After praying earnestly, we felt we needed to test the ground. I knew one of the owners, Mary, a little because she had invited me to go to the house one day and look at their goats and try the goats' milk. I also knew her as a champion of women's rights who had interviewed me for her book called *Fen Women* which was about the lives of village women.

The book caused a great stir in the village and there were angry scenes in the post office because everyone, including me, had spoken freely; not realizing the book would be a literal transcript of every word we said. I cringed when I read what I had said. In cold print it sounded awful. Mary's husband, the co-owner, was a charming man, the son of Rex Harrison and Lilly Palmer, who lectured at a university in the area.

I was convinced this was our house, but our parents all had the same gloomy reaction as Tony: how could we think of leaving our lovely home to buy this . . . well, this wreck! I think God has given me a gift of being able to see the possibilities for redemption in things as well as in people. I could clearly see the wonderful potential the house possessed to become a gracious residence.

I knew Tony was still not yet totally convinced, so I had a little talk with the Lord. "Lord, please will you sell our house within two weeks as a witness to Tony that it is definitely the right thing to do?"

I told Tony about the prayer and felt confident the house would be sold within that timeframe. We asked an agent to value the house, intending to advertise ourselves in the local paper. I refused his offer to put it on the market, but he was very persuasive and left with the brief. For some reason I completely forgot God's instruction to advertise it ourselves in the local paper.

Two weeks later, I was very puzzled. I was amazed the house had not yet sold.

"What is the problem, Lord? Why hasn't the house sold yet? I was sure you would sell it within two weeks."

He said clearly, "I did not tell you to put the house with an agent; I told you to advertise it in the newspaper yourself."

How foolish I had been. I could have kicked myself for being so careless and disobedient; quickly I rang the paper and dictated the advertisement, asking for offers over £14, 500 and cancelled the agent. Phew. What a relief . . . back on track!

The day the advertisement appeared, I watched an attractive young couple come to our gate; one of them carried the rolled newspaper under his arm. I thought, *It's our buyers!*

"Hello," they said. "We have come about the advert for the house. May we come in?"

They came in, had a brief look, and left quickly. The next day they returned, had another quick look around, and then sat with me in the drawing room.

"We would like to offer you £15,750. Would that be all right?"

I carefully held on to my facial expression, hiding the shock of receiving an offer £1,250 *above* the asking price. "Oh . . . £15,750 you say. Well . . . I will have to talk to my husband about it and let you know."

"Fine," they said, and then they left, leaving me a phone number.

I walked around in a dazed state, gibbering to myself and laughing. Could this be a hoax? Could this really be true? Who on earth offers so much more than the asking price? The answer, of course, is someone who has been sent by God and also someone who is astute enough to recognize a bargain when they see it!

Well, of course Tony agreed to the asking price! They had their survey. They then came back and negotiated for £250 less because of a little damp, finally paying us the princely sum of £15,500. We were now part of the way toward accomplishing our faith goal.

CHAPTER 10

Negotiation

The maximum we could afford to pay for the new house was £16,500, and even then it meant doubling our mortgage to the massive sum of eight thousand pounds. In today's housing market it is of course peanuts, but for us at this time in the 1970's it was a huge leap of faith.

Tony elected me to ring the owner of the house, and I called the number with my heart in my mouth.

"Hello, Carey. We are very interested in buying your house. We really love it." I began to explain why we wanted to buy it. "As you may know, we already have people living in our home who for one reason or another need a loving home. The idea of buying Sunbury House is that we will be able to offer a home to more people, as well as being able to accommodate our own family adequately. However, we can only make a low offer of £16,500, and it is not negotiable. It is really all we can afford."

He expressed his delight at our plans for the house, and after only a couple of moments of hesitation, he agreed to accept our offer, which we happened to know was less than they actually paid for it. His wife was not pleased with such a low offer, but being a man of integrity, he refused to go back on his word.

We were so happy! I was happy because I knew I had heard God. I was also happy because God had answered our prayers and once again had shown He was utterly faithful. Tony was happy because he felt God had clearly confirmed that we should buy the house. The children were happy, and even our dog, Bilbo, seemed happy! The new house would definitely be better for him. As a bouncy Labrador-collie cross, he had a lot of energy. At Sunbury House, there would be a large back garden for him to play in where he would not be able to frighten passersby as he had done to the unfortunate post lady. She had been terrified when he leapt the six-foot wall around The Old Dairy and chased down the road after her bike. We had a subsequent visit from a police officer, who Bilbo welcomed eagerly with a wag of the tail and a friendly woof. After Bilbo had licked him thoroughly, he lay down peacefully on the officer's feet.

"Is this the dangerous dog?" he asked.

Despite our abject apologies, the postal service took us to court, insisting that Bilbo was a dangerous dog and should be destroyed. Any hint that he was a dangerous dog would have been a disaster for him and us. It would have been an unbearable loss for our family and caused a stir among the twenty-four children who attended the playgroup in our house. Tony prepared to play the Perry Mason role in court; we also had two character witnesses: a playgroup mother, whose child had previously been terrified of dogs but had been converted by Bilbo into being a dog-lover and a friend named Ann who was a dog breeder. She testified that according to her experience with dogs, Bilbo was definitely not a dangerous dog. Bilbo was let off with a caution, and we were warned to keep him under control. The move was definitely necessary.

The house sale went through easily, and we moved in a couple of days before Christmas. The first night, just before we collapsed into bed, someone said, "Where is the dog?" Poor Bilbo! In the hurly-burly, we had left him behind. We raced to the old house to find a very miserable dog indeed sitting on the doorstep. He was overjoyed to see us.

The very next day, I swung into action. The dining room was a depressing bottle-green colour. It was a classic colour for a house of that age, but it made the room very dark, so I decided to wallpaper the room that day so we could eat Christmas lunch with everything looking new and beautiful. Tony thought I was quite mad and I had never wallpapered before, but I dashed to the shop and found some paper that looked just right. I finished the job at midnight, scrubbed the floor, and fell into bed exhausted.

At the new house, we reckoned we had £40 a month left over for food, clothing, holidays, and unexpected expenses after essential bills and the mortgage—definitely not enough for the five of us! Even thirty-six years ago, it was not enough money. We were going to have to pray and trust God for most of the things we needed.

It had been easy to buy the house, but now we had to live in it by faith. Thus began an extraordinary roller coaster faith journey. What we did not realise at the time was that it was merely preparation for bigger and much more difficult things God had in mind for the future. You could say we were merely cutting our baby teeth of faith.

A book called *Realities* by Basilea Schlink encouraged me in my faith walk. I knew God had brought this book into my life for just this time. This group of nuns prayed for everything they needed, from bricks for their building, which were impossible to get just after the war in Germany, to more insignificant things, such as paperclips for the office. I saw that God was interested in even the minutiae of our lives and He loved and honoured faith. I took to heart what Jesus said in Matthew 6:25-26:

> Therefore I say to you, do not *worry* about your life, what you will eat or what you will drink; or about the body, what you will put on. Is not life more than food and the body more than clothing? Look at the birds of the air, for they neither sow nor reap nor gather into barns; yet your heavenly Father feeds them. Are you not of more value than they?

After these exhortations not to worry, He goes on to say in verse 32:

> After all these things the Gentiles seek. For your heavenly Father, knows that you need all these things.

As God's people, we needed not to behave like the Gentiles, the Gentiles in this context meaning people of no faith and having no covenant with God. Greatly inspired by this book, I decided I would make a covenant with God. I declared, "While we live in Sunbury House, Lord, I will not purchase any clothing. Instead, I will pray specifically for items I need and trust You entirely to supply them or to supply the money specifically to buy them. The only items I will buy are tights because they are disposable."

That was that! I felt happy. I thought *My God is no respecter of persons; if He can do it for those nuns, He can do it for me.* I thought very little about it after that until one day when the sole started to come off my shoe. I knew I would have to have a new pair. *Momentarily* it crossed my mind that I could buy some shoes on a credit card, but then I remembered the solemn agreement I had made with God.

I felt I needed a picture of the shoes I was praying for, so I decided to go to Newmarket in my temporarily glued shoes and look in shop windows. I spotted a beautiful pair of black patent court shoes with little bows on the front that looked just right. They were my heart's desire! I leaned over toward them and under my breath said, "I would like some just like that, Lord, please. Thank You very much."

I went home rejoicing; it felt like a great adventure. I had no idea how God might do this miracle, but I was really expecting Him to do it.

Two days later, a woman named Freda knocked on the door. She was new to the village, and I barely knew her. She seemed a bit embarrassed. In her hand was a brown paper bag, which she proffered apologetically.

"My daughter was clearing out her cupboard and found these. They are a lovely, nearly new pair of shoes and she only wore them once because she did not really like them. I don't know why, but as we were clearing out the cupboard, your name just popped into my head. I wonder if you would like them. I do hope you don't mind."

"Mind," I said. *Mind?* "Come in and let me tell you a story!"

Trembling with anticipation, I took a quick look in the bag and was satisfied that God had truly come up with the goods. Can you guess? Yes! There in the bag was a beautiful pair of black patent shoes with little bows on the front, almost identical to the ones I had seen in the shop window. They were size five and a half—exactly my size. They fitted me like a glove, and I was utterly staggered by the similarity of these shoes to the new ones I had seen in the shop window.

I told Freda about my prayer and about how I had come to make it. She was so excited because she realised she had actually heard from God. She felt privileged to be used by God to answer someone else's prayer. We had a big hug and quite a party over a cup of tea.

Sometime later, I needed a new bra and a petticoat. I prayed my specific request, but I thought this might be a bit more difficult for the Lord because they are not the kind of things people would freely give away to someone else. This would definitely be more embarrassing than offering a pair of shoes. One night a week or so later, when I went to choir practice, a woman in the choir said, "My daughter has grown out of these; I thought you were about her size and that they might be useful to you. I do hope you are not offended." Again, in the bag were a lovely bra and a half-slip. They were my size exactly and just what I needed. They looked like they had never been worn. Thankfully she had braved the embarrassment!

As time went on, I began to realise that many of the things I was being given were much more expensive than I could have afforded naturally. They were lovely things such as dresses that had originally cost £70 from Harvey Nichols, a smart London department store. The Bible says that God knows how many hairs are on my head. He was now clearly showing me that He knew every detail of my life and really cared about me personally; He knew my shoe size, my bra size, and my dress size, and what is more, He knew my particular taste in clothes. How awesome is our God!

He always provided at just the right time. I was chasing around getting ready for Giles' birthday party when I suddenly realised I had been so busy that I had nothing clean to wear. I was looking frantically for something I could iron when Nana Maud said, "Oh, there's a bag in the hall from Aunty Dorothy. There is a nice dress in there."

I swooped on the bag and pulled out a gorgeous black silk dress with a large flower print that did not even need ironing. I threw it on and was instantly ready for the party. In the eight years that we lived at Sunbury House, I had a multitude of answers to prayer for everything I personally needed. God's love for us is so amazing.

Cars were also a feature of God's provision for us. When we moved to Sunbury House, we had a trusty green Austin Cambridge Estate—a vehicle fit for carrying numerous animals and children—but one day it was obviously ailing and finally gave up completely. With no spare money to buy a car, we prayed earnestly that God would supply one. As we prayed, the Lord said, "Don't go looking for a car. I will bring you a car. Put some money aside. You will know it when you see it."

I did not know how God would bring us a car or how we would recognize it when we saw it, but we started to put money aside as instructed and did nothing to find a car. One day when I went to the front door, there was a car parked right at the end of our path. As I looked at it, the Lord said, "That's your car."

I ran indoors and said excitedly, "Tony, Tony, our car is parked outside."

"Don't be so silly. How can it be? How do you know it's our car?"

"God spoke to me and clearly said that it was our car!"

There was no doubt; I knew! The owner turned out to be Jamie our American neighbour. I had not recognized it because it was not his usual car. He had just had a car accident and had bought this one as a stopgap while his own car was being mended.

"Do you intend to sell it after your own car is mended?" I asked.

"Yes of course," he replied.

"Well, we would like to buy it. Please would you give us first refusal?"

After a couple of months, Jamie was ready to sell, and we had saved two hundred pounds. He told us that he was willing to sell the car for £250. Disappointed, I said, "it's okay, feel free to sell it to someone else as we haven't got that much money at the moment."

I wondered what God would do. It had been very hard to save two hundred pounds, and God had clearly said it was our car! The following week, Jamie called me.

"You know," he said, "I just haven't got the heart to sell this car to anyone else. I don't know why, but somehow it's your car. How much can you afford?"

We told him we had £200, and he readily agreed to let us buy it for that amount. I told him what God had said and the reason he could not sell it to anyone else. He was flabbergasted that even though he was an unbeliever, God had prevented him from selling his car to anyone else.

The Lord keeps us on our toes by never doing things the same way twice, which of course stops us looking for formulas. The next time we needed a car, God said, "I am going to give you a car."

Lo and behold, one day a friend stopped outside and handed us the keys to a large grey Wolsey automatic. "Here you are," he said. "God has told me to give you this."

Heaven had again shown us grace and favor.

In our early days at Sunbury House, I had a funny incident with a car. God must have a sense of humour. He certainly seemed, at one point in this adventure, to be pulling my leg! It was January 20, Philip's birthday. We had invited a friend named Jill for a little party. When it came time for her to go home to Ely, it was snowing, so I suggested she should stay the night, but she declined because her little dog was alone at home. I set out to take her to Ely, but my car would not start. Not to be defeated, I rang the Baptist minister because he was the only one who might lend his car.

I got Jill home safely, but on the way back just before Stuntney, the car hit a patch of ice and spun around in the road to face Ely again. As the car gently slid sideways in slow motion down the steep bank, landing on its side in the snowy field, a myriad of thoughts passed through my head. My first thought was, *Oh well, if I die, I will go to heaven.* My second thought was, *If I am hurt, God will heal me.* My third thought was, *But I am not going to be hurt because God is protecting me!* Fear never entered my heart for a moment.

I turned the engine off and sat there in the car for a while wondering what to do. I tried to open the heavy car door, which was over my head, by balancing on the steering wheel, but I was just not strong enough or tall enough to keep the heavy door open while I climbed out. I thought that maybe if I rocked the car enough I could make it turn over onto its roof so I could open the door, but I thought that could be too risky. I was trapped. I sat back down again, earnestly praying for rescue. Unknown to me, a group of lads was coming along the road in a car. When they saw my car lights, which fortunately I had not switched off, apparently one of them, had said, "Oh look they are ploughing that field"

"Don't be daft," said his mate. They don't plough in January in the snow"

At that moment, they realised there must be a car in the field and came to look. I cannot say how glad I was to see all these lads come tumbling over the bank, who soon had me out of the car and into the warmth. As they drove toward Soham, I heard the words from Psalm 23 in my head: "The Lord is my shepherd; I shall not want. He makes me to lie down in green pastures; . . . He restores my soul."

"Well, Lord," I said with a chuckle, "thank You, but they were not green pastures, they were white ones!"

The lads asked me what I was laughing about and why I was so calm and happy when I had just come out of a ditch! I told them that I had prayed when I was stuck in the car and they were God's answer to my prayer. I gave them a testimony of God's grace in my life and what I thought God had just said to me. They seemed quite impressed. They were going to take me home to Isleham, but they could not get through because snowdrifts had blocked the Fen road, so they turned back and took me to a friend's house in Soham instead.

As they drove off, I was so thankful. I was conscious of how blessed I was that God had sent these rough angels to help me. What would have happened if they had simply driven past? I could have died of hypothermia in that cold night, and even in the daytime, I would have been invisible to people driving by.

Of course, I was shaken, but I was physically fine. However I felt terrible because Tom's car was now lying in a field, abandoned. When I got to my friend's house, I rang Tony to explain why I was not home yet. I also rang Tom and explained what had happened.

"Don't worry," he said, "we will get Charles's Land Rover and get it out tomorrow." Characteristically, all he was concerned about was that I was okay.

In the morning, they both came with the Land Rover. I took them to where the car was, and they pulled it out with no trouble at all. I was grateful to see that there was only a small dent. I promised that I would pay for the repair, but he would only let me pay half.

I told Charles and Tom the Scripture the Lord had given to me the night before.

"Ah," said Charles, "don't you know that land belongs to Mr. Green!"

He makes me to lie down in *Green's* pastures! What a joke. Was God pulling my leg?

CHAPTER 11

Giving Is Such Fun

A t this stage of our Christian lives, we were beginning to understand more of the Bible and we had heard about tithing or giving 10 percent of our income. We knew tithing was not a requirement as far as New Testament believers were concerned, but we felt it was a good guideline—a starting place for our generosity. But when we could hardly make ends meet using 100 percent of our money, giving away 10 percent seemed a monumental step to take. We were already trusting God for every penny. Money was not abundant, but we always had enough for our needs

I was once witnessing to a young woman who had come for a cup of coffee and some prayer. When I was telling her how wonderful life with Jesus was and how happy He had made us, she said rather sourly, "Well, I'd be happy if I lived in a beautiful house like this!"

I was taken aback. I did not know what to say. I thought momentarily that perhaps she had a valid argument, but in a flash God gave me the answer.

"Oh no you wouldn't!" I said. "It costs a lot of money to live here; if you did not know how to trust God, you'd be worried to death about how to pay the bills!"

I have always found it amazing that God can give just the right words to say when we wait for His answer to come into our heads.

Tithing had never been an issue, and the Anglican Church seemed reluctant to receive our money. When our old vicar had asked us to commit to giving a certain amount by monthly standing order, he refused the amount

I offered and insisted I give less! Eventually I realised that it was more to do with the parish quota than about being mean!

If the church did not want our tithe of £40 a month, we decided we would set up a tithing bank account and give out of it to the church and wherever else we felt led to give. However, we did not have the faith to set aside £40 the first month. We began with £20, then £30, and by the end of three months, we had worked our way up to putting aside £40. The amazing thing was that instead of having less money, we now seemed to have more; somehow our money stretched much further than it had before.

We took on our first Tear Fund child, one of many to follow, and gave to people we knew who had a need. One couple whose need we were able to meet from our fund came into our lives in an amazing way, but there is a lot to tell, to set the scene before I get to the end point which is about giving!

Tony had asked the vicar if there was any way in which he could serve, praying that he wouldn't ask him to swing the incense in the service! Anything but that, Lord! Surprisingly, he asked us both to visit a young man named Jonathan and his wife, Erica. We felt excited about our first mission for the vicar, but when we knocked on the door, Erica invited us in but did not seem terribly pleased to see us. As we sat talking to her, we were aware that her husband was in and out of the house, putting stuff in his car. She was polite but seemed a bit distracted by her husband's activity.

She quickly told us she was into witchcraft and had no interest in Christianity, and we thought this might be why she was so cool with us. What we didn't realise was that her husband at that very moment was actually packing to leave her and go off with another woman. That definitely explained why she was a bit uncomfortable and distracted.

I visited this young woman regularly after her husband left, but it seemed that nothing we said about Jesus penetrated her heart. We eventually lost touch with her because she moved out of the village. I carried this couple on my heart for a long while, feeling that God had a better plan for their lives than the one they were following. I prayed and believed that one day I would have an opportunity to have more input into their situation

For the time being, it seemed that all was lost, but I never forgot her. Imagine my joy years later when I saw her come into a convention meeting we were holding at the City College and watch as she gave her life to Jesus. She was wonderfully saved that day. When I visited her, she told me how she had come to realise the foolishness of witchcraft, and she now knew Jesus was the only way. God had been working in her life all that time, and we had been privileged to be a small part of it. It taught me never to underestimate God's ability to break into a life.

When I heard that Erica's original husband had returned to live in the village with the woman he had left with, I knew God had a plan for their lives too and was sure we were going to be part of it. It all unfolded like a dream!

I needed a cleaner, and I was sure that if I put an advertisement for a cleaner on the post office door, Jonathan's new wife would be the one to respond and bring both parties back into my sphere of influence. I heard nothing straightaway, but a couple of weeks later, I received the phone call I had anticipated. I had never met Sylvia and only just knew her name, but as soon as I heard her voice, even before she had introduced herself, I knew the person calling me was definitely her.

"Hello, has the post for a cleaner been filled?"

Of course, it had not, so she came for an interview. Over the early weeks that Sylvia worked for me, we actually talked more than she cleaned. In conversation, she let on that she had attended a Billy Graham meeting many years ago, and although convinced she needed to go forward for salvation, she had not done so. Within weeks she gave her heart to the Lord, and we set about praying for her husband. God always has creative ways to bring people into His kingdom, and we sought them for Jonathan.

God had just the idea! We needed a stud wall built in one of the bedrooms, and it just so happened that her husband was a carpenter. It was simple! We would employ him to do the work, have daily fellowship with him, and lead him to Jesus. I knew Jonathan was a Bob Dylan fan, and Bob Dylan had recently made a Christian record. We asked him if he would like to listen to it as he worked, and he loved it. We had many conversations during the week he worked in the house, and by the time he had finished the job, he had prayed a prayer to invite Jesus into his heart.

Now here's a further point of the story so far! We knew this couple needed a tape recorder. Jesus said, "Therefore, when you do a charitable deed, do not sound a trumpet before you . . . do not let your left hand know what your right hand is doing, that your charitable deed may be in secret; and your Father who sees in secret will Himself reward you openly." Our plan was to buy the tape recorder and sneak around secretly at the dead of night to put it outside the back door.

A few days later, I saw Sylvia, and she said, "Thank you so much for the tape recorder."

"What tape recorder?" I said as innocently as I could manage.

"Oh come on," she said. "You know it was you."

Of course, I could not lie . . .

We had another go at secret giving when a friend of ours told us his business was in great trouble. He needed a lot of money quickly or he would not be able to continue trading. Knowing that a dear brother and his family were in trouble stirred our hearts. When we got home from hearing this bad news, I stood in the sitting room and looked round at our beautiful suite of Victorian furniture. The delightful lady chair and the gentleman's chair were both upholstered in gold velvet. The very elegant, button-back, rosewood chaise-longue, which Tony had painstakingly upholstered himself in orange velvet were my pride and joy.

The two Victorian chairs had been given to us when we were first married. They came to us from an old lady Tony's mother had cared for. The chaise longue we had bought when it looked like sticks in a box from an antique shop on one of our many shopping trips, looking for old furniture. Tony had gone to upholstery classes to learn how to cover them, so they had more than just monetary value; they had sentimental value too. However, as I looked at them, I knew we should sell them as quickly as possible and give the money away to our friend.

I looked at Tony, who was also looking at the furniture. "Are you thinking what I am thinking?"

He said, "Yes I am . . . let's do it."

I had recently met a Christian antique dealer, so I rang her immediately and asked her if she would look at the furniture with a view to buying it. We told her what we wanted to do, and she offered us £1000 in cash—a very fair price. We put the money in an envelope and waited for nightfall. We walked down the road, crept up to the door, and slipped the envelope through the letterbox. It felt so good . . . such great fun. No wonder the Bible says, "It is more blessed to *give* than to receive!"

A few days later, a beautiful thank you letter came from Brian. *Oh no!* we thought. *How could he possibly have known we were the ones who gave it to them?*

He said, "I knew it was you because I do not know anyone else who would have the faith to do something like this."

Crumbs—we were so bad at secrecy.

We also helped other believers by lending them teaching tapes and realised that we needed a proper tape copier to make the copies more rapidly. We approached various ministries to ask if we could do that without infringing copyright.

We had learned about sowing seeds to release our faith for something. The argument was, if you want carrots, you must sow carrot seeds—like produces like—so we knew we needed to sow something like a tape copier. The tape copier would cost £300, which seemed like a fortune to us. Our seed was that tape player, which Jonathan and Sylvia needed. It cost £30, which was a tenth of the value of the copier. We waited patiently, firm in our faith for £300.

When we had received £50, we sent the deposit to the company. We wrote a check for the remaining amount of £250 and put it on the mantelpiece. The money came in so many different ways. We had agreed with the Lord that whatever extra money came in during the following weeks would be for the copier. A couple of people gave us money because they knew we needed the copier, but other money came from people who said, "God spoke to me to send you this money." They knew nothing.

By the time all but £50 of it had come in, the company was asking when we were going to take delivery, so we took the remaining money out of our account and sent it off immediately. We knew God would be faithful to supply the remainder before our actual point of need.

A week later, a young man rang us. "Have you got the copier yet?"

"Yes," I said, "we just posted the check for it last week."

"Oh blow," he said. "I am really disappointed because I was going to give you £50 toward it."

"Ah," I said, "you are not too late. We were actually £50 short!"

He was happy to give it, and we were most happy to receive it because that was half our mortgage money!

As we gave more, God began to bless us in greater measure. We used to have a running joke with Fred the husband of our friend Doris. He had a phrase he would trot out all the time: "Moderation in all things, dear boy. . . moderation."

"Nonsense Fred," Tony would say. "I am extreme: extremely blessed, extremely healthy, and extremely happy!"

Sometimes living by faith was scary. We loved the rewards and the benefits, but we did not do it for the benefits or the rewards. We did it because we knew faith pleased God. We simply lived to please Him.

CHAPTER 12

Being Naturally Supernatural

In Sunbury House, supernatural answers to prayer became the norm, mostly because we had *so* many needs we could not meet naturally. One of the first things I did was to find my fruitful mission field. I could not waste any of my limited time. As I prayed, God showed me a picture of the bungalow across the road, so I knew somebody there must need Jesus.

One Wednesday evening after tea, I knocked on the door and said, "Hello, I am Margaret, your new neighbour."

Dorothy greeted me pleasantly and invited me in. She turned out to be a new Christian who attended the Baptist church. I was disappointed she was a Christian, but I knew God had sent me there. I popped over every Wednesday after tea.

Her husband was an unbeliever who made himself scarce when I was there, but Wednesday was the night when her unbelieving son visited. He remained in the room with us, fascinated, while Dorothy and I chatted eagerly about Jesus and our answers to prayer. Every week he became hungrier and soon gave his life to the Lord.

Next door was a house rented by people from the Lakenheath American base. They changed often so they provided a constantly new and challenging mission field. One couple who came to live there were Mormons. We talked about God, but I did not press the issue. I felt very strongly that I did not want to get into a religious battle, entering into a doctrinal war of words, each trying to convert the other. The wife came to The Barn at Snailwell with me once and was somewhat fazed by it. In this instance I knew my life would speak for me louder than any words. During their tenancy, they saw many people come and go from our house and knew we had helped them.

When this neighbour came to say good-bye, she said, "Margaret, when I came here, I set out to try to convert you to the Mormon faith, but the more I saw of your life, which speaks so much of Christ, the more I decided I had nothing to say; it was I who needed to learn from you. Thank you so much for being such a witness."

Other families who came and lived next door received Jesus. We were thrilled when Claire, a daughter of one of the families who were already Christians, committed her life to Christ with us. She has since become a Presbyterian minister.

Our finances were so limited, and we had to pray for anything extra we needed. Fortunately we were able to avoid many vets' bills by prayer and as a result we had some great healing miracles with our cat, our dog, our goats, and even a hamster!

Bilbo, our dog, had a miraculous healing from what must have been food poisoning. One day he began to drag himself about and had lost his usual bounce. One minute he was listless, shivering, and miserable in his basket, and the next moment, after we had prayed for him, he was bounding about, his usual self. It was an astonishing result.

God also healed one of our cats of a condition that was causing her fur to drop out. We asked the Lord for a word of knowledge as to what was causing the problem. He told us it was an allergy to something in her food. After we prayed against this allergy, all her fur grew back and never fell out again, even though we didn't change her food.

Years later when we took three new kittens to the vet to be spayed, when we collected them, the vet apologized profusely. "If I had seen the state of this cat's mouth, I would not have bothered to spay her. She has cancer in her mouth, and she will not live. Perhaps you'd like me to put her down when you bring them back to have the stitches removed."

We were sad because she was such a pretty cat. We had called her Baby Zane Grey or Baby for short. We decided to ask God to heal her. We prayed over her fervently, rebuking the cancer, and thought no more about it until we went to the vet. As he took the stitches out, he said, "Which cat was it that had the problem in her mouth?"

"This one," we replied.

"Well there's nothing wrong with her now!"

He did not much like our idea about how it had happened and casually dismissed it.

Another time we needed a miracle for our beautiful brown goat, Gracie. For a few days we noticed that she was off her food, and then she began staggering about in a most alarming way, and also seemed to have become blind. The vet immediately diagnosed her with meningitis. Gracie was so very sick that the vet suggested we put her down straightaway. We were about to agree when I felt a check inside my heart and instead asked the vet to return in three days. I thought, *Hang on; if this was a person, we would not be thinking about putting them down. We would be praying for a miracle.*

We called our friends that evening and asked them to join us in praying for Gracie. We all solemnly knelt in the goat shed where she was lying down looking really poorly and laid our hands on her, fervently asking God to heal her. In the morning, we were amazed to see Gracie walking normally around the paddock, looking pretty okay. By the time the vet came back, she looked really well. The vet was amazed but heard our testimony skeptically, although the evidence was clearly there before all of our eyes. It is very strange though how reluctant people were to accept the explanation we gave as to why there was such a change! To us it was just a normal part of our lives because we had trusted God with everything in our lives.

Success with our animals boosted my faith for praying for people. However, I think it is probably easier to get a miracle with animals because although they do not have any faith they don't have any unbelief that blocks them from receiving! God never failed to show His goodness and kindness in using us to help those who mattered to us.

One instance stands out in my mind. A pregnant friend who was a backslidden Christian really did not want to talk with me about God at all so I began to avoid the subject. One day when I was praying for her, the Lord shocked me by saying, "If she does not repent, her baby will die!"

So I stepped up my prayer for her, knowing her heart was too hard to hear what I had heard from God and sure that her heart would harden more if I shared it with her. However, I was sure God was going to do something because otherwise there would have been no point in Him telling me about it. I knew that this dire warning must be a sign of His love and His desire to see her safely delivered.

One day, just before the baby was due, she came to see me. "Margaret, will you pray for me? I need to get right with God."

I was so relieved that she had come to me, but I still did not have God's permission to share the thought that he had given me. She repented and invited Jesus to take hold of her life afresh and we rejoiced together. The following week, she went to the hospital for a routine appointment. While she was there, she began to bleed profusely and was immediately delivered by Caesarean section. She had undiagnosed placenta previa, and if she had not been at the hospital at that time, both of them could have died.

When she next came to see me with the new baby, she suddenly said, "Do you know, Margaret, I believe that if I had not repented, my baby would have died."

I was then able to tell her what God had said to me and how much I had prayed for her to return to the Lord. We cried and again rejoiced together.

Our animals also helped to preach the gospel. We were asked by a friend to give a home to her beautiful donkey called Marigold. We were thrilled to add her to our menagerie. Marigold was cuddly, fat, and adorable but she was also rather willful. She was quite a personality and had previously taken part in nativity plays in Cambridge. One Christmas, in our village church, she trod the boards again. Later she took part in one of our musical productions, again carrying the precious cargo of the Virgin Mary. She seemed to enjoy it immensely, especially if there was a good supply of Polo mints in Joseph's pocket.

However, she was a mixed blessing. It was fun when I took the children to school on her back or for a walk down the drove, but I became rather nervous of her, especially after she chased and grabbed Ben by the flesh on his back. Our neighbours were not always so blessed by her behavior either. After one of our neighbours had come home one night from a party at three o'clock in the morning, Marigold had greeted him. . . loudly. In the daytime you could hear her very loud and friendly, "Hee-haw! Hee-haw! Hee-haw!" right across the village, so you can imagine that in the silence of the night, it was much worse. We didn't hear it because we were fast asleep on the opposite side of the house from the paddock, blissfully unaware.

We were soon made aware of her errant behavior because early the next morning, I was awakened by a call from a very irate neighbour, who before slamming the phone down yelled, "Your donkey woke me up at three o'clock last night, and your cockerel woke me up at four!"

Sometime later we found our cockerel dead in the yard. The angry neighbour had obviously had enough. We had to shut Marigold in the barn at night after that. She hated it and often made a terrible racket, braying loudly in protest and violently kicking at the door of the barn. She had wily ways and showed great intelligence. She somehow learned how to open the paddock gate herself and often escaped, but we always knew where she would be. Most of the time she would be found fifty yards down the road, talking excitedly to some local horses. Previously she had been kept with horses and loved being with them. One time when she escaped and after looking endlessly in all the usual places, we discovered that she had somehow found her way through the back garden, into the house and into our walk-in kitchen larder. There was hardly enough room for her to get in there, so getting her out was really difficult. She was firmly wedged and had to be persuaded to back out.

Marigold was quite an evangelist because she always attracted attention when I took her for a walk. Her presence certainly helped to start conversations and get to know people. I would take her and our dog, Bilbo, down the drove together. Preaching the gospel seemed just a normal part of life for us both. On our usual route was a house that had been empty for a while and Marigold helped me to meet the new owners

Jane, Rob, and their two children had moved into this cottage down the drove. Marigold and I met Jane one day as we were passing the cottage. I quickly realised that I had met Jane briefly about a month before they moved to the village. At the time, I knew it was not a coincidental meeting. God had clearly pointed her out to me, so I knew it was part of God's plan for us to get together, but I just did not know how it would happen. On the night when I had previously met her, I had been speaking at a women's meeting in Soham. I knew almost nobody in the room except the host, but as I scanned the faces in the room, I saw (in the spirit) a light appear over Jane's head. I asked the host, "Who is that lady?"

She replied, "Her name is Jane, and she is about to move to your village."

I was overjoyed to discover that the new occupant of the house was Jane. How convenient that she now lived a mere stone's throw away from us. She lived right on the donkey walk, and I knew I had a divine appointment to meet her.

They came to church regularly, but I could tell that they were not born again. When we got into a Marigold-led conversation, we found them hungry to hear about the reality of life with God. Tony and I visited them regularly. We talked to them about the Lord, and soon they were all born again. They became fervent Christians and good friends.

Our animals always seemed to have a way of attracting attention. Sometimes it was quite accidental. One day I went to the market in Bury St. Edmunds to buy some chickens. I had taken some big cardboard boxes to carry them home in. The day was absolutely sweltering, and I was a bit worried the chickens would be too hot shut in the boxes. Foolishly I decided to leave the lids undone a bit so they could have some fresh air. As I was driving along, suddenly a chicken landed on my head. Within seconds, others had landed on my shoulder, on my lap, on the wheel and on the dashboard. Then another one sat on the seat beside me. They all hopped out of the boxes until the boxes were empty and the car was full of chickens. They were everywhere!

Passing drivers were obviously entertained, and trying not to panic I prayed fervently that I would not see a police car. I dared not stop, and neither did I know what to do except concentrate as hard as I could on the road and ignore the distraction. When I got home, I had to drive as near as I could to the chicken run and hope that when we let them out, we could catch them and put them in it without losing any! I think I was much more hot and bothered than the chickens, who were reveling in their newfound freedom.

There were many wonderful spiritual lessons I learned at this time about how God works in our lives and how He organizes things so cleverly, but I also learned a painful lesson about submission to authority. The vicar had proposed putting a rood screen in the church to separate the chancel from the choir. There had been one there at some time in the past, and he was eager to see it put back so the church might be restored.

The Peyton family, who had massive and magnificent family tombs in the church but who now lived in America, had offered to pay for it. However, most of the church congregation felt it would spoil the lovely openness the building enjoyed and that it would make the officiating vicar, behind the proposed big screen, seem an awfully long way away.

I was quite an activist and felt militant about it, so I didn't think twice about getting signatures from church people and wrote a letter to the bishop to tell him we did not want a rood screen. I asked him not to grant the faculty. That felt fine until I realised that not only had I done this disrespectfully behind the vicar's back—an act that was sneaky and unkind—but that I had also usurped his authority. When God revealed this to me, I knew He was not pleased with me. I felt dreadful about it and felt even worse when the faculty was turned down and everyone rejoiced. My victory turned to ashes because I knew that I had acted in an unworthy way for a servant of God. The godly way would have been to pray and trust the Lord to work it out. It was not for me to take it into my own hands. God cares when we are disrespectful to authority, even when they do something we think is wrong, unless, of course, it is morally or biblically wrong.

I received a similar rebuke from the Lord years later in connection with a new vicar, whom regrettably I criticized openly. What is more, one day when I was busy criticizing him in my heart because I felt he was holding up the work of God in the village through fear, God broke into my train of thought. He said, "Margaret, change your attitude and stop being critical of this man. Trust me, I am able to make my servant stand."

Ouch! I was deeply convicted yet again! There seemed to be so many times when I was convicted of my ungodly attitudes. My mind obviously needed a great deal of renewing!

Our provision over the years came sometimes by supernatural guidance but also through natural earnings when I was able to use my gifting as a teacher. Various jobs came my way just at the right moment, but significantly, always after we had asked God to meet a particular need. On one occasion, we needed to get the ancient and fragile top-floor ceiling of our house re-plastered. It was old goat-hair plaster, and it was very uneven and wavy. It looked rather like a seascape, and it was slowly falling off. We knew it would cost a great deal because both rooms would have to be re-boarded as well as plastered.

I prayed and asked God how He wanted to supply our need. He seemed to be indicating that He was going to give me a job for as long as it would take to raise the money. I calculated that I would need a job for a year. I went down the road that day to have coffee with a friend. I was sharing with her my conviction that God would give me a job. She said, "Have you thought of asking Roger? He's the headmaster of a school in Newmarket, and he goes to our church. Maybe he has a vacancy next term."

I had not thought of it at all, but immediately I felt in my heart that she had given me the answer. I went home and straightaway rang the school. When I rang first, the number was engaged, so I waited ten minutes and rang again.

"Hi, Roger, I was wondering if you had any vacancies next term."

"Well, how strange you should ring just at this very moment," he said. "If you had asked me that question just ten minutes ago, I would have said that I haven't got any vacancies. However, I was just on the phone with a lady who was going to start teaching here next term, and she was telling me she is no longer able to do so . . . So, yes, I do have a vacancy. Send in your application, and I will let you know when the interviews are."

With unshakable certainty, I knew it was my job. I applied, and by the time the interview day came, there were actually two vacancies. I sat in the waiting room with three other women, and we made the sort of conversation one does with other applicants—trying to find out a bit about each other without being too obvious.

After we had all been in for our interviews, we were all waiting for the moment when we would know the panel's decision. At last the vicar came out and invited a young girl to go in. I wasn't bothered that it wasn't me because there were two vacancies. However, when he came out again and invited another woman to go in instead of me, I became somewhat perturbed. *What's going on, Lord?* I said in my heart. *This is my job!*

A few minutes later, Roger's head popped around the door. "Margaret, could you come in please?"

When I stepped into the room, he explained that the woman they had appointed was unable to start until Christmas, and he asked whether I would I be prepared to do the job until she could start. I readily agreed and started the term with a lovely infant class in a delightful Church of England school where God was honoured. The head and deputy, as well as one other teacher, were all lovely Christians. We had weekly prayer meetings to pray for the school, the pupils, and the other members of staff, which bore wonderful fruit. Teaching there was such a joy.

While I was teaching at the school, I had some remarkable answers to prayer. One little boy was so miserable every single day. When he came into the classroom, he clung to his mother until the very last moment and then continued to cry for ages. School life was obviously a great trial for him. I prayed and asked the Lord what to do. The Lord told me that I should pray against a spirit of rejection and that I should break a connection with his mother because she had been the same when she had gone to school. After that, I should ask God to heal him and bless him with a joy in coming to school.

I did all of these things, and it was so wonderful to see him come into the classroom cheerful. His mother remarked to me after a few days how amazed she was by the change in his behavior. I told her that I had prayed about it and asked her tentatively if she had been like that as a girl.

"Oh yes," she said. "I was just the same."

Jackpot! I told her that God had told me that she had been just the same but God had set him free from that inheritance. She was very grateful.

However, it was not all straightforward. One member of staff seemed very hostile to Christianity, and even though she tried to cover it up with a thin veneer of pleasantness, she seemed particularly hostile toward me. The design of the school was an open plan, which was pleasant but had some disadvantages, for example when other classes were noisy. Maybe she thought my class was too noisy.

Toward the end of the term, I wondered how God was going to keep me in there for the rest of the year as He had promised. The probationer who was appointed the same day as me was obviously in dreadful trouble and very unhappy because she could not control the children. Despite having help from other staff, we could all hear the children running rings around her.

During the school holidays, she suffered some kind of breakdown, and there was no time to advertise the post. Roger rang me and asked if I would complete the year in her place.

Later Roger admitted that he should have given the job to me all along, but he had not done so because he had felt threatened by my strong Christian witness. In the end, I stayed much longer than a year, and he was very glad he had employed me.

I did get into a bit of trouble though. During an RE lesson, one of my children asked me if God answered prayer. I felt I had to be truthful and say yes! A few days later, I had a summons to meet with the vicar and the headmaster because they had received a complaint from a parent. The child had told her mother that I had said God answered prayer and she was praying for her daddy (who had left them) to come back.

Sadly, Mummy did not want that and had complained to the one anti-Christian teacher in the school. This teacher took delight in shopping me, oddly enough, to the vicar! Hiccups aside, this lovely job was a great experience for me, and the extra income meant we could finally arrange for the re-plastering of the top story of our house. My very strong brother-in-law, who at that time was out of work, came up from Kent and ripped all the old stuff out for us, and the plasterer did a wonderful job. The whole top floor of the house looked really lovely.

CHAPTER 13

New Home; New Vistas

When we bought Sunbury House, one of the mortgage requirements was that we decorate the outside of the house—a big task. It wasn't easy to paint because it was pebble-dashed, which of course was not the correct period finish for the house.

St. Matthew's Thursday night Bible study in Cambridge had become an oasis for us because there was currently no Bible teaching in our own church. We mentioned to the vicar that we needed help to paint our house, so during the notices, he suggested people should come out to help us the following weekend.

Six people arrived that Saturday ready for action. As we set to, rain started to fall, so we all came inside and prayed and boldly commanded the rain to stop. We were reluctant to do this because there had been a drought and rain was needed badly, but we didn't want it to hinder our work that day. When we went outside again, we were amazed to find that it was still raining but not in the area immediately around the house; the house was in a rain-free bubble. We finished the painting with great joy, marveling at the grace of God, whose answer was ideal. At least we had not stopped anyone else from having rain.

Sunbury House was always full, and we could have taken twice as many people as we did. We did not seek people out. They just somehow turned up, and we simply trusted God to bring the right people. We had a constant trickle of residents of all shapes and sizes with varying needs and gifts. Life was certainly never dull.

A loving Christian family was so far our only qualification to help others and of course the love of Christ in us, which gave us the desire to see people set free. It was such a tremendous privilege to be part of the ongoing work of God in people's lives, but our guests often put a great deal of pressure on our marriage. They also competed for our relationship with the children.

We were far from perfect and knew we needed help too. One night God said to me, "Come into the sitting room." When I went into the room and sat down, He said, "Find Isaiah 61; this is what I want to do for you, and this is what I want you to do for others."

I was astounded because when I looked it up, I found that it said:

> The Spirit of the Lord God is upon me, Because the Lord has anointed me To preach good news to the poor; He has sent me to heal the broken-hearted, To proclaim liberty to the captives, And the opening of the prison to those who are bound; To proclaim the acceptable year of the LORD.

Puzzled, I said, "Thank You, Lord." I trusted that He would reveal how He would do it. I did not know this was the Scripture Jesus used in His first sermon in the synagogue to validate His ministry and that God was actually offering me the same ministry as Jesus!

Later that year at an NCT meeting in Ipswich, I met a vicar named Ian Davidson. In the morning I was speaking about breast-feeding, and he was to speak about counseling in the afternoon. As soon as I had opened the invitation letter, Ian's name jumped off the page. God said, "This man will show you what I want you to do with your life."

I waited for that day with a mixture of trepidation and excitement. Just as I had finished my talk, Ian came in. Immediately I knew he was the man, but how was I to approach him? What should I say—"Hello, God has told me you are going tell me what to do with my life"? I shrank from that direct approach!

We did have a brief conversation, but I could not bring myself to say anything about hearing God because sometimes people—even vicars— think you are mad when you admit God talks to you. Afterwards I felt foolish that I had been such a wimp, so I wrote to him. My letter began,

"Perhaps you will think I am mad, but I cannot help it." I then explained what God had said to me and asked him, "What is it that you are involved in that God wants me to do?"

No reply came, and I was tempted to think he had dismissed me as a crackpot. But when I could bear it no longer, I steeled myself and called him.

"Hello, Ian. My name is Margaret Cornell. Do you remember getting a letter from me?"

"Oh, Margaret, I am so sorry! I have been so busy moving, and I just could not find the time to reply. Actually, we are involved in two things. First, we are buying a big house and going into community with another family; and second, I am involved in a ministry of healing. The group I work with is called Wholeness through Christ. It is a ministry of healing of all kinds, including inner healing and deliverance. The Scripture we take for the basis of what we do is Isaiah 61, 'The Spirit of the Lord is upon me. . .'"

How incredible! I was completely dumbfounded! Community and *my* scripture! God had promised us that we would buy a big house and have a community. We also knew we would have a healing ministry to others that would make a great difference to their lives

I made an appointment to see him and his team to sample the healing ministry, but as the day approached, I was terrified because I needed to share many things about myself that I would never have told a soul. On the road to Ipswich, I nearly turned around and went home! But I need not have been afraid, because from the first moment I met them all, I felt unconditional love.

I left the session relieved, knowing I had been set free from some things that had been real difficulties in my life that I am sure created difficulty for other people too! I was so glad to untangle my heart. Tony also reluctantly went for counseling and came back very happy. The results of these sessions made me eager to learn how to do it for others, so when we were invited to go on a training course and learn how to minister to others, we gladly accepted.

We attended a couple of courses and then joined the team. The healing and deliverance ministry was a tool God was placing in our bag. For years we had had a constant stream of people coming into our lives who were bound in disastrous life patterns that were sometimes mental, sometimes physical, sometimes spiritual, and sometimes a combination of the three. At last we had a deeper way of helping that, combined with the family's love and support, was able to make a greater difference in people's lives. The ministry dealt with sin that was still a persistent problem in people's lives, demons that needed to be cast out, wounds that needed to be healed, and bondages that needed to be broken.

Mostly these sessions were very orderly and quiet, but occasionally deliverance ministry sometimes brought with it some pretty hairy moments when people freaked out. On one occasion a man in the grip of a demon suddenly grabbed a paper knife that was in the room and went for Tony, intending to stab him, but the name of Jesus stopped him in his tracks. Another time, when a demon manifested, the person tried to bite Tony's leg! We found that severe traumas in people's pasts often gave place to these evil influences. The devil always takes advantage of people when they are vulnerable, especially when they are children. Words of knowledge often showed the root of the problem, which made the job much easier.

At the end of each training course, everyone received prayer from the whole group with prophetic words. One such word came to us: "You will have a very large house and a community of people." Someone else said, "I see a large, oval dish. It has rice on it and new potatoes all around the edge of the rice. When you see a dish of food like this in your house, it will be a sign to you that you are in the right place."

My immediate thought was that this was very unlikely to happen because I would never actually serve rice and potatoes at the same time. However, we stored these words away in our hearts and got on with life. Once again community and that large house were mentioned!

Often we traveled to where the people needed our ministry. On one occasion I had mislaid the address and phone number of a family I was to visit in Ipswich as well as the instructions about how to get there. I decided to set off and simply pray that the Lord would take me there supernaturally. I knew God guided me in all situations, but one day I found His directions to be better than a GPS! When I got to the city, I listened carefully to what He was saying: "Turn left here, turn right there, go to the next T-junction and turn right." I carried on until He said, "Draw up outside the house on the right." I got out of the car and knocked on the door of the house where I had stopped. Amazing! I was at the right place.

God's instructions can save our lives. I was driving to the top of our road one day when I heard Him say, "Slow down and pull back." As I slowed and pulled back, a huge lorry came around the corner and crossed onto my side of the road in such a way that my car would have been hit by it. I am so thankful I heard God speak and even more thankful that I obeyed!

Another time I was hurrying home for lunch with three hungry boys. As I passed a friend's bungalow, I heard God say, "I want you to go and knock on that door."

The boys were hungry, and it was impolite to call at lunchtime, so I said, "Surely not, Lord . . . not now." However, I felt Him urging me insistently.

I knocked on the door and found Mary, who was heavily pregnant, in floods of tears. We settled the children, and over a cup of tea, she explained. She had been out walking the dog, and her dog had run off and killed someone's chickens. Being pregnant, she was probably more upset than she might have been. I explained that God had told me to call, wanting her to know He loved her. I was amazed that despite this demonstration of God's love and other opportunities in the years that followed, nothing seemed to touch her. As far as I know, she has remained an atheist to this day.

Since I was born again and filled with the Spirit, ministry has been a normal way of life. I always pray for divine appointments wherever I go, and airplanes and trains are ideal places to meet and witness to people. Several incidents stand out in my mind.

There was the Egyptian I met on a train going to London. He told me he was the curator of a museum in Cairo and would be returning to Egypt soon. In conversation I remarked that I was going to London to learn how to help women to relax during childbirth as part of training to teach antenatal classes.

Explaining that he had great problems with tension, he said, "Would you teach me how to relax?"

Without hesitation, I decided to trust him and said, "Of course I will. Here is my telephone number. If you would like to come to my home, I will teach you what I know."

I never imagined he would take me up on it. . . but he did! He rang and arranged a day to come. I taught him the relaxation techniques and of course, the gospel.

One day again on the train from London to Ely, I took out my Bible to read. After a while, a young woman sitting opposite me bent forward and with shining eyes said, "Are you a Christian?"

"Yes," I said, "I am."

"So am I."

There ensued an enthusiastic and natural conversation about our Christian experience. Out of the corner of my eye, I could see a young man on the other side of the carriage looking very interested. When the young lady got off at Cambridge, the young man immediately leapt over to the seat in front of me and said eagerly, "I couldn't help overhearing what you were saying. Can you tell me how to become a Christian?"

I could indeed!

Then there was the young woman who approached me as we stood in the booking line for the plane in Tenerife. I had gone to the ladies' toilet, and she thought she had seen me fill a plastic bottle with tap water, so she said, "Excuse me, do you know that it is not drinking water in the taps?"

I assured her that I did, and when we got into a conversation I learned that she was absolutely terrified of flying and had never flown without freaking out in some way. The airline staff had been made aware of her difficulty. She was obviously God's appointment for the day, so I said to her, "Sit next to me and you will be fine."

For the whole of the four hour flight I held her hand, talked to her, and prayed with her. God even gave me a word of knowledge about where the fear got into her, which I wove into the conversation. It was an ideal opportunity for the gospel witness and a demonstration of what God can do. She was very impressed that she was able to endure the flight happily and peacefully, with only a few moments of obvious anxiety when there was some turbulence. But as soon as she tensed, I said, "Look at me. . . look me in the eye. . . you are safe. . . you are fine." And she *was* fine.

Life is an adventure to be lived in Christ. We need to grasp it eagerly with both hands.

CHAPTER 14

A Significant Visitor

A young woman named Janet was sent to our home by the Mothers'
Union "Away from It All" scheme. I would never have called our
home a peaceful or quiet place, so the scheme's suggestion of
it being away from it all seemed like false advertising as far as we were
concerned. We gladly agreed to take her, but I wondered how we could live
up to Janet's expectations. At least she would have a rest from her children
because they were going to be looked after by somebody else.

On the day Janet was due to arrive, we received a phone call to say that
the arrangements for the holiday for her four children had fallen through.
We were asked if we would take the children as well. Well, that would
certainly not make it away from it all! But of course, our big hearts said yes!

At that time, we had five adult residents because we had three guests
and we also had three of our own children. With Janet and her four
children, there would be a total of six adults and nine children in the house.
When I voiced my doubts about the amount of peace and quiet she would
experience, they assured me that just being in a new environment, away
from the pressures of her own life's struggles as a single parent, would be a
wonderful rest for her.

Janet was a lovely young woman but wound up, tense, and lonely. She
talked nonstop, which was very wearing indeed because my ear was the one
most available to her. When I could get a word in edgeways, I talked to her
about Jesus. The children seemed to have a whale of a time and were what
you might have kindly called rambunctious. They certainly gave *us* no rest
or peace!

It might not have been so bad if it hadn't been such a roasting hot summer. Tony was also in the middle of laying a crazy paving patio outside the back door. For the first week, this conflicted somewhat with the free movement of the children in and out of the house, so we went to the park and did various things that got us all out of the way.

However, a crunch moment came when I wanted us all to go for a picnic on the Newmarket Downs. It was a bank holiday Monday, but Tony was adamant that he wanted to finish the job even though it was ninety degrees and the sun was beating down mercilessly on his back. That was not the only thing that got overheated. We had a rather angry exchange about the whole issue, which many would have rightfully called a row!

Nevertheless, in the end Tony worked on the patio, and I took everyone to Newmarket. I felt utterly miserable. *Well*, I thought, *bang goes our Christian witness*. When we got back, Tony and I had a hug and a kiss and apologized for our angry words. Life continued as normal and as harmoniously as it could in the midst of a whirlwind. Toward the end of her stay, Janet came downstairs after having been upstairs for a rest and said, "Oh, it's so peaceful here."

Peaceful? Was she on another planet?

"You know," she said, "I never sleep at home, but I have slept peacefully every night here. You have something so special in your home."

We happily agreed that indeed we had something really special. We knew the presence of Jesus in our home had made the difference. Whatever our imperfections may have been, Jesus, the Prince of Peace, was our peace, and He made His presence known.

Janet continued to amaze us when she said, "What impressed me most of all was when you had that row. If my husband and I had rowed like that, we would not have spoken for weeks, but you just forgave each other and carried on as normal, just being really loving and kind to each other."

Our amazement must have clearly shown on our faces because she then asked us to pray with her to have Jesus in her life too. We were so thrilled. What is a couple of weeks of extra noise and pressure and a few broken goat-shed windows compared to a soul won for Christ? Just after she invited Jesus into her heart, she also asked us to pray for the healing of her back. It had troubled her for years. God healed it instantly.

Janet also turned out to be a blessing to us long after her holiday. In June 1978, the year after she stayed with us, she invited us to her wedding. It was rather short notice, and it caught us at a point when Tony only had one old suit to wear, which had seen better days. I had nothing special to wear for a wedding and neither did the children. I was also feeling really exhausted. All those things made me dither a bit over the decision of whether to go. However, love for Janet won through, and we went, though I thought we all looked terribly scruffy.

We joined in the group photos, but when the photographer asked us if we wanted a family shot, I said a firm no. I did not want a permanent record of us all looking so awful. I could not believe the cheek and persistence of this man, who in the end asked us three times, the last time almost begging us to allow him to take the photo.

Reluctantly, we all lined up for the man to take the photo. It is a terrible photo, and we do all look terribly scruffy. Later events, however, made me want to hug this man and tell him how glad I was that he was so unashamedly persistent in wearing us down. We did not know it, but two weeks after he took this photograph, our lovely little family would change forever.

It was this photo that made Janet such a significant visitor for us.

CHAPTER 15

Sunbury Mixture

Our home's residents were many and various, and thus, we led a colourful life. Liquorice Allsorts have always been my favorite sweets.

Cynthia and Adrian had moved to Sunbury House with us, but they did not stay very long. Once Cynthia's mother had seen the beautiful baby, she changed from being a disapproving parent to a proud grandparent! Cynthia was soon reconciled to and reunited with her family. She then moved back to their area. We missed her a lot.

Jack was a single young man, a committed Christian, who was with us simply because he wanted to live in our village to attend the local Baptist church. He was great fun and became affectionately known as the greedy pantry owl because he would come downstairs for extra supper and cup his hands and blow through his thumbs to make an owl sound, saying, "Whoo! Here comes the greedy pantry owl."

Then there was Matthew, a lovely, gentle young man. He was grieving a broken relationship and much else in his life. We had met Matthew at St. Matthews church in Cambridge, where he was playing in the music group. He had only come to our house initially for the day with a group of others to help paint the house. He stayed for tea and then for the night. . . and then for another night. After that, he went home, fetched his clothes, and ended up staying with us for two years.

He had existed for years mostly on a terrible diet of black coffee and cigarettes. When he came to us, he was still smoking sixty cigarettes a day. God soon delivered him of that, but he was painfully thin, weighing about six stone. When he first arrived, I am sure he must have had anorexic tendencies because getting him to eat was quite difficult. I used to make him porridge every morning, enriched with vitamins, minerals, and an egg yolk. I would sit on the side of his bed in the morning until he finished it, whether he really wanted it or not. He did grow fatter and healthier in time. He also regained a normal appetite.

Another stumbling block to normal eating was his incredible politeness. As a boy he came from a large family where they were only allowed to have seconds if another member of the family invited them to have some more. The art of getting your own seconds was to ask another member of the family, "Would you like some more potatoes?" The reply was, "No thank you, would you like some?" Eventually we discovered that this was the reason he never helped himself to more and had gone without. We soon told him that this was definitely not the rule in our house!

Occasionally he would have bouts of kidney pain, which put him out of action for a while. However, he was a great cook and made some interesting but extremely smelly chutney. This was nicknamed Corvot chutney because everyone who came into the house would say, "Cor, vot a terrible smell!"

Matthew was a professional musician and a talented composer, so we had lots of fun writing songs. He eventually took over the church choir and turned many choruses into choir pieces, which made them acceptable to many staid Anglican people. He was a bit shy, so he would only practice his violin in the cellar. The sound came up splendidly through the floorboards, so we were able to enjoy the concert anyway. Eventually Matthew moved out into his own flat. He then married a girl in the church. It was a joy to see their blossoming romance and their happiness.

At the same time as Matthew was staying with us, a very large, adorable Canadian woman named Dolores who we also met at St. Matthews in Cambridge came to stay. She had a strong, expansive, loving, but slightly larger-than-life personality. She came with her two children, Francis, who was ten, and Stevie, who was two. Although she was an extremely beautiful woman, she was very overweight. She weighed well over twenty stone. At the same time as I was feeding Matthew up, I was also trying to keep Dolores from eating too much by helping her stick to a diet.

She was great fun, and she soon christened Tony "Beaver" due to his habit of always being busy. Dolores had come out of a terrible lifestyle. She was very broken, but after she became a Christian, she devoured the Bible avidly. She had a great intellect, which meant that although she was only a baby Christian, she knew a lot of stuff. She also loved talking to people about it. Sometimes she frightened people because she always made it clear to them what would happen if they did not accept Jesus Christ as their Lord and Saviour. My brother-in-law was especially nervous around her because she gave him a strong gospel message. It was what she called the straight scoop. She also loved talking late into the night, when her problems and her great sadness seemed to become magnified.

She was not the tidiest of people and at one time developed a bad habit of leaving Andrew's dirty nappies in the bathroom. She was the type of person who could dismiss you with a wave of the hand, so I think we were all a bit nervous to tackle her about it. We wanted to be firm, but we did not want to hurt her feelings. One day Tony was finally elected to broach the matter with her in a gentle way while we all stayed downstairs and prayed for a good result. She actually accepted it all with good grace and diligently cleaned them up after that. No doubt previously her mind had been on higher things.

Stevie, her son, was a curly-headed little darling and a real delight. His favorite food was cake and milk, which he called "coike" and "mawk"! His brother, Francis, did not stay with us long because he went to live with his father. In the end, Dolores left us and was given good council accommodation. She later found a partner, and when she married, she asked Tony to give her away. Over the years, Tony has been the dad, the groom, the best man, and the vicar. The only thing he has not been is the bride!

We never did manage to get Dolores thin, but we know that she received much and gave much while she was with us. She eventually went to America, and we were able to visit her in California, where she had gone to college and studied journalism. It was wonderful to see how much stronger she had become and how she was using her great intellect to her own and God's advantage.

Then there was a profoundly depressed girl named Caroline who was brought to us by social services. She was pregnant by her boyfriend, who was currently in Maidstone prison for rape and was later sent to Broadmoor. It was hard to see what attracted her to this man who had treated her so badly, but she seemed glued to him. She ran up a huge phone bill of hundreds of pounds speaking to him for hours when we were out. After that we got a payphone!

As the prison doors clanged shut behind me when we visited him and the keys were turned, it was a chilling feeling, yet I was only a visitor! I don't know what I expected, but I was taken aback that the prisoners looked just like those who were outside!

Caroline could not relate to us at all, but she could to Bilbo. He had such a sympathetic and attentive manner with anyone who was upset. It seemed like she resented us and hated us—despised us even. Some days I felt so oppressed that I had to run outside and breathe fresh air just to cope with it. We also had to hide the bread knife because a couple of times I caught her in the pantry trying to slash her wrists. She gave us no encouragement to love her, but we did.

Caroline allowed me to accompany her during her labour, something that did create some kind of bond between us. I knew how to help her due to my training with the NCT. Tammy, her baby, was undersized and unhappy, and the amniotic fluid was green; she had not had a good time in the womb. Predictably, the baby simply cried and cried and would not sleep, and Caroline became very exhausted. Part of the reason was the tension in Caroline herself. When I looked after Tammy at night, she slept right though. I did not dare tell Caroline about this because it would have knocked her confidence even more.

Bit by bit, Caroline marginally warmed up to us, but when she left to go to her own council flat, we felt we had really failed. Happily, though, she was reconciled with her mother and went to live near her. The second good thing about Caroline I will save to tell you later because it is connected with another story altogether.

Another young woman named Julia stayed with us for a while. Her children came to stay during the weekends. She was a lovely young woman, but she seemed a bit mixed up, tormented even. It looked like she was about to make a terrible mistake with a relationship. She did not attend our church, and our keenness to help her got us into trouble with her pastor.

One night we prayed with her for deliverance. At the time she seemed very willing to receive prayer, but when her minister heard about it, he was not pleased. He disapproved of us praying with her for deliverance. We suggested that if she did not need deliverance, maybe she was unsaved. This was even less popular with him. He was adamant in his defense of her. He said, "If she is not saved, neither am I!"

He invited Sidney Simms, the vicar of St. Matthews, to have a chat with us about it. Sidney listened to all sides and very wisely said, "Hmm, well if she is a Christian, it seems she could be quite a rebellious one!"

In hindsight, we should have spoken to her minister before praying with her. What we did was unwise. I have been in touch with her recently, and thankfully she has found stability and fruitfulness in her life.

A young man named Jeremy first came to us when he was nineteen after his mother had died, leaving him homeless. His mother had raised him and his brother by herself, which had been quite a struggle. At that time, he thought that his father was dead, though sadly he found out years later it was not true. His father was actually alive.

He was a brilliant pupil—the only one of Tony's pupils to ever get 100 percent in a math exam. He was a committed Christian and an intellectual—a deep thinker and very inventive. He stayed with us during his university holidays for the next eight years and gained three degrees, including one in theology. He then left to study theology in Germany. He was such a lovely chap, and we loved him dearly. We are still in touch with him thirty or so years later. He is now a Reader in Christian Origins at a Kent University and is married to a beautiful, talented woman!

Despite his brilliance and a sharp wit, he had zero confidence in himself. He suffered greatly with depression and could loom about the house like a black cloud waiting to drop its rain. When people are as lovely as Jeremy, it is hard to understand why they think so badly of themselves.

Having people to live with us, and seeking to help them in whatever way we could, often resulted in us getting the help that we needed too. The fellowship of believers can never be a one-way street. We are all in the process of helping each other to become more like Jesus. The Bible says in Proverbs 27.17, that "Iron sharpens iron." On one of his visits, Jeremy brought me one of the greatest revelations I'd ever had about myself, and it resulted in me receiving a great healing in my life.

He also found us a wonderful helper and friend who stayed with us in our hour of need. She was a beautiful and vivacious French-speaking Swiss girl named Giselle. Giselle worked with *YWAM* and stayed with us several times over many years.

For a number of years, I had a growing kidney stone, and the consultant was now saying it was time to remove it. I did not really fancy this. Healing was quite new to us, but we began to think that instead of an operation perhaps God could remove the stone. We decided to ask the new vicar to pray with me, so we met the vicar at the church building with a few friends and solemnly prayed that God would remove the stone. A week after praying, I was in terrible, agonizing pain—worse than any other pain I had experienced. Help . . . was this the stone moving?

This was not what I had expected from healing prayer. It seemed that I was sick *because* we had prayed! Do be careful what you pray!

I began to feel nauseous, and the pain was so terrible. I can only describe it as something like razor blades being dragged through my body. I went to the doctor and told him what I thought had happened. He said, "Nonsense, it cannot be the stone moving. You have a condition called medullary sponge kidney. The stone is in a blind-ended tube. It could never come out by itself."

He gave me some antibiotics. Twice I went back and then demanded an x-ray. On the day that I went to the hospital, I gave Jeremy a ride into Cambridge.

The x-ray showed a very unhappy kidney that was full of fluid and greatly distended. It also showed a large stone halfway down the urethra—stuck! No wonder I had felt so ill. All the toxins that should have passed through this kidney had been flooding back into my body.

The hospital doctor said I must come in on Monday to have it removed in just three days. I wondered how we would manage childcare during my stay in hospital, but when I picked Jeremy up again, the answer from God was already there. He said, "Do you think you could have a Swiss girl to stay with you who I met in Cambridge today? She is a missionary and a nurse and works with Youth with a Mission."

These glittering credentials seemed to be more than enough for our needs. We invited her to come to tea on Sunday so she could meet us. It was love at first sight for all of us! Giselle stayed with us and introduced us to things like real spaghetti and Swiss chocolate. She was so good at telling people the truth in the sweetest way possible, which often ended up with them making substantial changes in their lives. She became a strong friend and still is.

I was still a bit puzzled that a prayer for healing had resulted in me needing to take a trip to hospital. It was not what I had in mind at all. I went to church that Sunday troubled. Should I go to the hospital or trust Him to finish the job?

The Old Testament reading in the service was about Joseph being sold into Egypt as a slave. Because of God's ability in him, he was eventually put in authority over the whole land of Egypt. Later, when there was a famine, Joseph's brothers came to Egypt to ask for help. When they recognized Joseph, whom they had betrayed, they were frightened, but Joseph said to them, "Do not therefore be grieved or angry with yourselves because you sold me here; for God sent me before you to preserve life" (Gen. 45:5).

When I heard these words, I felt God saying, "Yes, go. I am sending you in there. Do not be afraid. There is someone in there I need you to help."

So early on Monday morning, feeling peaceful, I went to the hospital, sure God would show me who He wanted me to help. As I sat in the waiting room, I looked around; was she there? Suddenly a strange light appeared above the head of a woman on the other side of the room, and we exchanged a brief smile. I knew instantly she was the one God meant me to touch, but how would I get to minister to her?

God always has these things in hand! I was put into a ward with three beds. When I turned to look around, guess who was in the bed next to me? The very same woman, of course! Her name also happened to be Margaret. When the nurse had left us and we had both settled in, she turned to me straightaway and said, "Why has God allowed this to happen to me?"

An opening for a conversation about God had been handed to me on a platter. Margaret was very frightened because when her womb had recently been removed, a hole had accidentally been cut in her bladder. She had come back for the damage to be repaired. We talked, shared about God together, and prayed. We even had the chaplain come and give us communion. After the chaplain had gone, she said, "I feel such peace now. I can face it." Praise the Lord!

The next day I had my operation, which they said was simple because they were able to flick the stone out of the little tube leading to the kidney. However I felt very ill indeed and was in considerable pain. I don't know what I expected, but this was definitely not a standard healing!

I was still a bit hazy in my mind about healing, but one thing I had picked up was the power of saying what the Bible says because "faith comes by hearing and hearing by the word of God" (Rom. 10:17). I lay there half-heartedly muttering a few healing Scriptures. It felt pathetic and what I was saying seemed like the biggest lie I could have ever uttered, but I persisted. It went a bit like this: "Jesus bore my sins in His own body on the tree, and by His stripes . . . ouch . . . I am healed."

My mind said, *Oh really?* I had a huge cut across my midriff; there was no keyhole surgery in those days. I was attached to a drip, and a drain came from a hole in my side. I could hardly move. It hurt too much to move. Visitors went away shaking their heads because I was so ill. I had a visit from Jeremy, who kept making me laugh. I was glad to be cheered up, but I begged him to stop because it hurt so much to laugh with a large wound in my side. I received wonderful care from the staff. Being washed gently when I felt so ill by a skillful nurse with a sweet attitude was a wonderful experience.

Late on the third night, I was lying in the bed waiting for a nurse to come and turn off the lights when the most extraordinary thing happened. Jesus came into the room. He stood at the bottom of the bed and touched my feet. Suddenly I felt the power of God like electricity course through my body and leave out of the top of my head. At that very moment, I knew my body was completely healed.

The nurse turned the light off, and I dropped off into a peaceful sleep. In the middle of the night, suddenly I was wide awake. The operation had been on my right side, but now I had searing pain on my left side. Then I heard a sneaky little voice saying, "Aha! There now! Your other kidney's in trouble because it was under so much pressure when the other one was out of action."

I lay there dismayed thinking, *Oh golly, that's right.*

After a moment or two, I came to. Suddenly I recognized that this was the voice of Satan speaking an evil lie. In a moment of weakness, I had nearly believed it! A holy fire of white-hot anger rose in me when I realised the source of this torment. "Devil, in the name of Jesus, you can push off right now. I am a child of God, and I do not have to put up with you!"

The devil is real, and he "walks about like a roaring lion, seeking whom he may devour" (1 Peter 5:8). If we use the authority God has given us, he cannot devour us. I was determined that he was not going to devour me!

Instantly the pain left, and I went back to sleep. When I awoke in the morning, I felt wonderfully warm and comfortable and gloriously well and happy. I lay there basking in this lovely feeling and then decided to test whether it was just a feeling or a reality. I sat up in the bed without using my arms, just pulling up with my stomach muscles—a movement that would have produced searing pain and been impossible the day before. I swung my legs off the bed, stood up, and lifted my hands into the air. I bent down and touched my toes. I slapped the scar. *Wow!* No pain! Nothing!

My new friend in the next bed looked startled and said, "Golly! You *are* better today!"

"Yes," I said. "Jesus came into the room last night and healed me." Then I told the whole story.

I felt so full of energy that despite being still attached to a drip and a drain, I decided to change the water in the huge vase of flowers I had been sent. It was an enormous vase, and very heavy but I was able to pick it up at arm's length with no trouble at all, which again would have been unthinkable the day before. I walked out of the ward and past the nurses' station with the medical equipment I was attached to trailing behind me. I asked the nurse where I could change the water. Her mouth dropped open to see me mobile, smiling, obviously pain-free, and carrying this great big vase. "Over there," she said, pointing to a side room but not taking her eyes off me for a minute.

When I got back into the ward, she rushed to me and said, "My! You are better than yesterday."

"Yes," I said. "Jesus came . . ." And I told *her* the whole story.

At about ten o'clock, the doctor came around with his entourage. "Hello," he said. "How are you today?"

I said, "I have never felt better in my life! I am pain-free and fully mobile, and I would like to go home."

"Ah," he said. "Didn't we do well?"

"Oh no," I said, "I'm sorry, but it wasn't all your doing."

He was taken aback but as I told him the whole story, he was looking at me with a hard, discerning stare. There was a pause and then he said, "Hmm," Then, as if to give himself time to make a decision, he leaned over and looked at the little gold sticker on my Bible that said, "Born again."

"Born again," he said. "What does that mean?"

I launched into the gospel, but after a while, he politely cut me short. "Thanks, but we must move on now. Yes, you can get dressed right now and go home straightaway."

When they had gone the nurse came into the room, and I told her the doctor had just told me that I could go home straightaway. "Of course he didn't," she said. "You must have misunderstood."

She went off to check and came back amazed. "It's true . . . Well, let's get that drip and drain out quickly then."

I did not know how I was going to get home at that moment because Tony was at school and I knew nobody who could collect me at that time of day, but I said to Margaret, "Let's go over into the corner and pray right now because I am going home soon."

We prayed together. As we said, amen together, a third voice spoke. Startled, I looked behind me to see a church member who had come into Cambridge for the Cash and Carry. She had heard how ill I had been and decided on the spur of the moment to pop in and see if they would let her see me. You can imagine that I was really thrilled to see her. God had a plan to get me home

"Hello! I am so glad to see you. Could you give me a lift home please?" Rejoicing we left together

Giselle was shocked to see me back home so soon, especially when she saw how well I was. She said in her sweet French way, "Margaret! You are not behaving at all like a seek personne."

I said, "That's because I am not a sick person!"

What fun I had in the following weeks, witnessing to all and sundry, especially those who had heard reports that I looked as though I was dying. The next morning when the church bells rang for communion, I quickly sped up to the church building, astounding the woman I passed. She was the wife of the senior nursing officer at the hospital who, after visiting me the day before, had gone home with such a bad report.

Oops! I was in trouble though. The doctor called, and understandably he was furious that I wasn't there. Giselle made my apologies, but he frostily demanded that I present myself at the surgery as soon as possible.

A couple of days later, I *was* there when the district nurse came to remove the stitches. I gave her the active testimony—stretching, bending, and jumping. She laughed and said it was utterly amazing because she had never seen anyone behave like that so soon after an operation. I bubbled over with the joy of it all. I told people in the post office and in the streets; in fact, I spoke to anyone I could find who would listen about the goodness of God.

Our vicar was away on holiday, so a local vicar came to take the Mothers' Union service. Afterwards over coffee, I gave everyone my testimony. He looked so rattled that I thought he would run out of the room. He left as soon as he could, which I thought was very odd—that is, until a little while later, when I discovered his wife was a spiritualist medium. Their only son had died, and she told me she often spoke to her dead son. She was not pleased when I suggested as kindly as I could that I believed the Word of God forbade such thing

I had heard that the vicar was usually depressed, and I always wondered if his depression was due to his unresolved grief, or could it be that the spiritual activity in his home was the cause of his depression? Either way, there was certainly a clash of spirits.

My experience with kidney stones since then has always had a supernatural edge. The next time I passed one, I neatly avoided surgery twice because God answered prayer. When the same sick feelings and agonizing pain began, I knew my body was again being poisoned by a stone blocking the way of waste products getting out. For the first time ever, I asked Tony to take me to hospital, where I was admitted. X-rays revealed it! There it was, that little horror—a stone blocking everything up. Once again the kidney was distended.

After a few days of strong intravenous antibiotics, the doctor announced, "What we need to do is puncture your side with a long needle and enter the kidney to let the fluid out."

When he had gone from the room, I said, "Jesus I don't want this!" I was taken immediately to the operating theater, where the doctor scanned the area.

"Well," she said, with surprise "would you believe it! The stone has obviously turned and the fluid is now draining, so I won't have to do the operation after all!" Phew! Eleventh-hour stuff!

The next day after a further x-ray the doctor had another rather unpalatable bright idea. He said, "Ah! The stone is now right down near the bladder. What we will do is nip in through the bladder, go up the urethra, and hook the stone out."

"Jesus!" I said under my breath. "I don't want this either!"

The very next day before they had time to do the planned procedure, the sister gave me a container to wee into. After a few minutes, she returned triumphant with the stone in a little bottle.

"Well, Mrs. Cornell," the doctor said as he sat beside my bed. "You seem to have cured yourself." I was quick to assure him that it was not me and that I believed that God had done it

Earlier this year I recognized the familiar buildup of discomfort that I have come to associate with a moving stone. During that night I lay in bed tossing and turning unable to sleep, experiencing the now very familiar agony. I was just about to wake Tony up and ask him to take me to the hospital when a radical thought came into my head. God is my deliverer and healer, so I should just put my foot down in the spirit, and refuse to think of going to hospital and simply trust God to move this stone just as he had the others. I did not want to be presumptuous or to dice with my health so I asked the Lord for confirmation that this is what I should do.

As I was struggling to hear what God was saying, I suddenly remembered Jackie Pullinger and her book, *Chasing the Dragon*. I remembered how she helped people when they were coming off heroin by making them pray in tongues. While they prayed in tongues, the withdrawal symptoms stopped and they had a pain-free deliverance. Realizing that this was a prompting from God, I began to pray in tongues. I don't know how long I prayed, but as I prayed persistently, the pain lessened until it stopped altogether. I fell asleep, and the next day I woke up feeling great. I passed the stone from my bladder the very next day.

Phew!

CHAPTER 16

Day-to-Day We Work It Out

Another person came to stay in our house, and her name was Delia. She was a local girl and a single parent. She and her two boys stayed with us for a year or so. Delia was a strong believer, doing her very best to live for God. It was not the easiest mix because she was a very clean and tidy person with very strong ideas about how things ought to be. I always felt that our lifestyle didn't quite match up to her ideals. I have never been the most organized or tidy person in the world. However, she did leave us with a lasting mantra about the workings of life, which we have never forgotten: "If everyone *does* their bit, everything gets done."

Delia was not just a receiver; she was a giver too, and she helped in any way she could. She manfully looked after the children, the animals, and the house whenever we went away. She survived happily despite having to call the vet twice on one occasion when we were away because twice the goats had escaped from their pens—*twice!* Those greedy goats had broken into the pen where the food bin was and pigged out, giving them bloat, which, if not acted on promptly, could have proved fatal. It seemed that Satan was intent on attacking any weak point.

Another time, just as we were driving down the road as we returned home from a ministry trip, we watched, horrified, as a chicken escaped, crossed the road, and was run over. Why on earth did the chicken cross the road?

Delia's time with us overlapped with Giselle's for a while. Giselle's accent and English pronunciation caused some laughter. Giselle asked Delia, "Do you like to eat the mice?"

"*Eek!*" screeched Delia. "No!"

"Oh, it is very good. You should try it."

After some exclaiming, spluttering, and laughter from us all, Giselle explained that she meant maize. "You know, like *la farine?*"

We also had a shaggy-looking young man named Mikey stay with us for quite a while. He was a lovable ex-drug addict. No wonder people thought of us as bohemians and wondered if we too were druggies! He was very amenable and cooked and looked after our plants. He christened our cheese plant Elizabeth and talked to her regularly. He was no trouble, but eventually we came to the conclusion that we needed to ask him to move on because he had not shown any interest in Jesus and we needed the room for others who would respond. He accepted it calmly and moved out almost without a word, and as I watched him walk up the road, I felt so sad.

While he was with us, Helen, a young woman who had just tragically lost her husband, came to stay for a few weeks. Early one morning she burst into our bedroom clutching an empty bottle of pills, proclaiming hysterically, "I have just taken all of these."

In one second we were wide awake sitting bolt upright in bed. The ever-resourceful and practical Tony said, "Helen, go to the bathroom and I will come and help you to be sick."

However, she stood there completely transfixed refusing to budge. At the time Tony never slept in pyjamas and was reluctant to get out of bed naked with a lady in the room. But true to his nature, my action man, never one to be lacking in initiative, said, "Oh blow it!" He leapt out of bed and dived across the room to his walk-in wardrobe to find his dressing gown. She didn't bat an eyelid! He took her firmly by the arm, led her to the bathroom, and dispatched me to the kitchen to make a strong glass of warm saltwater, which when she drank it made her very sick.

When Mikey looked at the label on the bottle, he shrugged his shoulders and said, "She's okay. These pills are harmless." We knew he was knowledgeable about drugs because when Dolores had some slimming pills, he said, "Cor, I could get ten bob each for these on the drug market."

During this time, we also privately fostered a little girl called Rene for six months whose lovely mother was a drug addict. She got on well with our boys and fitted into the household very well. Eventually her grandmother came and took her to live with her in Australia, and we kept in touch with them for some time.

David was a very sick and depressed man who stayed with us for about year. David wanted God to help him, but we felt he never really broke through his problems. The heart of his problem seemed to lie in the fact that he only wanted enough of God to be able to get back to what he thought was normal life: the pub and snooker. We saw that people needed to have a bigger vision than their own personal safety or comfort to have breakthroughs of any magnitude. People have to want to glorify God and be part of His answer for the world. He was with us at a time of great upheaval in our lives, which he weathered surprisingly well. A number of years after he left us, we were very sad to hear that he had committed suicide.

David relied heavily on a medication for depression, which caused problems when he took too much of it. On one particular day when he took too much, he fell asleep in the bath with the taps running. It was not until the water came cascading through the ceiling that we realised what was happening, and we had to break into the bathroom to turn off the taps. Despite us making a terrible racket, shouting, banging, and breaking the door down, he was still fast asleep and remained so even after we had drained the water from the bath. We simply covered him with a blanket and let him recover in his own time.

David's forgetfulness also caused a fire. I was away on a course, along with the vicar and his wife, and the first I knew of any problem was when the vicar approached and asked to have a word with me. Since school days when teachers pulled me aside to have a word with me, that phrase has always had the power to strike terror into my heart, so I trembled a bit when he said it. He took me aside, and once we were seated, he said, "Don't worry. Nobody has been hurt . . . but . . ."

The pause between "hurt" and "but" was just long enough to set every alarm bell ringing within me. I thought, *Argh! Nobody hurt. . .* **but what?** *What has happened!*

"There's been a fire at your house."

He explained that the chip pan had exploded and set the kitchen alight. Now something clicked. The previous night when I had called home to talk with Tony, I had heard all sorts of strange noise in the background. I could hear clattering and laughing in the kitchen.

"Who is that?" I said.

"Oh, it's just Mavis and Doris. They have come back with me after the Mothers' Union service and are doing some washing up."

A voice said, "Bye."

"Bye," said Tony

"Who's that?" I said

"Oh, it is just the electrician. He came to fix the kitchen light."

I must be the most unsuspicious woman in the world because I just accepted what he said at face value. I had thought no more about it, but as the vicar spoke to me, it all became crystal clear.

David, the boys, and the babysitter had been upstairs watching TV in the television room directly above the kitchen. David had cooked a meal with chips and had forgotten to turn the chip pan off. Suddenly they all saw smoke coming through the floorboards and heard, "*Boom!*"

David ran downstairs and found the kitchen ablaze. Fortunately, he did the sensible thing; he phoned 999, grabbed the fire extinguisher, and went into the kitchen through the back door. Shutting the outside door behind him first, he opened the inner door to the kitchen and sprayed the stove and other areas that were alight before quickly shutting the door again.

Tony had been leading the Mothers' Union service in the church. When they heard the fire engine go through the village, they all prayed for whoever might be in trouble. Our friend Fred walked into the service and said in his characteristic dry way, "Tony, I thought you ought to know that your house is on fire."

As one man they all dropped to their knees, prayed, and quickly abandoned the service. It was about an hour later that I had called. Tony did not tell me the truth because he did not want to spoil my time away.

The only rooms really badly affected were the kitchen and the dining room, but the whole house was covered with a layer of greasy soot, which took some shifting. God bless insurance companies because they paid for redecoration as well as for someone to come and wash everything from the top of the house to the bottom.

David was still with us when real tragedy struck our lives. Saturday, June 23, was a day of great significance. I was doing a jigsaw puzzle. My parents were with us for the weekend, and I felt tired, bad tempered, and completely out of sorts.

That day Tony had an appointment with the bishop to have an interview about becoming a lay reader. For a long time, I knew very little about the content of Tony's experience with the bishop because events happened that totally overshadowed it.

When we got up that day, we were tired and irritable with each other. Our joint mood ended up escalating into a full-blown argument, though what it was all about I can't even remember. However, my heart locked into a state of stubbornness. When Tony left the house, he wanted to be reconciled, but I would not have it. I suppose it would not have looked too good if the bishop had asked, "And how is your relationship with your wife?"

Tony would have had to say, "Oh fine, but we are not speaking to each other at the moment."

It is to my shame that I did not want to be reconciled and continued to be angry well into the day.

Philip, our eight-year-old son, had been given a beautiful bicycle for his birthday. He asked if he could ride down the road to visit his friend. I thought this would be fine because he was a sensible boy. Besides, he could ride on the pavement most of the way. The village felt like such a safe place that the boys were able to have quite a bit of freedom to come and go.

I decided to pop up to the village hall to attend a fête. I came back to find my mother standing outside the house, anxiously wringing her hands. "There has been a phone call. There's been an accident. Daddy's gone to help."

We waited anxiously until there was another phone call. "Philip has been knocked off his bike. He is unconscious, and he has gone to the West Suffolk Hospital in Bury, St. Edmunds."

As I heard those words, in the spirit I felt a blow to my head and heard a peal of demonic laughter. From then on, there was no doubt in my mind as to who was at the bottom of this act. Then I felt the words form deep down in my heart: "He is dead." I tried to shake them off and think positively, but they would not go away.

We drove to the hospital, praying all the way. I was nervous about what I might see and dreaded seeing him in terrible pain or badly damaged. We arrived at the hospital, where Philip had been put on a life-support machine. He had stopped breathing on the way to the hospital in the ambulance. To all intents and purposes, he had died. I don't suppose it helped that the ambulance took twenty minutes to arrive; it took a further twenty minutes to make its way back to the West Suffolk Hospital.

We discovered the story of what had happened jointly through my father, who had arrived at the scene of the accident soon after it happened, and from Philip's friend—the one he'd been out riding his bike with.

When Philip had gone down the road to see his friend, they had asked his mum if they could go out for a bike ride. She had said yes, never dreaming that they meant to ride very far. They had set out to ride to Mildenhall along the winding fen roads. They had played by the river there until they had felt they should head home. On the way back through West Row, the wind was so strong that they decided, sensibly, to walk for a while and wheel their bikes beside them. After a while, Philip decided to get back on his bike. He rode across the road to get to the side he should ride on.

However, an American car came round the corner at just that moment. Because it was an American car with the wheel on the left side, the driver did not see Philip until it was too late, and she hit him. The car tossed him into the air, causing his head to meet the roof of the car with such force that it cracked his skull.

We walked quietly into the intensive care ward. As I approached the bed, I felt nervous, wondering what I would see, but apart from a mass of tubes, there was not much to see. I went close to Philip. He looked pale and very still. He was breathing evenly, aided by a life-support machine. It was very silent in the ward apart from the eerie sound of his rhythmic breathing. With some relief, I noted that he looked totally normal and unhurt except for a bump on his forehead. He looked as if he was simply fast asleep. He was wrapped entirely in a foil blanket because his temperature was dropping rapidly. We looked hopefully at the monitors that beeped as they monitored his progress, hoping to see some evidence of normality.

The doctor explained that his skull was cracked and the brain was swelling, his leg was broken, and he was gradually losing temperature.

"We are very sorry," the doctor said quietly. "We do not hold out any hope for his recovery."

When we heard the doctor's news, we felt an unnatural calm come over us. We prayed and felt God was very close. The only course we seemed to have available to us was to trust in the one we knew loved Philip and loved us. We truly had such supernatural peace come upon us. It was amazing.

We also knew God is good and He answers prayer, so we did not feel able to accept the diagnosis at that moment.

So we prayed and asked others to pray too. We did not realise at the time quite how many others were praying for us, but eventually we heard that people all over the world were supporting us in prayer. Soon our vicar came to see us at the hospital, along with the Isleham Baptist minister and his wife. It was wonderful to feel their support.

When the vicar arrived, he was quite agitated. He found it hard to understand our peace. It was clear that he had come to the hospital in some trepidation, expecting to find two grief-stricken parents in a situation that would be very difficult to handle. I think he was as surprised as we were by our calmness.

Hour after hour we did everything we could possibly do to help Philip recover. We sat and talked to him and held his hand. I talked to him about everything I could think of and reassured him of the love Jesus had for him and the love we had for him. We read the Bible to him. We played his favorite music tapes with the Christian songs he so enjoyed. Even when people are unconscious, it is said that it is still possible for them to hear. We wanted to take advantage of every possibility, however small.

I was somewhat comforted at this time by remembering a conversation I had had with Philip two weeks earlier. He had said to me, "Mummy, I do love Jesus, and I pray and read my Bible every night."

This was typical of my eager, loving little boy. He was full of enthusiasm for life. He loved cricket and football, climbing trees, and all the normal things little boys love. He especially loved church, where he sang in the choir. He loved going to school. He loved his Bible, and he loved the children's club he attended at the Baptist church, where he shone in his ability to remember Scriptures.

Church was a favorite game of the children at home. They would dance around in the sitting room and sing choruses. Sometimes they would sing an old Baptist hymn:

> Oh happy day, Oh happy day,
> When Jesus washed my sins away.
> He taught me how to watch and pray
> And live rejoicing every day . . . Hallelujah!

I can never hear that hymn without wanting to cry remembering them all and those sweet moments.

They would get the Bible out, and one would pretend to preach. Church was in their blood, and God was real to them. It was fun too. A session like this would often end up with them rolling on the floor in fits of giggles. Those memories were such balm to my soul. We knew Philip had invited Jesus to be his Lord and Saviour. What a comfort to know that even at eight years old, he had his own connection with Jesus, and even if he died, he would go to heaven.

I stayed the night at the hospital, snatching a couple of hours of sleep, and Tony went home to comfort the other two boys. We were praying hard, fervently even, but in hindsight, I am not sure what we really believed. I think we were so young in the faith and so ignorant of the Word of God and the things that belonged to us in Christ that we were probably praying with much more hope than faith.

The true believers we knew and trusted at that time seemed to put great store on the sovereignty of God, which I came to understand later was rooted in Calvinism. They said that God, in His sovereignty, wanted to heal some people and not others, and so we had to find out what His will was in the matter. Therefore, although they were very loving and encouraging to us in one way, in another way they left us with the dilemma of finding out what God's will was. I did not want to go against the will of God, but apart from receiving a direct word from heaven, I did not know how to find out what His will was. At that time, I only knew what I hoped His will was.

God had so often spoken to me, but He seemed distinctly silent at this crucial moment. I told the Lord that if He wanted to take Philip home, it was fine with me because I trusted Him and knew that He knew best. However, I tempered this by telling Him that my preference would be for Philip to be healed and restored, and that if he was restored, I wanted him to be fully healed so he could live a normal life and not a crippled one.

Having slept briefly that night in a hospital room provided for me for a couple of hours, I returned to the ward at about 3:00 a.m. to find that Philips's temperature had continued to drop. The only sign of life he displayed was the flexing of a toe when they stroked the bottom of his feet. I looked at the charts by the bed, eagerly scanning them for some sign of improvement. They were not at all encouraging and only showed deterioration.

Standing by the bedside, I suddenly felt a strong heat come into my hands. I put my hands onto Philip's head, and he immediately began to move. He lifted his head up three times off the pillow, pushing up my hands and pulling his sound leg up. For a second or two, it looked as if he was trying to wake up and get up. I panicked, not really knowing what to do. I knew I was experiencing the power of God, but I just didn't have a clue what to do with it.

However, as suddenly as he began to move, he fell back again, completely still and lifeless. My heart was thumping with excitement; perhaps there was still hope. The nurses who were standing at the bottom of the bed were shocked to see a sudden and unexpected reaction from someone who was so comatose. I found out later that one of those nurses standing there came to Christ because of our witness.

I am so glad the nurses were there to witness this event because otherwise I might have thought that I had imagined it. If I had known what I know now, I would have loudly commanded Philip to get up in the name of Jesus. However, I had no knowledge of our authority in Christ to exercise the gift of healing or miracles.

On the Sunday afternoon, I decided I must go home to see Ben and Giles. Goodness knows what they were thinking and feeling. When I opened the front door, they both ran to the top of the stairs, asking, "Mummy, Mummy, is Philip coming home?"

I felt like I was in a difficult position. We believed God could raise him up and that he could come home, but what should I say? I was reluctant to tell them a lie or mislead them, and I was not sure enough that God was going to heal Philip to say yes. After a moment, I said falteringly, "I don't know . . . I don't think so. He might not come home."

Ben said, "Is he going to die?"

My heart was heavy. I wasn't ready to answer such a confrontational question, especially since we were still holding out hope for a miracle. Perhaps my silence gave him the answer, but what Ben said next immediately changed everything and put a totally new perspective in my heart. Before I could answer his question, it seemed that he had made up his own mind. His face lit up and shone as he said eagerly, "Does that mean he is going to have abundant life?"

Immediately, I felt my heart lift. "Yes, darling, I think he is."

I ran to the top of the stairs, and we laughed, hugged, and cried together—tears of joy mixed with sorrow. I desperately did not want him to die, but in that second, I knew that the only people I would need to feel sorry for in the event of my son's death would be me and the rest of us who were left behind without him. He was going to be fine because he was going to be happy in heaven with Jesus—completely safe with the person I loved most in the whole world. He would be free from the prison of his natural body, free from suffering, and full of the abundant life of God forever. Even more wonderful was the knowledge that we would see him again. One day we would all be reunited in heaven.

When we returned to the hospital, a doctor invited us into a side room. He wanted to talk to us. I felt extremely sorry for him. Obviously he had the unenviable task of delivering bad news. He was nervous and agitated. He asked, "Do you smoke?" We shook our heads. "Oh that's a pity," he said. "It would be a help to you."

"Don't worry," we said. "We are perfectly at peace. We are fine. We have Jesus as our comfort. We do not need cigarettes."

"Oh yes . . . yes . . . er . . . well . . . I can see that . . . Well, what I need to say is that if your son continues to deteriorate, we are planning to turn the life-support machine off at nine o'clock tonight." We received the news like a cold stone dropping into our hearts. After a silence, he said, "If this does happen, we wondered if you would consider donating your son's kidneys."

We gladly agreed. If Philip could not be restored to us but was going to die, then we had no hesitation in wanting someone else to benefit. The doctor explained that it would mean they would have to take the body away immediately and perform an operation as quickly as possible to remove the kidneys and it could be difficult for us.

Suddenly, an inappropriately superficial thought came into my mind. *Oh no, he can't die. I have nothing to wear for a funeral!* In view of the seriousness of the events, it was a ridiculous but very human thought because I did have nothing appropriate to wear! Of course, it would not have mattered to me at all what I wore, but the funeral would be in the presence of all the people of the village, so I knew it was a detail God would take care of.

As the evening wore on, Philip's condition did continue to deteriorate, and so at nine o'clock, with our permission, they turned off the life-support machine. He had breathed his last breath, and his little life was officially gone. Staff members suddenly appeared as if from nowhere. Carefully and quickly they wheeled him away. People spoke in hushed voices, and the room without the machine's noise was eerily silent.

As we stood there in that room, holding hands and watching as the staff disconnected him from the machinery, I think they were a bit worried we were too calm and we might suddenly freak out in some way. I noticed that one of the doctors was watching us quite carefully out of the corner of her eye. We watched sorrowfully, our hearts torn as the staff wheeled him away straight to an operating theater to remove his kidneys, which thankfully would offer someone else quality of life. Later we went into the mortuary to check that Philip looked all right before the boys came in to say their final good-byes. I felt that, for their benefit, they needed to see that he was really gone, even if it was painful; reality is always better than imagination.

When we all went into the room where he was laid out and looked at his body lying there, it was so obvious that he just wasn't there anymore. His body was just an empty shell. We knew the real Philip had gone; his spirit had already gone to glory. It was a bittersweet opportunity to touch his little body lovingly and say a final good-bye. It was very quiet in the room. We could hear just our hushed voices as we reminded Ben and Giles that we would see Philip one day when we all went to heaven. When we came out, they gave us the useless shreds of his clothes in a carrier bag that had been cut off his body after the accident. To them it was just a necessary formality, but to us it was a stark reminder of the reality of our loss—not just the loss of Philip but the loss and enjoyment of everything his future might have entailed in the way of career, marriage, and children. In many ways, the true effects of this loss remain with us to this day. He is still gone. For the boys it was the loss of an irreplaceable brother and a new structure in our family. The loss goes on and on.

Many years later, I suddenly felt curious about what had happened to his two kidneys, and I called Addenbrooks Hospital to see what I could find out. I was so thrilled to find out that two different people had received a kidney from him, and both were now living normal lives.

CHAPTER 17

More than Survival;
Enduring with Joy

I do not know how, without God's presence, my mind and body might have coped with this cruel and terrible blow. Physically, I felt heavy and very tired. Emotionally I felt drained. The pain in my heart was almost physical almost unbearable and threatened often to overwhelm me, but spiritually I felt vibrantly alive.

I had put a Scripture on my kitchen wall soon after we moved to Sunbury House, and I would often read it and wonder if it could possibly prove to be true for me. It said:

> As you live this new life, we pray that you will be strengthened from God's boundless resources, so that you will find yourselves able to pass through any experience and endure it with courage. You will even be able to thank God in the midst of pain and distress because you are privileged to share the lot of those who are living in the light. (Col. 1:11)

I was about to either prove it or disprove it. We wept, but we were also at peace. We were deeply sad, but we also had deep inner joy. My big question to the Lord was, "How will I get through this time, Lord?"

Clearly, He said to me, "If you look at Me, keep your eyes fixed on Me, and keep your heart full of thanksgiving to Me, I will keep you in perfect peace."

Mercifully, He did. Although I was not able to thank the Lord for Philip's death, I was certainly able to thank the Lord for Philip's life and for the wonder of all the care we had received. In fact, I sat down the day after he died and wrote a whole sheet of the things I was thankful for. My intention was to add to it day by day.

I found that thanksgiving was such a cleansing tide in my heart. You can perhaps imagine that at the top of my list of thanksgiving was the fact that I had been reconciled with Philip when he was four years old; I was grateful to know that for the last four years, I had loved him as much as I loved the other boys. I cannot imagine how much guilt and condemnation I might have felt if he had died and I had not loved him with all my heart.

- I thanked God for the peace He was giving us.
- I thanked God for the privilege of the life I had shared with Philip.
- I thanked God for Philip's generous nature.
- I thanked God for how he loved his brothers.
- I thanked God that he suffered so little in his death.
- I thanked God for all the people who had shown they cared.

It went on and on. I was able to fill the whole page without even stopping to think. Although I felt like a part of my own flesh had died or that I had actually lost a limb, despite those terribly bleak feelings, I could witness to all we met of the very real joy and peace Jesus' presence was giving us moment by moment.

A flood of visitors, cards, letters, money, flowers, and gifts of other kinds began to arrive daily. After the report in the local paper, even more letters and cards came. It was amazing how many people cared about us. Particularly important to us were the gifts people gave to Ben and Giles. Thankfully, people did not forget the children. They needed signs of love too. They were grieving in their own ways.

We had no clue how we would manage to pay for the funeral or a headstone, but by the end of the week, we had received sufficient gifts of money to pay for the funeral, a buffet meal after the funeral, and a beautiful headstone. We were able to have the headstone inscribed with our chosen design. Philip loved wildlife and animals of any kind, so we put a carving of a bird on the headstone, along with the words of Jesus from John 17:10: "All Mine are Thine and Thine are Mine, and I am glorified in them."

The funeral director blanched at the number of words in the inscription for the headstone, but he promised to do his best. I suppose he thought this because the stonemason charged by the letter. By having such a lot of words, we had chosen to run up the cost a good deal more than we might have. But for us, it was the perfect Scripture that admirably described our sentiments about Philip, who belonged to Jesus and had glorified God in his life as well as in his death.

How we needed the love of friends and family at this time. My friend Mavis promised to drop by every day, and she did so for weeks, simply to give me a great big hug. How I needed and looked forward to that comforting physical touch from a dear friend, which made me feel so secure. My doctor also visited and was the nicest to me that he had ever been. His usual irascible demeanor was completely absent. Very kindly he said, "I am so sorry about your loss, Mrs. Cornell. Can I help in any way? Would you like some sleeping pills?"

I thanked him profusely and told him Jesus had given us complete peace and I was sleeping very well indeed. I could see that he believed me, and he knew I was not just in some sort of crazy denial. I discovered from a friend who was a health visitor at the medical centre that after visiting us, he had told people how impressed he was with us and with our obviously genuine faith.

Other people came and ended up crying because it brought their own unresolved grief to the surface, so I ended up praying with them and comforting them. Some people came with questions about how we could possibly be the way we were. Why were we able to be so strong? We were able to explain to them that it was only by the power of God and the presence of the Holy Spirit that we were remaining at peace. We then led them to the Lord or prayed with them for the baptism of the Holy Spirit. What a tremendous privilege that was! They were glory days!

I suppose one of the most precious moments of all was when the vicar came to see me the day after Philip died. He asked if he could speak to me privately. We went into the sitting room, and he said, "Margaret, I am so sorry that I have thought so many mean things about you. I am so sorry that I discounted what you told me about the Holy Spirit. You *have* got something I haven't got, and I need it."

Falling to his knees in front of me, he continued, "Will you pray for me to be baptised into the Holy Spirit? I really want what you have."

It was my great, great, great privilege to pray with him and to see him receive exactly what we prayed for. This was a wonderful beginning of a new journey with him and the whole church. Things had previously been so difficult with him because, sadly, someone had warned him about us before he came to Isleham. Suspicion had been put into his mind even before he had actually met us that we might cause him trouble. Thankfully, this distance between us was now gone.

He had been so sarcastic about our claims that the baptism of the Holy Spirit was a genuine experience that enabled Christians to live an overcoming life. He had said, "Well, Margaret, I can't see that you have anything I haven't got. You have character faults just like anyone else."

I could only admit that, of course, we did have faults. It was as if he thought that by saying we were filled with the Spirit, we were somehow implying we were perfect and therefore better than others. Of course that was just not true!

When he had come to the hospital after the accident, he said he had been so surprised to see how peaceful we were. He saw how much the Spirit of God was enabling us to stand strong. Our behavior convinced him of the reality of the baptism of the Spirit as nothing else had done. Many years later, when this vicar was promoted to rural dean, he invited us to the deanery meeting to speak to everyone about stewardship. He instructed us, "Tell it how it is. Give them the Bible truth about giving, and tell them of your experiences of God's faithfulness to you over the years."

Before we started to speak, this lovely man said, "Now, you may not like everything you are about to hear, but I have invited Margaret and Tony here to teach the Word and to tell of their experiences. From personal experience, I know they are people of integrity, and everything they tell you of their experience is true. They have lived it. I know because I have witnessed it."

This felt like a massive reward for living our lives transparently before men. We gave them a no-holds-barred explanation of what the Bible says about giving, along with lots of testimony of God's generosity to us. We told them about our lifestyle of faith when we lived in Isleham and about how God had always answered prayer faithfully. I think they were astonished.

The Sunday after Philip died, as a matter of course we went to church as usual. People in our congregation were amazed we were at church again so soon. We were just as amazed at *their* reaction and said, "Where else would we want to be other than in God's house, where His presence is tangible, where His precious people are? It is the very place where some of our comfort comes from."

Another precious moment that day was when a young man we knew had previously mocked and despised us approached Tony as he came away from the altar rail after communion, saying, "Please forgive me, Tony. I have hated you. I thought you were just crackpots. I now know you do have something so special and that you are truly genuine Christians."

Wow! The funeral was almost a village event. Over three hundred people came. The church was packed with family, friends from everywhere, work colleagues, and village people, some of whom we barely even knew, as well as ministers from both the other churches.

I had not been sure about what I should wear for the funeral. I did not want to dress somberly, but neither did I want to cause a stir by looking too jolly. The day before the funeral, God's provision came for clothing. When Tony's mother arrived, she said, "Oh, there's another parcel here for you from Aunty Dorothy."

And there it was—a beautiful bouclé wool dress and jacket! It was dark purple with narrow pink stripes around the jacket sleeves and the bottom of the dress. It was both tasteful and suitable because it was neither too somber nor too colourful. Truly, it was a marvelous provision for that sad moment when we knew many eyes would be on us.

The church was a mass of flowers, and the perfume was so beautiful; it smelled like a summer garden. Church people had done us proud; they had spent hours cleaning everything until it shone and arranging masses of flowers for us. A man who lived in the village who was a professional photographer went in to take photographs of the church with its flowers and wreaths all arranged around the coffin. This gave us a lovely record of how beautiful it looked.

A couple of friends sang a beautiful song during the service. Its theme was "Trust in the Lord," and they sang like angels from the organ loft. The vicar did us proud and preached the gospel more boldly than we had ever heard him preach it before. We had triumphant hymns, like "Thine Be the

Glory, Risen, Conquering Son," because we were determined to celebrate his life rather than mourn his death. We wanted people to know that we believed in Jesus, the true Resurrection and the Life, and that death was not the end for a believer; death is but the gateway to a wonderful life in heaven with Him.

I had never been to a proper church funeral before, so I really did not know how we were supposed to behave. It was only when I went to a funeral a few months later and saw the relatives follow the coffin in, weeping uncontrollably, supported by others that I realised how odd our behavior must have seemed. However, I am so glad we did what we did.

Before the service, the coffin was put at the front of the church, resplendent with flowers, rather than us processing in behind it. We welcomed people at the church door as they came in and thanked them for coming. People were surprised but also pleased.

When some people heard about what we had done, they disapproved. They thought we should have at least been weeping and showing more grief. When they knew about the service being a celebration, a horrible rumour went round the village that we could not really have cared much for our son because we were not showing any grief. How could people understand that Jesus Himself was our strength and that He was bearing our grief?

After the wonderful service, we walked in solemn procession through the streets behind the bier to the cemetery, and there we finally committed Philip's body to the ground. It was only at that moment that my composure failed. As I saw the coffin being lowered into the ground, a great wave of grief swept over me. The realization dawned with full force that from this moment and forever Philip was truly gone, and I would never hold him or speak to him again until I was reunited with him in heaven.

After the funeral, we went back to the house for refreshments. Many people came back with us to bring gifts and to offer comfort, which was a very healing experience. One very surprising person who came back to the house after the service was Caroline, the deeply depressed girl who could only show us great hostility when she lived with us!

Caroline came into the room, hesitantly hugged me, and gave me a bunch of flowers, saying very sweetly how sorry she was about Philip. Her awkwardness was acute but her sincerity evident. Tilda, the social worker who had originally brought Caroline to us, decided to inform her about

Philip's death and had been very surprised when Caroline asked to come to the funeral. She felt that Caroline's reaction was a sign of a tremendous breakthrough in her life, as well as an indication of what we had been able to give her despite how it appeared. What a precious gift to us that day! What balm to the soul. It had looked like we had been able to accomplish so little with Caroline. I was so moved and encouraged by her presence.

A few days after the funeral, I had a sudden thought about *that* photo! That awful photo the photographer had virtually forced us to take at Janet's wedding! I could not wait to find the photographer to order ourselves a copy. When it came, it was as awful as I had thought it would be. We did look dreadful—like a group of scruffy orphans straight out of *Oliver Twist*. Nevertheless, that photo was precious because it was the last one ever taken of Philip. It is now a treasured part of our memory of him and of our family at that time. How I thanked God for that annoyingly persistent photographer.

When I look back, if I had to evaluate the experience I have described of Philip's death, I would have to say that I treasure it a great deal. Of course, I cannot say I am glad it happened. That would be foolish as well as a lie, but in so many ways, it *was* a wonderful experience. It is a mystery to me—a paradox. How could something be so absolutely horrible and so painful and yet be wonderful at the same time?

The answer is this: it was the precious presence of Jesus, who enveloped us and girded us up within to be able to meet the challenge. This is what made the difference. It was His strength, His wisdom, His love, His people, His church, His Word—just *Him*!

We discovered that whatever happened in our lives, *He is more than enough*. I cannot imagine anything happening in my life that could be worse. Strangely, the experience of our God and His workings in our lives at that time gave me a confidence in God that I believe nothing else could have done. That extreme experience removed a lot of fear from my life. Now nothing could shake my knowledge that He is truly El Shaddai—the God who is more than enough. Our God is truly who He says He is.

Another blessed aspect of this time was the way that God drew Tony and me closer together in a way that enabled us to really support each other. In many cases, marriages break up because of disasters, especially a child's death. Guilt, condemnation, accusations, reproaches, and anger often alienate a couple from each other. If a couple starts the blame game, it's all over. Mercifully, we were able to avoid doing that. Without God, our own human nature might have certainly led us down that pathway. It is the pure grace of God that we did not do so.

Thankfully, Tony and I were able to give each other a lot of comfort. We somehow managed to break down at separate times so each of us could take turns in comforting the other. I only remember one day when Tony was grieving that I just could not cope with it. That day my own grief was raw too. Miraculously, at that very moment, our friend Brian called at the house. He was able to help Tony instead of me. He hugged him and prayed with him. How hard it is to see people you love suffering like this!

In fact, Philip's death began a small revival in the church. People seemed to wake up and see that there was more to Christianity than they had previously thought. Suddenly we had a voice, and they had ears to hear. We had talked to so many of the church people during the time of Philip's accident, death, and funeral, and so many people had been to visit us. We knew we had made a great impression on many. People were astonished that we could be full of peace instead of anger, grief, and unforgiveness. The fact that we could forgive the lady who had effectively killed him was an enigma to many. I think people just do not realise the personal cost of *not* forgiving. Unforgiveness is guaranteed to damage our health and our relationships. Unforgiveness would have ruined our lives!

A prayer meeting started in the tiny church vestry every week. Many crowded in there, and the church rang with joyful singing! Unbelievably, or perhaps believably, opposition arose against these meetings. One of the church wardens met Tony in the street one day and said aggressively, "I heard you in there alleluljahing and all that. It's disgraceful!"

It was some people's jaundiced view that we Anglicans were becoming just like the Baptists. Ancient feeling had always run high in the village between church and chapel.

After the funeral, though I knew our experience of God had been wonderful, I had the nagging thought that somehow we ought to have had the faith and the ability to stop Philip from dying or even to have raised him from the dead. I knew Jesus would have done so. I said to the Lord, "Lord, why couldn't we raise him up? There must be something missing from our Christian life. Whatever it is, Lord, will you please provide it?"

CHAPTER 18

The Bible Becomes Our Rock

A bout six months before Philip's death, a couple named John and Stella had contacted us because they wanted to give us some tapes and books. For various reasons, we had just not been able to meet up with them. In hindsight, it was obvious that Satan prevented us from meeting up with them. When they eventually came to see us, they left us with a whole load of tapes by Kenneth Copeland, Kenneth Hagin, and Derek Prince. We had never heard of these people, but our faith life was about to be changed forever.

I began to listen to one of the Kenneth Copeland tapes about prayer and fasting. I thought, *Oh Lord, I can't listen to this. I cannot even understand what he is saying!* Who says Americans speak the same language as we do? However, deep down in my heart, I knew these tapes were the answer to the prayer I had made about the missing element in our Christian lives. I realised our understanding of our authority in Christ, of our covenant with Him and His ability to work in us, was pitiful. We simply did not know what the Word of God said.

So I gritted my teeth and persisted. When I eventually got a handle on what Copeland was saying, I became so elated and excited that I plugged into each new tape with eager anticipation. Every day I got my Bible out, looked up every Scripture he quoted, and made copious notes. I may even have listened to each tape about ten times to make sure I was missing nothing.

I checked and checked the Word for myself because the things I was hearing about the Bible and what it promised us seemed almost too good to be true. Could I really take the Word of God literally and believe every word in it? Was the Bible truly the inerrant Word of God? Did God really promise financial blessings, healing, and a life that was abundant in every way?

Of course, I already knew God would meet my needs because all the time I had lived in Sunbury House I had prayed and trusted God for clothing and everything else imaginable. I had learned this from a German nun called Basilea Schlink, whose theology was very different from these faith teachers, and proved it to be true. These tapes raised new questions. Would God do more than meet just our needs? Could I really expect abundance?

God, they said, was the El Shaddai who is more than enough. They said Jesus has given us all authority in His name. We can lay hands on the sick and expect healing. The list of good things went on and on, but I did not tell anyone else what I was hearing. I wanted to study the Bible carefully and check it out thoroughly for myself.

We became serious Bible students. We became excited about the Bible and our faith in God. We came to believe it was God's will to heal—full stop! We learned that prosperity was God's will—full stop! We learned that we were the righteousness of God in Christ. We learned that the Holy Spirit moving dynamically in our lives was actually just the normal Christian life. We learned that we had a covenant with God. We learned that faith was the key to release everything God had given us by His grace and our faith could grow and develop as we heard and decided to believe the Word of God. We learned that Jesus' reference to the Word of God as seed (Mark 4) meant we could actively plant that seed into situations in our lives. As we watered the seed by faith and thanksgiving, God would act on our behalf, causing it to grow and bear fruit.

It was so exciting to have the Bible opened up to us in this wonderful way. We believed that through this teaching we would be able to see greater results for the kingdom and for the glory of God. We began to develop faith in a *big* God whose love and compassion was bigger than we had ever dreamed. How dearly I wished we had received this teaching sooner; then maybe. . .

I knew that I must immediately cut off this kind of destructive thinking. 'If only' is a dead end and a steep road downhill toward misery and torment.

I recognized that road of regret for what it was and absolutely forbade myself to go down there. Instead I only allowed myself to think of the grace of God, which was now enabling us to build precious faith and trust into our hungry hearts!

We were soon visiting John and Stella regularly, getting more tapes to fill our hearts more and more with the truth. John was a mine of information about the Bible and the history of the Pentecostal movement. They had both been in Christ for the Nations Bible College in Dallas, Texas, for a year, and they were always studying and growing in the Word themselves.

We would sit for hours with them over endless cups of tea, avidly drinking in what they both knew. They were key people in our development because they were some of the few who were on fire for God and full of the Word, and we wanted to be just like them. They were also instrumental in influencing us to go on a life-changing trip to America. We could never be grateful enough to them. Sadly, John died in his early sixties. I wish he was alive today to read this and to know just how much we appreciated his input into our lives.

We made sure our children understood what the Word of God could do for them. We knew the Bible said, "The word of God is living and powerful, and sharper than any two-edged sword" (Heb. 4:12), and also, "Faith comes by hearing, and hearing by the word of God" (Rom. 10:17).

When Ben was seven and caught measles, we set the tape recorder up with a tape of healing scriptures and left him to listen to it repeatedly. He had a comic, which I said he could read as long as he had the tape playing in the background.

I was having coffee with a friend in the kitchen when Ben appeared to get himself a drink. I said, "What have you learned Ben?"

In a matter of fact way he said, "Well, I have learned that according to Deuteronomy chapter twenty-eight verse sixty-one that measles is a curse under the law . . . but according to Galatians three thirteen, I am redeemed from the curse of the law by Christ Jesus who was made a curse for me. Therefore, I do not have measles."

I was amazed! We were hardly into the day, and he was completely well! The next day he went back to school. A while later, Giles got measles, and when the school found out, they said that he had to stay away from school whether we thought he was healed or not! Ben was obviously glad to be well but was peeved that he did not get the same amount of time off school as Giles.

Praying for healing became routine, and we expected God to do it. Many times I have received my healing when I relaxed and listened to the healing Scriptures. Rather than *trying* to receive my healing, I just let the Word wash over me. I can remember one particular time when I had come home from being away, and I felt very ill with severe flu symptoms. I staggered upstairs, flopped on the bed, and put the healing Scriptures tape on to play quietly. I lay there in a semi-doze. Suddenly I heard Malachi 4:2 with more than just my ears: "But to you who fear My name the Sun of Righteousness shall arise with healing in His wings; and you will leap like calves let out of a stall."

As the Holy Spirit made the revelation of that Scripture go off inside me like a rocket, instantly every symptom of flu left. I lay there thinking how strange it was that I no longer felt ill, and it took me a few minutes to absorb the fact that I was completely well. Since I was no longer sick and I could not think of any good reason to stay in bed, I got up, went downstairs, and began to fill the dishwasher. Someone who had seen me come home looking very ill came into the kitchen and expressed surprise. "Margaret, when you came home, I thought you were ill!"

"I was, but now I am healed!" I wish all healings happened so instantly!

In due time, Tony qualified as a lay reader, and he undertook his duties with enthusiasm, even the preaching, which he had never wanted to do. It seemed that the church had accepted him wholeheartedly. However, when we arrived on the first Sunday he was due to lead the service, we were dismayed to find nobody there except a close friend. Oh dear! Maybe people had really disapproved of Tony's appointment and decided to boycott the service. We stood around sheepishly outside the church, desperately hoping for someone else to turn up.

Suddenly I noticed that the whole street was quiet, and there was nobody at the Baptist chapel either. Their service was an hour later than ours, but by that time people were usually there. Then it dawned on us. The clocks had gone back, and we had arrived an hour early. What a relief; we had not been boycotted! Laughing all the way down the road, we went to our friend's house for coffee, returning at the right time to find the entire congregation there ready to enjoy Tony's first sermon. *Phew!*

Qualifying as a lay reader gave Tony greater boldness, but his boldness got him into trouble straightaway. Tony went and prayed with a man who had glaucoma, and as he was praying, he felt the Holy Spirit say, "You will not need the operation."

That's what he told the man. When the vicar heard about this proclamation, he was horrified. He said that Tony must not say such things when they were simply not true. As it turned out, the man received his healing, and he did not have the operation. Thankfully, Tony's faith was vindicated.

The Word was certainly producing fruit in our lives, but a new crisis arose with my parents, who were practicing as spiritualists. What I had dreaded happening after Philip died happened. My father rang up and said, "We went to a séance last night, and Philip came through. He sends his love. He told us that you have a lock of his hair in a little pouch in your dressing table drawer."

I knew how much this would have meant to my parents, but I felt sick, cold, and full of despair. What he said fell into my heart like a stone. I had hoped this would never happen. I said to him, "Well, Daddy, I am really sorry. You must know how we feel about spiritualism. Do you understand that this is a problem for us? If you cannot refrain from mentioning these things, how can I have you in my home again? We need to talk."

We had been thinking for some time about the real danger of my parents visiting our home. Before Philip's death, there were three occasions when something violent had happened because of their presence in our home. It could not have been a coincidence that my parents were present. We were sure these events occurred because of the evil spirits my parents were unknowingly bringing with them. Those invisible visitors had caused us a lot of trouble.

Naturally speaking, my parents were lovely, generous people—good people who were wonderful to us. As I write this, my mother is still living in our home alive at the ripe old age of ninety-one, and I hope anyone who reads this will be tactful with her because I would hate her to be hurt. All of this is in the past as far as we are concerned.

On one day when I was in the kitchen washing up with my mother, the first of these high-impact events happened. The children were playing in the garden. I knew I needed to be honest with my parents about their involvement in spiritualism. As part of my conversation with her, I said, "I think spiritualism is evil."

My father walked into the room just in time to hear this, and his countenance became as black as thunder. He was shaking with anger. He lifted his arm and pointed his finger at me threateningly. "Don't you ever say anything like that again!"

Before he finished speaking, we all nearly jumped out of our skins because there was a great explosion. *Boom!* The football the boys were playing with in the garden came crashing through the large kitchen window at great speed, scattering shards of glass everywhere. It was as if my father's words were backed up by hell itself. We were shaken because it did not feel in the least like an accident or a coincidence.

On another occasion when they were with us, one of our cats Ina became very sick and died. The vet could not save her because before it was too late, he had no idea why she was so poorly. Later we realised that Ina must have gone into the cellar and had eaten the rat poison that had always been hidden in there. Could it have been a coincidence? We began to question, why did she find it that day and not any time before?

The third incident was during Christmas festivities the following year, and the effects were potentially far more serious. Both sets of parents were with us for a few days. On Boxing Day morning, Tony's mother suddenly felt very ill. She said, "I have a nosebleed. I don't feel well. I'm going to have to have a lie-down."

When she had gone upstairs, I felt alarmed and when I prayed I felt sure that it was a demonic attack so I called some friends whom I knew would pray too. I spoke briefly to Brian's daughter on the telephone. I said, "Would you please ask your dad to pray? My mother-in-law has been suddenly taken ill." This was the sum total of what I said; nothing dramatic at all because I wanted clear confirmation of what I was thinking and did not want to put ideas into their heads. Just as I was serving lunch, we had a phone call from our friend asking us to go to their house immediately.

Hurriedly, we made our excuses, telling everyone that we needed to go to a friend's house and that we would be back in a while. It seemed rude, but I knew we had to go. When we got there, he shared with us what God had said as he had prayed. He said, "Your parents are not aware of it, but every time they come to your home, they bring with them a spirit of death."

I thought of my father's rage and the extraordinary timing and the violence of the broken window, the timing of the death of the cat, and also what I had felt about Nana's symptoms being demonically produced. He said, "I think you will have to think twice before having them in your home."

That was terrible news which I did not want to hear at all; I loved my parents very much and felt that surely if we were careful and if we prayed for protection, we would be okay. After all, isn't God bigger than the devil? Isn't the devil defeated? Of course he is. We immediately prayed together, bound the spirit of death, and commanded it to leave Tony's mother.

We returned home and a few minutes after we got back to the house, Nana Maud came down the stairs looking perky. "Thank you," she said.

"What do you mean 'thank you'?" I asked.

"Well, I heard you go out, and then about ten minutes ago, I suddenly felt better and I knew that you must have gone to pray."

Wow, that was clear enough proof of the source of the trouble.

Then on that fatal weekend when my parents were with us again, Philip was killed. Despite our love for them and all their natural kindness to us, we knew that we could not invite them to our home again if they would not give up their spiritualist activities. We knew that we were not fighting flesh and blood and there was no way that we were blaming them personally for Philip's death. If anything as parents we bore the responsibility because we had not reckoned with the sneakiness of the evil one and had not heeded the warnings. We sorrowfully concluded that Satan's assignment against us was more than we were ready for.

I had never asked God belligerently, "Why have You done this?" because I knew *He* hadn't taken Philip. I knew He was my loving heavenly Father who had forgiven me and loved me unconditionally. But it says in the book of James that if anyone lacks wisdom, he should ask God for it, so I asked Him, "Lord, why did this happen?"

He said clearly, "Satan sought to steal your ministry."

I was puzzled at His reply because a ministry to us, at that time would have meant some kind of leadership position, like a vicar. Although Tony was going to be a lay reader, I knew this was not what God meant. I just tucked the statement away in my heart for future reference. Other people said, "God took your son."

Immediately I would say, "No, I don't believe that for a minute. God is good. God is love. He is my loving Father. The Bible tells me that children are a gift from God. He gave Philip to us, and I do not believe He would take him away again because the Bible in Romans 11.29 says, "The gifts and the calling of God are irrevocable." God does not take away what he has once given.

Others said, "God allowed it."

I said to the Lord, "I know You did not take Philip, Lord, but is it true that You allowed it?"

"No," He said. "I didn't allow it. You allowed it."

Astounded I said "What do you mean. . . *I* allowed it?"

Then came an answer that has produced controversy between me and others over the years, but I cannot help that because I know I heard the Lord loud and clear say. "When you refused to be reconciled to Tony and were in deliberate unforgiveness with him, by that willful and deliberate sin, you opened the door to the evil one. Satan was prowling about as a roaring lion, seeking to devour, and he found the door wide open."

When I sought God for further understanding I remembered that in 2 Corinthians 11, Paul linked unforgiveness with Satan being able to take advantage of us. That afternoon, I had definitely been in a state of deliberate unforgiveness and turmoil. I also realised that Satan's desire was to separate us from God. It has been the same since the Garden of Eden. Although we do not lose our relationship with God through sin because it is secure in Christ, sin does break our fellowship with God and clouds our minds. We are then out of position to hear Him and receive any warnings He may need to give us that there is danger about. This is certainly how it was for me that day.

It was, of course, a very sobering answer and one that people have almost forbidden me to believe, fearing I would feel condemned. However, instead of being negative, it was, as far as I could see, a completely positive answer. I was very relieved and very glad. A weight fell off my shoulders. I did not feel in the least bit condemned, and I never have. It is my hope that nobody reading this will feel they need to fear Satan, that they brought some disaster upon themselves in the past, or that they might do so in the future by some kind of sin.

Actually, I was greatly comforted by God's reply to my question. If my sin made me responsible in any way, I knew there was a simple answer.

I knew that every sin, however horrible it might have been, was forgiven because the cross had dealt with it completely. I knew I could repent at that very moment and by faith, receive afresh the knowledge of God's precious blood-bought forgiveness in such a way that I would be immediately and completely released from all sense of guilt.

I truly felt a new gratitude to God for the cross because through it He had enabled me to walk free and move on with my life without the crippling condemnation and guilt many people bear when they lose a child. People who do not even believe in God feel these things. One of the biggest keys to the peace, love, joy, and freedom from disabling grief, which I experienced, was the knowledge that I was forgiven. I was able to affirm this fact to myself.

I think it would be true to say that much of people's grief is compounded by the toxic addition of guilt. However, if God had told me that *He* had done it—that *He*, according to *His* sovereign will, had chosen to take Philip from us—I think it could have greatly damaged the deep trust I had in Him. How could you trust somebody who might take a loved one from you at any moment because of your sin?

I know for sure that God is not a thief. As children of God, we know that the Father's will toward us is good. He is a giver, not a taker. In John 10:10, Jesus clearly identifies the devil as the thief. He states, "The thief does not come except to steal, and to kill, and to destroy." In contrast, Jesus then says of Himself, "I have come that [you] may have life, and that [you] may have it more abundantly." If God has already given us heaven's best (Jesus), "How shall He not with Him also freely give us all things?" (Rom. 8).

Does this mean I believe that when we are out of sorts with our partner, something bad will happen to our children? No, I do not believe that is necessarily true because bad things happen to good people. Plenty of bad things happened to St. Paul because he was doing God's will.

I believe there were many factors in play that day, some avoidable and some not, that somehow culminated in our terrible loss. On that day, I believe Satan intentionally conspired against us and won a victory, even if it was only temporary and short-lived.

Life is often unpredictable. At times we may face what appear to be hopeless situations, but Romans 15 tells us that we are in covenant with the "God of all hope" who fills us with "all joy and peace in believing' that we may abound in hope by the power of the Holy Spirit."

Satan is defeated; Jesus gave us authority over him, but he still has some ability to wound us if we foolishly give it to him. First I think I had drawn Satan's attention by entering into some unwise spiritual warfare. I had set myself, some months previously, to pray and fast against the demonic hold that was over my parents. Soon afterwards I was overjoyed to receive the news that indeed it had been successful and my parents' spiritualist circle had been broken up. In hindsight it was a lack of wisdom for me to pray in this way alone.

Second, there was an open door because of my refusal to be reconciled with Tony when truly I knew better. Surely that too was the work of the enemy. If we keep ourselves from sin by walking in the love of God that is in us, 1 John 5:18 gives us assurance that *the wicked one does not touch [us]."*

Third, after my mother-in-law was ill during the previous Christmas, Brian had warned us of the danger of inviting my parents into our home. If we had been more aware of the dangerous, demonic influence my parents brought with them, we would either not have invited them, or we would have been much more spiritually vigilant. If we had realised that we were in such a fierce spiritual battle, I know Tony and I would have taken preventative steps to stay in unity.

We were, of course, reluctant to believe this particular warning because we loved my parents and did not want to hurt them. However, because we understood very little about spiritual things at that time, we were ill-equipped to deal with the demonic. It would have made sense to act on a warning and be alert to what was happening behind the scenes. The main problem was that we did not *realise* that we were lacking in understanding and ill-equipped!

I am also sure that if I had been walking in harmony with God on that day, I could have heard Him speak to me, and He could have warned me of the danger, just as He has done on many occasions since then. Unfortunately, because of the foul mood I was in, I was not listening to Him, and I was not receptive.

When I reported to Tony what I felt God had said, we vowed that we would never allow unforgiveness to flourish in our lives again, and we would never allow ourselves to part from each other while still in unforgiveness.

We would not "let the sun go down on our wrath," nor would we ever "give place to the devil" like that again (Eph. 4:26-27). This has done wonders for our relationship! Realizing our accountability and our individual part in keeping ourselves free from the evil one has produced wonderful fruit in our lives, and knowing who the thief was made us more determined to defeat him at every turn. I said to the devil, "Well, Satan, if you think you can turn us against God, you need to think again. I promise to wipe you off the face of the earth wherever I see you!"

We then reluctantly faced the issue of what to do about my parents because of the danger. We soberly considered how the demonic influences they carried had brought damage to us on previous occasions, and we concluded that because we were still baby Christians—innocents abroad— we were not ready for the challenge of the demonic.

Taking his courage in both hands, Tony went to see my parents. He explained how much we loved them, but then he told them about the four recent instances when violent things had happened at our home while they were staying with us. He took great pains to express love for them and to make it crystal clear that we were not blaming them or saying that it was their fault Philip had died. We knew according to Ephesians 6:12 that it was not flesh and blood we were fighting against but evil spirits. These accompanied my parents because of their involvement in spiritualism, and it was these that were causing the problem when they came to visit.

Tony tried to explain this in the gentlest way he could, but understandably they could not see it. We asked a minister friend, Frank, who had a church in London, to try and explain the problem to them. However, he found them equally unyielding. I knew they would say, "Well there is spiritualism and spiritualism. There are evil spirits, but we are involved in something that is completely different. We only work with good spirits."

Of course, they were ignoring all the promises spirits had given them that had never materialized as well as the very unpleasant and frightening experience we had when I was twelve years old when my father became possessed by an evil spirit. He began to read the Bible obsessively and behave very strangely. He washed constantly and would no longer sleep with my mother because he said she was unclean. He went about declaring like an Old Testament prophet, "I am the Christ. You must follow me."

It all ended one dreadful day when he locked himself in the bathroom and was raving like a madman in a hot bath about all sorts of religious things. At one point, we could just make out that he was crying out, "Go and get Lynn . . . Go and get Lynn."

My mother sent me to find Lynn, her spiritualist friend who lived just down the road, and she dispatched me to the telephone box to ring the doctor. That telephone call was such a traumatic experience that till this day I still don't enjoy using the phone. The doctor's receptionist kept making me repeat what I was trying to tell her over and over again. I suppose it could have sounded like a hoax, so although I started very calmly, I was nearly hysterical by the time she agreed to send the doctor.

When I got back to the flat, Lynn had taken charge and somehow had got my father to open the bathroom door. I was sent into the care of the lady in the flat downstairs, but the floors were so thin that I could still hear what was going on. The doctor came, and of course nobody let on that they knew it was an evil spirit at the bottom of it all. If they had I don't suppose the doctor would have believed it! My father was committed to a mental hospital for six months. Before he left he was calm and seemed to be in his right mind and apologized for frightening me.

What amazed me was that a few days later when we attended a séance, the spirits admitted he had been possessed by an evil spirit, but of course they said it was his own fault because he had invited it! It makes me so angry to know that the devil had deceived my parents by presenting his activity as something good when it was actually so evil. Of course, I shouldn't have been surprised because deception is Satan's chief weapon, and the Bible clearly says he "transforms himself into an angel of light" (2 Cor. 11:14).

My parents believed in healing and would send out thoughts to heal people. They laid hands on people and counseled them. If they had thought for a minute that they were involved with evil, I am sure they would never have done it. They truly believed that they were doing good but the Bible is clear God tells us it is wrong to try to contact the dead so even if we do not understand how can we, with partial knowledge, be wiser than He who knows all?

We did not invite my parents to our home for many years, and when God eventually told us we could visit them, the enemy was obviously not willing to give up without a struggle. Both boys were happy about going to see my parents, but as we drove along the street where my parents lived, we had to stop the car for both of the boys to be violently sick. Satan was certainly maintaining his threats over us as a family, but now we were ready for battle.

Right there in the street, we took authority afresh over the spirits of darkness that were threatening our family. It felt like a last ditch stand from the enemy, a final but powerless threat to destroy us, which Satan could not carry out because we now understood our authority in Christ and had learned how to master him.

It was a relief to reconnect with my parents because being separated from them for so many years had been a kind of bereavement. I had also agonized over the grief that my mother must have felt because she could not see her grandchildren, whom she adored. I had hated doing it to them.

CHAPTER 19

We Need Help Too

After Philip's death we knew that our marriage needed urgent attention, so when we heard about a marriage seminar weekend, we decided to go. We set off one Friday night for what we hoped would be a great weekend away. On the way the car broke down, which meant we got there late and were feeling fed up because we had almost missed the evening session.

I felt nervous about Christian teaching on marriage, and I felt sure they would go on about wives needing to be in submission to their husbands. The idea of submission, which sounded like control and domination, put the wind up me! When we walked into the room and the leaders greeted us, the wife said cheerfully, "Oh my! You're an independent one, aren't you?"

I was in no mood for any kind of confrontation and I was shocked that *anyone* would speak to me like that the moment they had just met me, even if it was true. What a nerve! I went to bed disgruntled, wishing we had not come to the beastly course. But after a good night's sleep, I felt much better, and we settled into the weekend.

We learned a major life-changing technique during this weekend: how to communicate with each other and avoid rows over hot topics. This was called "Describe and Dialogue" or D and D for short. We had to decide on a topic we needed to discuss, and then we had ten minutes to write down our feelings about the issue. Then we were allowed ten minutes to share what we had written and talk *but* only for ten minutes, and each little passage had to begin with, "What are my feelings about. . .?"

A strange thing happened. Because our communication had been poor about difficult issues, we had always assumed we felt very differently about things, but we were amazed to find we didn't feel differently at all. When we talked properly, heart-to-heart, and listened to each other, the lights turned on!

I was very shocked by the things Tony told me during that weekend about how he felt about my behavior and our lives. I never knew. Sadly, I also knew that in the past, I would probably not have cared about how he felt either because I was too selfish and hurting too much myself. What a reversal we were able to make, and what a difference to our relationship! What wonderful harmony began to come between us.

During the weekend, something Jesus said penetrated my heart in a completely new way, searing through layers of selfishness. Jesus said to me, "Inasmuch as you did it to one of the least of these, My brethren, you did it to Me" (Matt. 25:40). I was gutted! It hit me like a sledgehammer: *If every time I treated Tony badly or carelessly, I was really doing it to Jesus, it was just terrible.* I was aghast! What had I done to Tony and to Jesus, my Lord, the two people I loved most?

I said, "Jesus, I have been so mean to You. I have treated You so badly. I am so sorry."

I apologized to Tony too and resolved to be more thoughtful about my words and actions. That simple revelation did more to guard my heart and my mouth than anything else could possibly have done. Every time I was tempted to speak rudely to Tony, remembering that saying stopped me in my tracks.

I had read Ephesians 5:33 many times, but when I read it in the Amplified Bible, it was much more convicting. After it instructs a husband to "love his own wife as himself." It also says, "Let the wife see that she respects and reverences her husband, that she notices him, regards him, honours him, prefers him, venerates him, and esteems him; and that she defers to him, praises him, and loves and admires him exceedingly."

When I realised I needed to take this Scripture seriously as well, I told the Lord, "You have to be joking!" However, as I prayed about it over a period of time, I knew God had worked a miracle in my heart and I could do those things in all honesty. Of course, when a husband loves his wife in the way the beginning of that Scripture tells him to; as Christ loves the church, it is no problem for a wife to do the things that Scripture says! The Bible encapsulates such deep truth in this verse because it seems that a woman's greatest need is for love, and a man's greatest need is for respect.

We promised to practice D and D every day for a month, which we did gladly because we found it so helpful. I was continually astounded by how much we had hurt each other through total ignorance of each other's feelings. There's that word again: ignorance... yuck! No wonder God says, "My people are destroyed for lack of knowledge" (Hosea 4:6).

There was another dynamic moment during the course that had far-reaching effects in our relationship. After the final teaching session, we were given two hours to write a piece entitled, "What are my feelings about spending the rest of my life with you?" As we went our separate ways to write the description of our feelings, I wandered out into the sunshine feeling a wave of despair. *Oh dear,* I thought. *This is where everything will come horribly unstuck.* I was really troubled about what I could say. My feelings about spending the rest of my life with Tony were not *at all* positive. I was horrified because I knew that if I told him how I really felt, in cold print, he could be hurt. I loved him enough not to want to hurt his feelings on purpose.

As I have said, I loved Tony, but I knew that I was not in love with him. Through fear I had always kept part of my heart closed to him. I had never really dared surrender myself to him because after my experience of rejection by divorce, I was too frightened of being hurt.

I walked around the garden of the conference centre and sat out there on a bench, praying and agonizing for the first hour, feeling at a total loss. What was I going to say! I cried out to God for His help, and He said, "Just start to write."

With some trepidation, I began, "Dear Tony, when I sat down to write this, I did not know what to say. I am so sorry, but I felt a real dread in my heart about being with you for the rest of my life, which says a lot more about me than it does about you. I knew I couldn't write that. I wanted to be honest with you, but I did not want to hurt your feelings. As I write now, I actually feel . . ." When I got to the word *feel,* I felt a release in my heart, and miraculously I found myself writing, "a new hope and a new love rising in my heart for you, and I am looking forward in the coming years to building something really special together."

Whew! What a relief! I couldn't believe I had written those words and really believed them. It was a God moment; right then, as I wrote the words, a great new and unexpected onrush of love came into my heart for Tony that had not been there before.

At that moment, I know I fell supernaturally in love with Tony, and I am still in love with him over thirty-five years later. God enabled me to take all the barriers down and open my heart to Tony completely. You may imagine that this made an enormous difference to our relationship. We still had to work it out, bit by bit, but our marriage was definitely on a new page. We returned home with new hearts, determined to work on our communication skills and to listen to each other. The course leaders contacted us after the course. They asked whether we would like to attend another course and train to be leaders. God had used the course to make such a wonderful change in our relationship that we were eager to do so.

One of the consequences of being involved with these courses was that we met the most troubled peopled with seemingly impossible marriages. Sometimes you just wanted to say, "Okay, why don't you just quit! This marriage is impossible!"

But it was wonderful to see what God could do for people and how He wasn't at all fazed by the impossible. Some of the people we met remained in contact with us, even playing a major part in our lives as dear friends in future years. This has been, to me, one of the greatest thrills of the Christian life. It's not a setup like doctor and patient or the helpers and the helped. Each of us has the capacity to minister to one another. It is a mutual operation. We are a body, each with skills and abilities and anointing from the Father. Every person is able to help others, no matter how wounded we are or whatever difficulties we face from day to day.

There have been difficulties in our relationship over the years, of course. We did not ride off into the sunset and live happily ever after because our emotions fluctuate. However, I am so glad that with God's help we stuck it out. We worked at our marriage and pressed on to make it the wonderful, mature, and close relationship we have today.

I think Tony is lovelier and more handsome today than I ever thought in the past, and our relationship brings us great joy. He is the kindest man I know. Today we have been married for forty-five years, and we really do love each other more now than we did last year. What a journey it has been! By the grace of God, we have been immeasurably blessed, and even disaster brought us closer, making us more tender and thoughtful toward each other.

Of course, our relationship was greatly helped because we fed our hearts with the Word of God and learned to rely on the Word rather than our feelings. We realised, too, the importance of praying the Word of God. He showed us how to put the words of the Bible into the first person and pray. We organized a prayer room in our house. We put Scriptures on large pieces of art paper and stuck them onto the walls; then we went into the room and read the walls! We knew that when we spoke it with true faith that the Word could have as much power as when God spoke it Himself. We relied on the Scripture that says "no word from God shall be without power or impossible of fulfillment" (Luke 1:37). And that any word He (God) speaks "shall not return to [Him] void, But it shall accomplish what [He] please[s], and it shall prosper in the thing for which [He] sent it" (Isa. 55:11)

We took this message to heart and knew we were breaking exciting new ground in our spiritual walk. Faith began to grow in our hearts, and our spiritual strength increased. Being stronger spiritually helped our life in many practical ways.

It was then that another exciting, life-changing book came into our hands called *Chasing the Dragon* by Jackie Pullinger. It was the story of a young music teacher who felt God was calling her to go out as a missionary even though she had no training or experience in ministry. She boarded a ship and ended up in Hong Kong, where she got a job. Over time she began to work with drug addicts. She had no success until she met some Americans who talked to her about the importance of praying in tongues. She had been baptised into the Holy Spirit and had once spoken in tongues, but she had never bothered to use the gift. They instructed her to begin to pray in tongues for fifteen minutes a day.

Even though she did this reluctantly, she was amazed because the addicts started listening to her and were being drawn to Jesus as she spoke to them. Eventually she had a huge work in the walled city, where drug addicts came off drugs without withdrawal symptoms because they prayed in tongues until they were free.

It was clear to us that we needed to follow suit because we needed more of the power of God in our lives and ministry. When we prayed together each morning, we would pray in tongues for fifteen minutes whether we felt like it or not. To begin with, even five minutes seemed like an eternity, but we found a new power and grace flowing into our lives. We then understood how it was possible to "pray without ceasing" because we could pray in tongues easily while going about our ordinary daily tasks. "Pray without ceasing" became attainable, and we had broken through an invisible barrier in the Spirit—and in our own flesh!

CHAPTER 20

Another Move?

Coping with needy people was heavy work for a couple. We could see the need for a team. The vicarage in our village would soon be up for sale. We wondered if God was saying this was to be our community house, but the more we considered buying the house, the more we got into strife about it and the more confused we seemed to become.

Events seemed to be falling into place. We had come to know a lovely couple who expressed an interest in living in community. They were friends of a lady called Virginia, or Ginny for short, who ran the Cathedral Bookshop. I had come to know her because I ran our own church bookstall. It seemed more than a coincidence that soon after we met them the lovely old vicarage became vacant. We had talked with them about our ideas of community, and because we wanted to explore the possibilities of going into partnership with somebody, they decided they would come and stay with us for two weeks to give us time to get to know each other and explore our options. During that time, we all went to view the vicarage and thought it had possibilities, but during the time we spent together talking and praying, none of us had any positive leading to go ahead as a team. It seemed that we were at a dead end because Tony and I were not in agreement about buying the house anyway. We decided to ask a trusted minister friend to pray about it and see what God spoke to him. Immediately he sent back a Scripture from a Psalm 43:2, which said, "Why do I go mourning because of the oppression of the enemy?"

The scales fell off my eyes immediately. I saw it clearly. Purchasing this house wasn't an Isaac; it was an Ishmael. We were just trying to make something happen ourselves; like Abraham did when he was desperate to have the child God had promised him. The last thing we needed was a project out of our own minds because it would be sure to fail! The world is still suffering a few thousand years after Ishmael and Isaac lived after Abraham foolishly fathered Ishmael by his own plan and effort instead of waiting for God to fulfill His plan by giving him Isaac, the real promised son. We did not want to make the same mistake, and I felt so grateful that the issue was settled.

Working in the established church had always been hard because there was opposition to any change. There was even opposition to the gospel and the Holy Spirit. We were often tempted to be downhearted and to throw in the towel, but God would never let us. Just when we felt we could not possibly stay any longer; there would be a small breakthrough. Then we would be back on track and enjoying ourselves. In hindsight, the opposition we experienced could have been God's way of preparing us for what was just around the corner, which was going to be something much bigger and much more difficult. It would require large amounts of grit and determination.

When the new vicar, Dennis, came to our village, he said to us quite bluntly, "I don't think I will do things the way you would like me to, and I think you will leave."

We assured him we would not be going anywhere unless God spoke to us directly about it, and we meant it. We were totally committed.

In the few years after Philip's death, things had changed so much until there were now about thirty people who were filled with the Spirit or were at least born again and assenting to wonderful change. New life had come to the church, and the whole atmosphere was different; it had a new friendliness, a new spirituality, and a new joy. God showed me how to express the new life in the church and beautify it by making eight massive banners with bible verses on them. They hung on the organ loft, the pulpit and on the pillars. Everyone loved them including the bishop when he visited who said they were a sign that the church was alive. At last it felt like we were going somewhere.

When we led people to Jesus in the past, we sent them to the Baptist church because we knew that, as baby Christians, they would never weather the hardness and the deadness of the Anglican church as it had been. Except for the staunch churchgoers or the radicals like us, it was too hard. Now we could invite them into our own church, and the congregation grew.

However, the tensions did not cease. People wanted us to lead, but you cannot lead from behind; you have to be a follower. We found it hard to follow where we did not feel God was leading. We were impatient for things to move on to a more radical expression of the Holy Spirit's work. Dennis was not prepared to go that far and seemed always to be worried about displeasing people. Others who wanted things to change faster were criticizing Dennis to us, and we did not want to be a ready ear for dissidents.

However, one day I was in crisis, and I said to the Lord, "Lord, I am not happy. We are causing division, and I do not want to do that. From today, I am going to give it six months, and then if nothing changes, I am simply going to attend church, sit in the congregation, and cease making any waves."

This was in October. At Christmastime, we always put little paper doves with Scriptures inside them on the Christmas tree. At our Christmas party, we invited people to pray and ask God lead them to take a particular dove, believing God would speak to them. We were careful not to put Scriptures in the doves that represented any kind of direct guidance so it was not a fortune-telling kind of thing. It was meant to just be spiritual encouragement. On this Christmas, when I took my dove off the tree, it stopped me short: "Do you not say, 'there are still four months and then comes the harvest'? Behold, I say to you, lift up your eyes and look at the fields, for they are already white for harvest!" (John 4:35).

I gasped . . . I was just two months into my six months! Was there an imminent harvest? On New Year's Eve, God gave me the Scripture, "For you will go out with joy, and be led out with peace" (Isa. 55:12). But no guidance came as to when or how. I knew God did not lead you out of something without leading you into something else.

In the New Year, I decided that I wanted to be baptised by immersion in the Baptist church. I had been baptised by sprinkling many years earlier, but I felt for some it was not what the Bible taught about baptism. Tony and I talked about it, but he was not too sure that the quantity of water really mattered. It is certainly true that baptism is an outward sign of an invisible and spiritual grace.

In his lay reader's training, he was obviously presented with the Anglican way of thinking. He had to write a number of essays as part of his reader's course, and one of them had to be about baptism. I could not believe he was going to defend the Anglican party line in his essay by advocating baptism by sprinkling. He stoutly declared he would definitely not be baptised again.

I spoke to the vicar about my desire to be baptised by full immersion in the Baptist church, and he gladly gave me his blessing and attended the service to support my stand. Of course, Tony and the boys came, along with many friends.

When I gave my testimony, I completely forgot the boys were there because they were up in the chapel balcony where I could not see them. They heard me speak about my previous involvement in the occult, and I explained that we could not invite my parents to our home anymore because of their involvement in the occult that brought demonic influence to our home. We had explained to the children that we could not see Nana and Granddad for a while and promised that one day we would tell them why. I had shown them a big, heavy suitcase and asked them if they could pick it up. Of course, they could not. I explained that, just as they would be able to carry this suitcase when they were bigger, so they would one day be big enough to carry the real explanation. They seemed satisfied with that.

After the service, they bounded up to me and said, "Now we understand why we cannot see Nana and Granddad!"

Children! They are smarter than you think! It was such a wonderful moment, and I was really glad I had forgotten they were there.

Soon after I was baptised, Tony was driven to ask God if he should be baptised too. The word that came to him was, "When you are baptised, I will reveal your ministry to you." So of course he then wanted to do it and it was arranged for the following month. All this talk of ministry was extremely tantalizing because although we were always busy ministering to people, there seemed to be no official openings for us at all.

I was so thrilled that we would now both be baptised, but there was a funny moment during Tony's baptism service. The worship service was lively, and many people were raising their hands in true charismatic style. I was standing next to Tony's Aunty May; a staunch Baptist, her face showed extreme disapproval of all she could hear and see. She was utterly incensed by what she thought was such unseemly behavior in church. In high dudgeon, she reached up and pulled my arms down to my sides, saying loudly, "Put your arms down, Margaret!" It was a bit of a shock because I had my eyes closed!

Because of the effect that being baptised had on me, I understood that there was much more to being baptised than just going through a rite or quibbling about an amount of water. There is actually real spiritual power released by it. I felt entirely different afterwards. I was inwardly clean and new. The symbolism in baptism of dying and being raised from the dead as we go under the water and come up again is such a powerful picture of what happens to us when we are truly saved.

It is clear that the enemy hates baptism even more than he does the baptism of the Holy Spirit. In a way, our baptism was the beginning of the end of our time in the Anglican Church.

CHAPTER 21

Out of the Nest

At the beginning of 1981, there was a landmark event. Tony became involved in pioneering a Full Gospel Businessmen's chapter in Ely (FGB for short). A group of Spirit-filled men had been to an FGB chapter in Norwich and were keen to start one in Ely.

At that time, there were no Spirit-filled ministers in Ely, and there was only one who was born again and preaching the gospel. He had even lost many of his congregation preaching a radical gospel. However, the born-again man was not open to the baptism of the Spirit at that time.

When a visiting minister gave a gospel message at the Anglican Church in Ely, some people were incensed. They said, "We don't need to hear that kind of preaching, thank you very much!" It seemed so strange to me that churchgoers were offended when they heard the good news about salvation or about the baptism of the Holy Spirit. They always seemed to resent it, particularly the baptism of the Holy Spirit. Somehow talking about the Holy Spirit made them feel as if you were saying they were not really Christians. Of course, *if* they were like me when I was a churchgoer, I was not really a Christian!

How could it be that I was a churchgoer for nearly twenty years, attending church nearly all my life, yet I failed to make Jesus Lord of my life? I have heard many preachers say, "You could live in a garage all of your life, but it wouldn't make you a car." By the same token, it seems you can go to church all of your life, but it doesn't of itself make you a Christian. After the initial shock of realizing that I was not the real thing, I sought

God with all of my heart and found a reality beyond my wildest dreams, so I could never understand why these people rejected what I had come to love.

In 1981, an FGB began in the Lamb Hotel. After a meal and free worship, there was a testimony from someone about how God has blessed his financial affairs, and they took an offering. Then another man gave his testimony about God's dealings in his life—in particular the story about how he met Jesus or how God healed him. God uses these testimonies to bring salvation. In Ely it seemed that people were unaware of what God could do and did not want to know either. People thought we were very strange or some kind of a weird cult.

The press came to one of the meetings, and the headline in the local paper the following week read: "Moonies Grab Ely Cash!" Hmm, not very promising for the FGB!

Tony was secretary for the group, and we persevered with meetings for about a year. It was really hard going. When we gave people invitations, they were very suspicious and nearly always refused even though we were offering them a wonderful free dinner. Then something happened that finished the FGB in Ely off for good. Core members of the group found it increasingly difficult to go back to their own churches. If they had been dissatisfied before, they were increasingly so now.

There was brief excitement when the Countess of Huntingdon Connection church invited some Americans to come over to do a mission about the Holy Spirit, but hopes were cruelly dashed because the men who spoke trashed both the baptism of the Holy Spirit and speaking in tongues as a heresy and of the devil. In hindsight it was to be expected because they were Southern Baptists, who were well known at that time for this anti-Holy Spirit stance

Consequently a small group of friends began meeting to pray and seek God, and in October 1981, an Australian named Barrie said, "Well, I am going to hire the upper room at the Maltings down by the river and have a praise meeting. I will be there after the six-thirty church service every Sunday, even if it's only me, my wife, and my cat, Plonky!

We all met at eight o'clock, and a young couple named Peter and Virginia led the worship on their guitars; it was all very informal, and we had wonderful free worship. Tony, who had usually preached a sermon that day anyway, preached it again for the evening group. There were anything from ten to twenty of us, and we had a ball and formed good friendships.

We also met a radical young woman named Isobel Chapman who came to our FGB to give a testimony about her missionary work in the Philippines. She had an amazing testimony she recorded in a book called *Arise and Reap*. Her missionary trip was full of healings, miracles, and salvations. I particularly remember her telling how she prayed for people with goiters and saw the goiters disappear beneath her hands. She was such a young Christian, but she had simply given up her job in insurance and gone out on a limb for God. She strongly encouraged us to start a church and gave us a beautiful communion set.

We very soon lost touch with her but not before her visit caused a stir in Tony's school life. Tony was a physics teacher and the head of the Christian Union at the local college. He invited Isobel to speak at the lunchtime meeting. They had a whale of a time, with lots of children being baptised in the Holy Spirit and falling under the power of the Spirit. It seemed that everyone loved it except one particular girl, who was not actually upset by the demonstration of the power of the Spirit but upset because she did not receive anything! In the afternoon, a member of staff discovered her crying and reported it to the head. The cat was now among the pigeons. Tony was taken aside and reprimanded even though the girl told the head she was not upset about what had happened but about what did not happen. The headmaster closed the Christian Union, and Tony was given a black mark on his teaching record. Newspaper reporters called us, and even though Tony said, "No comment" to all of them, the *Daily Star*, a communist newspaper, still ran the headline: "Christian Union Banned."

When they pressed Tony further he told them that the headmaster had the authority in the school, and he therefore had the right to do whatever he decided was right. There is no real news in that! Everyone thought Tony had leaked information, but he hadn't. In hindsight, it was a case of power released without sufficient protection through the backup of intercession.

After some months, the core of the group who were meeting in Ely each week at the Maltings called a time of prayer and fasting to seek God's will for the future. They met at Barrie's house in Chapel Street on the last evening to share what God was saying. Many of them said, "We believe God wants us to start a full-gospel church in Ely, and we believe Tony Cornell should be the pastor."

Privately I said to Tony, "Oh no, the last thing I want to do is lead a church."

I knew I had been a hard person for our vicar to handle, and thought, *What if I have members of the congregation who are just like me. How will I handle them?* I was scared! Pastoring a church would not be a picnic. Tony and I agreed that we would take a week to pray and fast to ask God what He was saying to us. *Perhaps*, I thought hopefully, *God will just say no.*

We both decided we would expect God to speak in our normal Bible reading times and agreed that we would not discuss anything during the week but come together at the end of the week and share what God had said to us. There were Scriptures that stood out to me as I prayed that week. God led me to 1 Corinthians 2 and highlighted verses 12 and 13:

> Now we have received, not the spirit of the world, but the Spirit who is from God, that we might know the things that have been freely given to us by God. These things we also speak, not in words which man's wisdom teaches but which the Holy Spirit teaches, comparing spiritual things with spiritual.

Through this Scripture, I felt God was saying clearly that we would be teaching spiritual truths to those who had the Spirit. I found that exciting! God then directed me back to Isaiah 61, saying, "Look at our Scripture again. Look at verse 6 and then 8 and 9."

> But you shall be named priests of the Lord; they shall call you the servants of our God. . . . I will direct their work in truth, and will make with them an everlasting covenant. Their descendants shall be known among the Gentiles, and their offspring among the people. All who see them shall acknowledge them, that they are the posterity whom the LORD has blessed.

As I sought God, I had a growing sinking feeling, mixed with a tentative excitement, that God really did want us to start a church. Did God really think we were qualified to do that? Did we have any idea how to do that? I felt dismayed about leaving our village. We loved Isleham and its people. It had been the seedbed of our life in Christ and the place where we had been born again and filled with the Spirit. We also had lived in two exceptionally beautiful homes. It was a bittersweet place of great joy and tragic loss. People had been saved and baptised into the Holy Spirit through us, and we had built some great and treasured friendships. This was the place where our precious son was buried. We had made huge personal deposits into this village, and the thought of leaving it all behind was very hard. We had told the Lord that we would not leave the Anglican Church unless we were thrown out.

However, alongside the misgivings and sadness I felt in my heart about leaving Isleham, there was something else quite new growing in my heart. It was a rising sense of adventure, of destiny being fulfilled. I began to look forward to the time at the end of the week when Tony and I would share our guidance with each other. I hoped he had heard similarly encouraging things from the Lord.

Tony was using the Church of England lectionary. He had questions for God like, "Should we start a new church? Is it right for me to be the pastor? Should we move to Ely?" Quite extraordinarily, the answers to those three questions came back to Tony from his daily readings: Yes. . . Yes. . . Yes! One of the Scriptures Tony had received was:

> Go out of the ark, you and your wife, and your sons and your son's wives with you. Bring out with you every living thing of all flesh that is with you: birds and cattle and every creeping thing. . . (Gen. 8:16)

This seemed a very fitting Scripture because we had ducks, hens, and a donkey we wanted to take with us. If we were going to take all of them with us, God was going to provide a place that had ground big enough for all of them. I wondered how we would find that in a city.

The Scripture that had been most telling for me during the week was 1 Corinthians 2:4, which really excited me. The opportunity to teach about things of the Spirit, once I had accustomed myself to the idea, was a tantalizing prospect. I was certain that if Tony knew it was right, it was right! At the end of the week, of course, we shared the things we felt God had said to us, and we concluded that it was a definite, *"Yes . . . Go!"*

Tony went off to the group prayer meeting in Ely that night to report our decision. I always love to be in the thick of things, wherever the action is, but quite uncharacteristically, I felt I needed to stay at home that night with the children. I soon found out why God had led me to stay at home when during the evening, a letter came through the letter box. I heard it plop into the wire-letter cage; I knew it was an important letter. I knew it was the reason I had felt led to stay at home that night. I ran to the door and recognized the vicar's writing on the envelope. My heart sank. Oh dear . . . I had been expecting some trouble after what had happened on the Sunday, and I knew in my heart this letter was connected with that.

Tony had preached a great sermon on healing. In the course of the preaching, he had asked people to raise their hands to indicate if God had healed them of anything. Many people raised their hands. On their way out of the church, several women shook Tony's hand warmly and said what a wonderful word it was and how much they had enjoyed it. Those of us who wanted so much to see the gift of healing used more in the church were overjoyed because it looked as though the door was opening.

However, as I sat in the choir stalls, I had a bird's-eye view of things I might have preferred not to have seen. I could see the congregation's faces lighting up, but I also noticed out of the corner of my eye some stiffened faces and some disapproving looks, which spelled trouble.

Holding the letter in my hand, I rang Tony. When I telephoned, Tony had just finished sharing the guidance we had received, so there was a very joyful atmosphere in the room. I said, "A letter has come tonight, and I am sure it is from the vicar. Shall I open the letter and read it to you?"

"Yes," he said, "do."

Trembling, I opened it. I was right; it was from the vicar. I cannot remember the exact words, but it read something like this:

Dear Tony,

After you preached this last Sunday and what you did during the sermon—asking for people to raise their hands, which offended some people—I feel that I must ask you to tone down your sermons; otherwise, I do not feel that I can continue to let you preach.

Yours sincerely. . . etc.

I said, "Tony, we have been released to go. We have been shown the door."

I did not know whether to laugh or cry. There was no way that we could even begin to think of toning things down because we were just beginning to tone up! When Tony reported his release to leave the Church in Isleham, there was a tremendous whoop of joy. This final word completed everything; the vicar had propelled us into our new venture.

When we shared our guidance with him, Dennis was horrified. "Oh no," he said. "I was not meaning to throw you out. I don't want you to leave."

However, it was too late. We reassured him that we loved him and his letter was not the primary reason we were leaving. We explained that we genuinely knew God had called us to start a church in Ely and that the group there had called us to be pastors.

Telling others, especially our close friends, that we were leaving was hard. Some people were disappointed and hurt, and some of them blamed the vicar for us leaving. I was so glad we had received such solid guidance of our own before the vicar's letter arrived because we could tell them firmly that our exit was certainly not the vicar's doing. Some felt we were abandoning them. I am sure many people thought that we were completely crazy. Start a church?

We planned to start the church, christened Ely Christian Fellowship, on Palm Sunday in just two weeks, which seemed appropriate because it was the day when Jesus rode into Jerusalem on a donkey. Jesus was certainly coming into Ely in a new way on that day.

The vicar went to every church member, told them we were leaving, and collected money for a sending-out gift. He was very surprised to find that people were genuinely sorry to see us go and were very generous. We might have been a thorn in his flesh, but the majority of the congregation also loved and respected us.

As we stood in front of the congregation on our last Sunday, Dennis led prayers for us, blessed us, and sent us out. What a precious moment that was, and how much we loved and respected him for it. We were very happy that we were able to leave the church in peace with all men and in good standing with the church congregation. Thus we were ready to start afresh in Ely with a clean slate. Perhaps Dennis breathed a sigh of relief that we were going, but he did not say it!

God had fulfilled the Scripture beautifully that was written inside the dove I had taken off the Christmas tree: "For you shall go out with joy, and be led out with peace."

CHAPTER 22

Flying by the Seat of Our Pants

We were raw recruits, and we had no practical experience with running a church. We were bewildered by the various models of church government, and our inexperience in this area caused some problems. Because people joined us from all sorts of different churches with experience with different models of church government, they all had slightly different expectations of how a church should be run.

All we were sure of was that there needed to be power sharing. Tony would lead and guide the group in consultation with others. People varied in their responses from, "Just tell us what to do and we will do it," to "We think we should be involved in all of the decisions." It was not an easy situation to handle, and it took some working out.

In the period coming up to our first official Sunday morning meeting, we had a meeting to share what we believed about communion and when we thought we would have it; how, where, and when we would baptise people; whether we would adopt a pattern of formal membership as some churches do; etc. We did our best to follow what we felt God was telling us to do and tried to take others along with our decisions through Bible teaching and inspiration rather than discussion. I imagine the early church was the same.

The first Sunday meeting was tremendously exciting—positively euphoric! Everyone prayed over us, and we all made a corporate confession of what we believed, which Tony and I had composed. It was a vision for a Bible-based church that would honour God the Father, God the Son, and the work of God the Holy Spirit. We all declared it as one, and all fourteen of us signed it. Thirty years later, it is fascinating to see how little we have changed our minds.

Our dear friends John and Stella Hughes came to one of our early church meetings, and John gave us an interesting prophetic word about a large house. He said, "You will have a very large house. It's a mansion. I can see a picture of it."

I asked, "Is it a heavenly mansion or an earthly mansion?"

He was sure it was an earthly mansion and proceeded to describe it in detail: "It is an oblong, cream-coloured house with white pillars across the front. It has a large lawn in front of it with a semicircular drive. There are large, wrought-iron gates and square gateposts with pagoda-like tops."

It seemed a very concrete description, but where was it? Later on, I heard that someone had mentioned to a friend that a huge property called Egremont House was for sale in Ely, and her friend had laughed and said, "Oh, the Cornells will buy that!"

When I heard this reported conversation immediately something was alert, and I had a strong urge to find out more. I jumped into the car and drove to Ely. As I drove down Egremont Street, I saw it! Well at least I saw the wrought iron gates and the gateposts with pagoda-like tops. I could not see beyond because by the time I got there it was dark

In the morning I hurried back, and there was the lawn, the house, and the pillars, just as John had described it. It was indeed a mansion and looked empty! We found out that the estate agency was a large Cambridge firm and eagerly made inquiries. It was on the market for a lot more money than we could afford, but we had been in that situation before!

We both knew we must buy this house. We also felt Peter and Virginia, our worship leaders, a couple we barely knew, should join us there. When we were having our midweek meeting in Peter and Virginia's home, we said, "We are going to buy Egremont House. All we need is someone with twenty-five thousand pounds."

"Okay," said Peter. "If we sell our house, we will have twenty-five thousand pounds. Can we buy it with you?"

"Peter, are you serious?"

"Yes, absolutely."

"That's a deal then."

"We are not trying to push you into anything, you know," said Peter.

"We know you aren't," said Tony. "Just get your house on the market."

Then it was *their* turn to ask if we were serious, and we assured them that we were completely serious. We did not know them very well in the natural sense at that stage, but we knew by the Spirit that they were the people who should move in with us.

Apparently they had already been aware of the house and had discussed buying it themselves. They also had an interest in community living and had discussed what community living might mean for them. We had no idea that Peter and Ginny had been looking at this house for years and had felt they would like to buy it and that they, like us, had guidance from God that they would have a large house and a community. We made an appointment to go and view the house together on March 1.

This house was big and bleak. It obviously needed a lot of money to fix it up. It had a massive hall with an elegant staircase. It had ten huge bedrooms and two large downstairs rooms, which were obviously a sitting room and a dining room. It had a massive kitchen with an AGA; a huge cast iron four oven stove, a utility room, and a breakfast room. There was a study, which was referred to in the sales details as the morning room. There was also a large cellar, two acres of grounds, sheds, and a large garage.

I felt gloomy. Frost damage had cracked all the toilet pans. Plaster was falling off the walls in places, and the plumbing was antiquated. The kitchen had no sink, just some musty old cupboards and an old boiler, which looked like one of the first ever invented. The cracked kitchen ceiling was like a parched desert; the tiled floor looked as if an earthquake had taken place, and it was also covered with thick, white mold; and the cellar had three feet of water in it. The whole place was depressing. . . except for the Aga. I could be excited about the Aga. I had always wanted an Aga, and we had already been to a demonstration on how to use one. I could also feel warm about the elegant staircase. I could imagine sweeping down it in an evening dress. I could see the goats being happy in the sheds. I could also see how sumptuous the front of the house could look if we renovated the pillars and the double doors.

Tony did not appear to be overjoyed either. We were both looking at it soberly, counting the cost. Peter and Ginny, on the other hand, were excited. While they were oohing and aahhing with delight, I went and sat on the elegant staircase and had a serious chat with the Lord. "Lord, if you really want us to buy this house, you need to make it very clear to me. We have already renovated two properties at great personal cost. I do not want to take this on if it is not Your will."

Odd, isn't it, that even when you know something is God's will, if it looks too hard, you always ask Him to tell you again just like Gideon did with his fleeces? The problem was that I *did* know it was His will, so when I got home, I prayed about it a lot.

One day I said to the Lord, "This house is very expensive." He replied to me with Genesis 22:14: "Abraham called the name of this place, The-Lord-Will-Provide."

I had known the next house we would buy would have an Aga, and a few months earlier, before we knew we had Egremont House, an unsought invitation had arrived in the post for an Aga cookery demonstration in Cambridge. Believing that we would have a house with an AGA Ginny and I had attended it eagerly.

After some time we were dismayed to find that Egremont House was now "sold subject to contract" for a price that was far above our modest means. The survey that we had on the house was very frightening. It said that it needed at least thirty thousand pounds to bring it up to a habitable condition. We asked the agent to let us know if the house came back on the market, but he was not hopeful. He also was not impressed with the fact that, so far, we had not been able to produce any money.

On February 25, I asked the Lord, "What are you going to do now that the house is sold?"

In response, He spoke to me and said, "Look at Genesis 8:14." It read, "And in the second month, on the twenty-seventh day of the month, the earth was dried." He also gave me Jeremiah 10:18, which said: "Behold, I will throw out at this time the inhabitants of the land."

I rushed in to Tony and said, "The house will be back on the market on Saturday. It's ours!"

The following Saturday was February 27—the second month. On that day, we were standing in the hall when, *plop*, through the letterbox came a long, white, official-looking envelope. The letter said in so many words, "Egremont House is back on the market. Are you interested?"

We were indeed interested but had no money. It did not make us look like genuine buyers. The agent was pressing us to put down a deposit.

Members of the church group in Ely were pressing us to get a bridging loan in faith that we would sell. However, we did not think we should do anything but wait.

In the previous March when we had viewed the property, Ginny had asked the Lord, "Lord, when will we move in?" She was confident that God answered her by saying we would be moving in May. It would not be long then. Peter felt he should walk around the house praying in tongues every day for six days and then seven times on the seventh day, just as Joshua and the Israelites had marched in faith around Jericho. Ginny said that after Peter did this, she had a picture of the big wrought iron gates with padlocks on them.

We had both put our houses on the market, and we had sought planning permission for the land at the back of our house, which was valued at ten thousand pounds. Naturally speaking, we did not stand a chance of getting the permission because the council classed it as back development. Predictably, the council refused the permission, but we appealed. Isleham is *full* of back development, and it is part of the character of the place. We knew we would get the permission because God gave me Isaiah 61:7. The verse said: "In their land they shall possess double . . ."

When we did not have Egremont House by May that year, we were puzzled. We asked God what was going on. He said, "Do nothing, and in September you will know."

We had no buyer but Peter and Ginny had sold their property immediately, so they moved in with us at Sunbury House. It did not seem to make sense that there were now six of us going back and forth from Isleham to Ely day after day. What it did, though, was give us the opportunity to get to know each other better. We tried to establish the habit of praying together before the upheaval of actually moving into Egremont House.

Before we could come up with any money, another buyer loomed up for Egremont House. The agent rang us and in his posh, drawling tones rather condescendingly told us that he needed to decide whether to sell to us or to this new buyer. Dryly, he said that he hoped he would make the right decision. Tony told him that he had no doubt which buyers were the right ones, for as far as we were concerned, and despite what it might look like, God had told us the house was ours. The man chortled and said, "You sound just like your wife."

Tony replied, "We are absolutely agreed about it!"

After he had put the phone down, we were the probably the laughingstock of the office. Well, predictably the agent made the wrong choice. He decided to sell it to the other man. I am sure our faith talk just sounded like hot air, and I do not think the agent ever considered us as a real prospect. In wobbly moments it even sounded like hot air to me too! Even the local paper told us and the rest of the world that the house was sold. The plan was for a small hotel. The new buyer even published detailed plans for the adaptation. On paper, it all looked good.

Everyone bombarded us with this bad news. A friend of mine crowed over the article, seeming almost glad we had not got the house. I told her in no uncertain terms that whatever the paper said, God had told us to buy it and the house was ours. She never spoke to me again. It hurt, but I understood perfectly. It did sound outrageous.

People must have talked about us because a girl in our church had a visit from a relative in another village who said, "Do you know who this mad woman is who lives in Isleham and says God has told her to buy a big house in Ely?"

During this waiting period, we were very attracted to a large, immaculate house we saw on the market. It looked like my heart's desire. We all went to have a look at it and even told the owner we were interested. The next day, I was stricken that we had been foolish. I rang the owner of the house and apologized for misleading him. We could not buy any other property.

At this point, our whole family went off on the trip of a lifetime to the States.

CHAPTER 23

American Adventure

In 1982, in the midst of preparing to move and seeking to buy Egremont House, God had spoken to us about taking the boys to America for the whole of the school summer holidays to attend conferences run by the various people whose ministries we had really grown to love and respect, such as Kenneth Hagin and Kenneth Copeland. It was due to their teaching that we had grown so much in our understanding and operation of faith.

It seemed completely the wrong time to be going away and spending so much money, but I have learned that God does not work or think as we do. It says in Isaiah 55:9, "His ways are higher than our ways and His thoughts are higher than our thoughts."

We kept the idea of the trip alive in our hearts by a simple faith action. We stuck a little card on the kitchen window that had been given to us by our dear friends John and Stella Hughes. The card read, "We went to Camp Meeting 1981." We edited the card so it read, "We are going to Camp Meeting 1982." I would look at this every day and thank the Lord that He was going to make it possible. It was a confession we used daily to prepare our hearts for a whole year before we planned to go.

In the spring, we began to pray in earnest about the trip. As soon as we did that, gifts of money began to arrive. Anonymous envelopes came through the door with notes in them—two hundred pounds and three hundred pounds. People sent money by post or gave it to us personally. Very soon we had accumulated enough to pay for four flights with Braniff Airlines. This was a brand-new airline that was cheaper than all the others.

We bought the tickets and planned our itinerary. We had no budget for accommodations and very little spending money, so we asked the Lord to supply that too.

In the first week, we wanted to be in Tulsa, Oklahoma, for Kenneth Hagin's Camp Meeting. In the second week, we wanted to be in a place called Broken Arrow, which we thought was fairly near Tulsa, for Hagin's Prayer and Healing School. During another week, we wanted to be at Christ for the Nations Bible College, and for the last week, we wanted to be at Kenneth Copeland's convention in Fort Worth, Texas. We prayed and trusted God to make all of this possible. All we knew was that the favor of God was upon us for this trip. The first two weeks were easy; John and Stella had a friend who was going to lend us her flat in Tulsa. Apart from that, we had no idea where we were going to stay for the next three weeks.

A few weeks before we were due to go to America I went to a Women's Aglow meeting at the Mildenhall Military Base. A young blind woman from California came that day and gave a remarkable testimony. Her eyes had been removed from their sockets but God was re-growing eyeballs in her empty eye sockets. Feeling a bit squeamish, I forced myself to look into her empty eye socket. It was a strange sight, but I could clearly see that there was what looked like a growing eyeball in there.

An older woman accompanied this interesting young woman, and we chatted together. In casual conversation with absolutely no agenda, I mentioned that we were going to America and staying in Tulsa for Hagin's Camp Meeting and then going on to meetings in Broken Arrow the week after.

"Oh," she said, "that's amazing. Next week my son and his family are moving to Broken Arrow. I know they would love to put you up. It's quite a long way from Tulsa to Broken Arrow. Would you like me to ask him if you can stay there?"

I said I would be thrilled if she could arrange it, and I left her my telephone number. True to her word, she rang me and gave me her son's telephone number so we could contact them once we got to Oklahoma. Miraculously, we had now sorted out the first two weeks of our trip. John and Stella had attended Christ for the Nations College in Dallas for a year, and so they asked for us to be offered the missionary flat there for our third week. We heard it was unlikely to be given to us, but nonetheless God arranged for us to have it.

Our provision for the weekend after that was a weekend stay with some other friends of John and Stella in Duncanville. The final week, we knew, was a little less clear. Well . . . actually not just unclear; we actually had nothing fixed at all, but there was no doubt in our minds that God would provide for us.

One morning I was horrified to read in the *Times* that the airline had gone bust. I asked the travel agent what that might mean for us. He said, "Well, it almost certainly means you have lost all of your money."

"Oh no," I said. "We have not lost it. That's God's money. He gave it to us for the trip, and He will certainly look after it."

He laughed unbelievingly and said, "Well I hope for your sake that you are right."

I said, "I am."

We prayed earnestly that night, believing that the money would be reclaimed. It would have been easy for us to believe we had lost the money because a friend who had booked flights with Freddy Laker's airline, which had gone bust, had lost every penny.

A day or so later, the travel agent rang me. "Well, Mrs. Cornell, you were right. I am very glad to tell you that you have not lost your money and you can rebook with another airline. However, you will need to pay another forty pounds each for the fare." Instead of losing over one thousand pounds, this little bit extra seemed like chicken feed. Whew! This was rescue indeed, but our success made me feel worse about our friends' loss.

We flew off on our great adventure, which we knew would be full of wonderful, new experiences. In the United States, the intensity of the heat was quite shocking—like nothing we had ever experienced before. As we stepped out of the plane, it felt like we were walking into a hot oven.

The flat in Tulsa was stiflingly hot because it had very noisy air conditioning that kept us awake, so we turned it off, choosing instead to sweat through the night. We had planned to do without a car, so each day we had to walk to the convention centre. Going in the early morning was hot, but coming home late at night was easier.

We were truly innocents abroad. We had no idea at all about how far it was to travel anywhere in the States. Everything was so different from England. Everywhere is so far away from everywhere else. We drew some interested stares as we walked along. It seemed that nobody walked anywhere in America.

The convention was so good. We loved every minute of it and took copious notes. Kenneth Hagin was marvelous preacher who built our faith and made the Word come alive. His experience and spiritual maturity were so evident. The children went to the Willie George meetings for children and seemed to have a ball. We were thrilled that there was good, solid Word teaching for them too.

One day we met Kenneth Hagin and his wife as they walked among the people at the convention. We felt privileged. We met some lovely people, especially a man named Mark Meiners who worked with Norvel Hayes, one of the other conference speakers. Mark later played an important part in our lives.

I have come to appreciate Norvel Hayes's ministry a great deal, but at that time, because of his odd accent and the way he ran all his words together, I had such severe difficulty understanding a word that he was saying that I opted out of some of his meetings. He may as well have been speaking Chinese for all I understood of what he was saying. However, afterwards, when we listened to the tapes at home, I loved him! Perhaps it was jet lag!

Soon the conference was over, and it was time for us to move on. At the end of that first week, true to her promise, the son of the woman I met at Mildenhall picked us up. He took us to his home in Broken Arrow. He was so thrilled to have us to stay. He introduced us proudly to his beautiful Korean wife and his two lovely daughters. They were roughly the same age as our boys, and they, too, were overjoyed to have new friends to stay.

We were so blessed by this family's generosity because the wife lent us her car every day for the whole week. Tony braved the American roads and drove the wife to work so we could use the car for the rest of the day.

The prayer school meetings were in the mornings and the healing school in the afternoons. While we were at the meetings, all the children went together to a local holiday club run by the Salvation Army, where there was swimming and games.

We took the girls out with us one day to the amazing Oral Roberts campus. It is a wonderful place. We walked around awestruck. Oral Roberts had built the most wonderful hospital. In the foyer was a beautiful fountain.

It is a place where they minister to the body, the soul, and the spirit at the same time. They actually employed staff to minister to people in all of these different ways.

Next to the main building, they had built a massive prayer tower. It was open around the clock, and a constant team of people were in there taking phone calls for intercessory prayer. We went up to the large viewing area, where we saw a film about Oral Roberts's vision and how he conceived and built the complex. Seeing a place that was built by the faith we coveted for ourselves was so encouraging.

The two girls thought that it was great fun being with their English speaking friends that week. They said to me, "Aw gee, you're just like Mary Poppins."

When we were walking along complete strangers who passed by would stop us and ask us to say something to them just because they loved the sound of our English accents. Someone actually thought that I really *was* Julie Andrews! I was flattered!

At prayer and healing school that week, we were so blessed. The worship had such a sweet, gentle spirit, and there was such an atmosphere of love. God imparted so much faith to the congregation to receive healing through Kenneth Hagin that day. One afternoon during the worship, I saw what looked like a beautiful, shimmering cloud hovering over the congregation. After the meeting had finished, Hagin said, "Did anyone see the glory cloud today?" I was so excited because I did! I saw it shimmering and hovering over us! We insisted that the boys give up playing one day and come to receive prayer from Kenneth Hagin. They came under protest, but we could not let them miss out on being in the presence of such a great man of God.

Our next port of call was Christ for the Nations. We arrived as a three-day meeting was in full swing. We entered into it with great enthusiasm, especially the vibrant praise and worship. There were people signing, or using language for the deaf and dumb, and dancing during the worship. In fact, we noticed that wherever we travelled to in the States, there was always a special section for the deaf and dumb. The section was always full of people. Where on earth were these people in England?

The boys were thrilled about Christ for the Nations. I would love to be able to tell you their enthusiasm was because of the spiritual quality of the place but principally it was because there was a McDonald's just up the road and a swimming pool just outside the apartment block! Tony and I had already been in over sixty hours of meetings, but we were not in the least bit fed up with them. Each one of them had given us something different. It was like collecting the pieces of a jigsaw puzzle. We were so spiritually hungry and so inspired by all we were hearing that it was pure joy.

We had a little free time at Christ for the Nations to relax and go swimming, and in the lovely pool, we had the privilege of meeting Freda Lindsey, wife of the famous founder of the college. Meeting this woman of God who had weathered the storms and pressures of being a pioneer was wonderful. When she heard that we too were pioneers, she insisted that they would send us a complete set of her husband's books.

The missionary flat was lovely and more than enough for our needs. We easily made friends with some of the students who had cars, and they took us to the shops when we needed to buy food.

We also visited a church that week with a couple of students. We knew one of them had just been diagnosed that very week with cancer. At the end of the service, and she went forward for prayer and was obviously in great distress, travailing at the altar rail, obviously doing business with God. A couple of days later, we heard that she had been completely healed! She had no cancer in her body anymore! We felt we were treading a miracle trail each day. Miracles were happening to us and to those around us.

Next we moved to where John and Stella had arranged for us to stay with some of their friends who lived in Duncanville. It was a wonderful time with them because as they helped us, they received help themselves. We had deep conversations with them and found that they were greatly discouraged because they felt rejected by their denomination. The husband had been divorced a number of years previously. When the church found out about the divorce, they were told that they would never be able to become leaders in the church, just as Tony had been told he could never be a vicar or a non-stipendiary priest because I had been divorced. It was almost as if the church thought divorce was the unforgivable sin. It was such an encouragement to them that I had been divorced and that God was calling us to be pastors despite it.

It was soon time to move on to Fort Worth, where we still had to find accommodation for the final week. There we were, in a strange place, knowing nobody but absolutely sure God had everything in hand for our stay.

One of the students at Christ for the Nations had recommended that we go to a particular church in Fort Worth because they were strong supporters of Kenneth Copeland. We telephoned the pastor, who said he would certainly find us a family to stay with during the convention. We arrived at Fort Worth in time for the service, during which a notice was given out that they needed accommodation for a family of four—two pastors and two children—as well as for another couple.

One family had already been asked tentatively if they could accommodate us, but they intended to refuse us and accept the couple because they were intimidated that we were pastors. However, the other family who had volunteered to have guests only had room to take the couple and did not have room for us. She told us how horrified she was when the pastor pressed them to take us instead. However, God knows what He is doing. She needed us as much as we needed her. Our visit was a great blessing to her and her husband. God was sending the troops in because their marriage was in deep trouble.

I had prayed and asked God very specifically for what we needed that week. There was no child care or children's meetings at the convention, so wherever we stayed needed to provide a good experience for our boys. It needed to be a safe place for them to play, with, of course, a swimming pool. I asked God to find us a family with some sensible teenage children who would love to look after our boys while we were at the meetings

When we got into their car, we knew we had found the right place. There were the two lovely, teenage children, a boy and a girl. On the journey home, they told us they lived in a new complex with its own pool by the side of Eagle Mountain Lake. The husband was a wealthy executive who owned a share in an airplane and worked all over the country. Their house was indeed a beautiful property, and it and its surroundings lived up entirely to every word I had prayed. It was safe, and its location, beside Eagle Mountain Lake, was just beautiful. The teenagers were pleased to be with our children. My list was ticked!

Casually the dad asked us what we wanted to do for the rest of the day. Did we want to go to church that night, or would we prefer to go out on the lake in the speedboat and try water-skiing? I think they were considerably heartened and less intimidated when we chose the boat and the water-skiing! They did not realise that we had attended such a great host of meetings in the space of four weeks that we needed some relaxation! We had done more than enough for anyone to demonstrate that they were spiritual!

We soon broke the ice that first night and had a deep conversation that lasted long into the night. We did not realise they were very prejudiced against the Copelands, having heard all sorts of gossip, which we assured them was untrue. The next day the wife drove us to the convention, and with some difficulty, we persuaded her to stay

After she had been to a few meetings, she could hardly bear to stay away. By the end of the week, the husband was coming too, and they began to see that by faith in God there was a way out of their difficulties. It was wonderful to see how the Word of God inspired them to think quite differently about their problems.

We flew home on Ben's eleventh birthday. The crew found him a tiny birthday cake and a candle and sang happy birthday to him. He was then invited to go into the cockpit to watch the pilot. When they asked him if he would like to do that, we all looked so wide-eyed and eager that they let us all go. It was so awesome seeing the wide circle of the earth. The colour was incredible, and the view of God's beautiful world spread out beneath us was a glorious sight.

What an adventure! We got home with books full of notes, our minds full of the Word, and hearts so full of gratitude for all the loving-kindness and care we had received. We had blessed the people who had blessed us, and God had so obviously planned it all. Better still; the teaching had filled us with faith and confidence, equipping us for the daunting task of pastoring a church. I think we had enough notes to fuel our preaching for at least a year.

CHAPTER 24

It's On!

While we were in America, we had a phone call from Peter and Ginny, who told us that . . . wait for it—yes! Egremont House had come back on the market yet again! The previous buyer had paid his deposit of eight thousand pounds but had been unable to find the money to complete the purchase within the agreed time. Consequently, he lost not just the house but his deposit as well. It was sad for him, and we prayed God would bless him in some other way.

We were waiting in faith for the completion of the sale, but we knew we should do nothing in a hurry. It would very soon be September, the month when God had said we would know. God showed me that we should get in touch with the executor of Mrs. Evan's will instead of the agents. We had definitely had enough of condescending agents.

I wrote a very simple and chatty letter to the solicitor, telling him the whole story from start to finish, sparing nothing. I had the collywobbles as I dropped the letter into the post box because there was a risk he might dismiss us out of hand as loonies, but faith said otherwise.

The solicitor replied to us in heart-warming terms. He was thrilled that we wanted to use the house for Christian work because the previous owner, Mrs. Evans, was a Christian, and he was the son of a local vicar. It seemed that he too was fed up with the agent. He said, "Make me an offer!"

Thinking that we needed to spend thirty thousand pounds to renovate the house, we offered a low amount and gradually increased our offers by ten thousand at a time until he said, "Look, I already have eight thousand pounds toward the house from the previous sale. Offer me seventy-eight thousand pounds, and I will square it with the owners." The amount we paid for the house was a lot less than the amount we had offered the previous year.

The eight thousand-pound deposit became ours. Proverbs 13:22 came true: "The wealth of the sinner [was] stored up for the righteous." (The righteous being those who are accounted righteous before God because they have faith in Jesus Christ). Rejoicing, we realised it was September, and we knew!

Our faith had been tested and proved, and there were many signs that God was watching over us closely all of the time. One example of his watchful care was our contact with a young man named Mark Meiners.

We had met Mark in America and spent some time with him at Camp Meeting, where he had had shown a lot of interest in our plans. Out of the blue he telephoned and woke us in the middle of the night.

He told us that he was on his way to India to preach and asked if he could visit us on his way through. He said we had been on his mind a great deal and God had given him something very important that he must share with us. I drove to Heathrow airport to pick him up. We shared a few days of great fellowship. He listened attentively to Peter, Ginny, Tony, and I when we explained our plans. Then he said, "Now I really know why God sent me here."

He expounded some scriptural principles about authority that, had we ignored them, could have destroyed our ministry at the house. He explained that although Peter was head of his own family, Peter and Ginny needed to let Tony have the headship of the house. Although we would discuss things, Tony should be allowed to have the final say about the running of things.

He also said we should have no legal agreement or safeguards about ownership like a contract or a joint mortgage but that we should base our relationship and the whole enterprise entirely on trust and faith. Peter and Ginny, he said, should pray and consider whether they still wanted to go ahead with the deal under those terms. He said this might seem to put Peter and Ginny in a dangerous position, but if we all had integrity, it would not do so. The question was, could they trust us enough? Did they believe we had that much integrity?

Mark said that if we did things this way, it would ensure the safety of the ministry of the house, but it meant that if Peter and Ginny wanted to leave and we did not want to sell the house, they would have to leave taking nothing out. Since they had sunk all of their money into the property, this was a very big decision to make. To their credit, they wholeheartedly agreed to these terms. We were so impressed with their faith and integrity that we made a pact with ourselves to always live up to the trust they'd placed in us.

After months of waiting, it seemed that Egremont House was again in danger of slipping through our fingers. Rumours reached our ears that someone had made a better offer for the house, and even the kind solicitor was getting impatient because we were still unable to produce any money. He must have also been a man of integrity who would not go back on his word.

Interest in our lovely Queen Anne house was very low, but during the autumn, at last, we seemed to find a prospective buyer. A family came to view it a couple of times and made encouraging noises. They made us a good offer, but I was strangely uneasy. I prayed about it and asked God why I felt so uneasy. He said, "Look at Jeremiah 9:6." I was shocked because it said, "Your dwelling place is in the midst of treachery and deceit."

Somewhat alarmed, we prayed that this deceit would not succeed. We soon discovered that the prospective buyer had written to the council opposing our planning permission for the building land hoping to get both the house and the land for the same price. This was of course legal but did not show much integrity

When they came to view the house again, I displayed the notice we had received from the council regarding their objection in a very prominent place where they would be sure to see it. I wanted them to know we knew what they were doing. Needless to say, we did not sell the house to these crafty people.

At Christmastime, we had a very handsome offer for the house. We were so excited because this offer would give us much more available cash. The prospective purchaser also planned to restore the house completely to its Queen Anne grandeur, which sounded like a great idea. However, on the day when we had tentatively agreed to sign contracts, again I felt uneasy, so Tony rang to check that all was well. My uneasiness was justified; the buyer had changed his mind due to a very bad surveyors' report.

Help! If, as the man's report had suggested, our house was in such a bad state, it did not simply mean we had lost a buyer, but it might mean our house was unsaleable. Fortunately we had a surveyor friend and asked him to come and look the house over. He examined it with a fine-tooth comb, and all he could find was a few loose roof tiles and a small patch of damp in a cupboard at the side of the chimney breast in the dining room. There was nothing terrible at all.

What on earth was all that about, we wondered! But it did not take much wondering. The answer was easy: Satan did not want us to sell our house and buy Egremont House. However, the disappointment left us reeling. Later on when we were praying with some friends about it, the Lord gave us a gentle rebuke for our response, which really indicated unbelief. Our friend Brian said to Tony, "You have an apple in your hand, but you can have the whole orchard full of apples. What are you going to do?"

"Well," Tony said, "I suppose I should put the apple in my pocket and leave my hands free to pick the rest."

"Precisely."

God was using the apple as a metaphor for our house. The apple of Egremont House must remain safely tucked away in our pocket and instead of fretting and worrying, God simply wanted us to get on with building God's kingdom and leave the rest to Him.

"Oh Lord," I said, "How on earth will I know the genuine buyers when they come?"

He said, "Trust me! You will know them when you see them."

In January we had a breakthrough. The solicitor for Egremont House suggested that we give him the largest deposit we could muster and sign contracts immediately. He then offered us a year to complete the transaction. In that year, we could get into the property and start the work that so badly needed to be done. A year! What a miracle; I am sure it must be completely unheard of to get a year to complete a sale!

We gladly accepted the solicitor's generous offer and parted with our twenty-five thousand pounds on the clear understanding that if we made any changes to the house but failed to complete the sale, we would have to put it all back as we had found it. Now we could move into the property, clean up, chip the plaster off the walls downstairs, and deal with the damp. We could replace the rotted joists in the morning room and attack the now vastly overgrown garden.

While Peter and Ginny were staying in Isleham with us, they had conceived a baby, which was due in April. The stalwart Ginny did not want to be left out of the effort to get things shipshape and made gargantuan efforts, staggering about heavily pregnant, knocking down walls and pulling up trees around the garden. Their wonderful little girl, Zara, was born on April 14, and we sent Ginny off to her mother's house to rest and recuperate.

A week or two after we had paid our deposit and made a start on the house, a young man came to view the Isleham house, and at once I knew he was our real buyer, just as the Lord had said: "You will know them when you see them." The man took a perfunctory look at the house and poked his head around the doors to each room, saying, "Yes . . . yes . . . yes."

When he reached the front door after his lightning tour, he said, "I'd like to bring my wife to look on Saturday. Is that okay?" As promised, she came on Saturday and also looked around very quickly. She said, "Yes, we love it; we want to buy it." I think I must have looked a bit puzzled because by way of explanation, she smiled and said, "We have a house just like this in Derbyshire."

The sale swung into action with completion at the end of April, and just as the Lord had told Ginny, we would be in Egremont House in May. The only difference was that we thought He meant May 1982, not May 1983! God's timing is very often so different from ours. It's odd, but I just happen to be writing this sentence on Zara's birthday twenty-six years later!

Everything speeded up. The planning permission for our land at the back of the house came through. We instantly had three good offers from people who wanted to buy it. The offers were so similar that we had to ask the Lord which one to accept. We really needed to know which one would be the most reliable purchaser because we could not afford any more hold-ups. Miraculously, the money for the land arrived at the perfect moment, on May 6!

On the Wednesday before the completion day, we had a call from our buyers about some minor matters. "See you on Saturday," I said.

"Saturday," he said, "what do you mean? We are coming on Friday."

How foolish of us to have forgotten that a purchase completes on a *weekday*, and you have to leave the property by midday. I tried not to panic, but we needed to speed up the packing process. Mercifully there was no problem with the removal firm because they "just happened" to have the Thursday free.

CHAPTER 25

Behold How Good and How Pleasant It Is . . .

W e had to move in two stages with two vanloads, and one had to go the very next day. When the van arrived, we were still throwing things into boxes at top speed, just slightly faster than they were loading them into the van. It was a frantic rush, but my stalwart helpers, Irene and Sylvia, sang and laughed with me as if we didn't have a care in the world. We were pushed beyond our natural strength, but we were enjoying ourselves AND praising God. The removal men could not understand why we were so cheerful when the circumstances seemed to dictate that we should be bad-tempered and fraught. It was the grace of God!

The full vanload was taken to Egremont House and was rapidly unloaded with everything left in the downstairs for the sake of speed. That night, dozens of fellowship members arrived, and instead of the usual Bible study, they swarmed all over the house, moving things where they were wanted. Everyone chipped in, heaving, sweeping, and scrubbing everywhere with great gusto. It was wonderful to have such help. The mess was overwhelming because there was still a lot of rubble from removing the plaster.

As the light began to fail at about half past nine, it was hilarious to see people working on the top floor by torchlight because the electrician, one of Barrie's lame ducks, whom he had taken pity on and wanted to help, had a drinking problem. Due to his drinking habit he had not yet completed his work. What a mixed blessing to have such friends!

The animals had to come with us too, so that night we also moved our large chicken coop. We put it on a trailer and trundled it slowly all the way to Ely. The goats and chickens traveled in the back of the estate car. When we stopped at a junction, a passing driver shouted, "Oy, mate, I like your caravan!"

The next day it was back to more frantic packing and cleaning in Isleham. Just as our last load was pulling away from Sunbury House on Friday morning, the new owner's removal van came into sight. We had finished all of our labours in Isleham in the nick of time. I felt very tearful leaving our lovely house where we had made so many happy and sad memories. . . bittersweet indeed!

The next day at Eggy, as we had lovingly christened the new house, it was straight on with the clearing, cleaning, and sorting. We were hoping to get things straightened out before Sunday. We felt we must get a move on because we were so busy with the church, and we did not want to live forever out of boxes.

During lunchtime, various people brought food for us to eat. Suddenly, there it was. . . there, before our eye was the picture we had been given at the healing and deliverance course many years previously. On one of our large, oval dishes was a mound of rice surrounded by new potatoes! It was a clear visual affirmation that we were in the right place at the right time.

We were obviously a matter of public interest because a reporter soon called at the house to interview me. She asked me, "Are you a refuge?"

The answer, of course, was yes *and* no. "It is my home," I told her, "but it is indeed a refuge for many."

Of course, if we had been a refuge, we were following a tradition set up in previous centuries; Ely has been a city of refuge from its conception. Queen Etheldreda started a monastic community there. She was fleeing two political marriages, one to an old man and another to a youth. Then the monks of Ely sheltered Hereward the Wake while he was fleeing from William the Conqueror. However, there seemed to be quite a stir in the city about what and who we were. Some thought we were a hippy commune. They were shocked when they visited and found that the house was actually clean and ordered. What were we really? Simply two families that wanted to share resources to benefit others.

God's grace was really evident in our midst. We were a true community and had to work hard to make it work. There were endless opportunities for strife. What do you do when someone has just run the bathwater out, which you have only just run for yourself? What do you do when people do not fulfill their household duties? What do you do when people are irritating? What do you do when someone breaks your favorite vase? What do you do when someone eats the last morsel of something you were saving to eat another day? As a way of life, it was not an easy alternative. It took determination and self-discipline. It built character if you let it. We shed many tears. We felt a lot of pressure We laughed a lot. We had to allow, as the Bible says "love to cover a multitude of sins." It would be a place where romance developed. It was a place where people found healing. It was a place where God was at work in us and around us.

In some ways, now that the purchase was complete, it seemed that we could relax because the battle was over. But of course, the truth was that the battle had only just begun. It was just a new kind of battle—a new phase of struggle. The early days were so tough. Despite some help, we were still in a terrible muddle. There was no electricity on the top floor, no boiler, and no kitchen, and everywhere needed our attention at once.

On top of all that, we had brand new baby Zara, and a baby church to attend to. Some days it seemed as if the whole world was on top of us, and we had to fight feelings of despair. Alongside the practical difficulties were the mental attacks. Some nights I would find myself lying awake, and Satan would say to me, "You will never afford to live here. You'll get into horrible debt and fall flat on your faces. You'll be the laughingstock of Ely." Since we had no idea how much it would actually cost us to live in such a house, and because we had very little income, those words were very easy to believe and panic about!

One night I lay in bed and wrestled for about an hour, worrying about how much gas the Aga was gobbling up as it ran day and night. To combat this worry, I spoke God's promises from Philippians 4.19 about His provision. "And my God shall supply all your need according to His riches in glory by Christ Jesus." God had given us a specific word from Genesis 22:14 about the house: "And Abraham called the name of the place, The-Lord-Will-Provide."

Half of me knew this fear of lack was just the devil's lies, and the other half of me believed it. It was just like the night when I had been in hospital and had my kidney stone removed. I believed, but I was just like the man in the Bible who said to Jesus, "I believe but help my unbelief!"

That night was sheer torment, so in the end, to get some sleep, I got up, ran downstairs, and switched off the Aga. I had imagined it was burning gas day and night, faster than we could possibly pay for it. In the morning I felt a bit sheepish about my silliness in the night. Of course, I switched it on again when the light of day dispelled my doubts, and I never worried about it ever again. The Word of God that promised His provision became more real to me than all my fears.

Initially it seemed that much of the cleaning and decorating work landed on my plate. Ginny was, quite rightly, busy with Zara. Tony and Peter were both at work, and the people we had taken in were actually more of a hindrance than a help. I can clearly remember a particular day when I was scrubbing the parquet floor in the hall on my hands and knees, weeping because I was in a state of total exhaustion.

After months of unremitting work, we prayed earnestly that God would send us some extra help. A young man who was an out-of-work painter and decorator turned up. He came every day for several weeks, and we zipped through wallpapering and painting the dining room. Our first completed room encouraged us no end. Another big plus was also that he got saved while working with us

One day in the spring, when I was in prayer about needing more help, God gave me a picture. Just as I was on my way out with Zara in the pram, I turned to shut the big double entrance doors, and in the Spirit, I saw the hall filled with young people painting. They were up ladders, on the stairs, and all around the hall and landing. It was as if He was saying, "They are on the way!"

That summer, a friend named Giselle came to visit. She had lived with us previously in Isleham. She was quite shocked by the amount of things we needed to do. She went home and told her household at YWAM that we needed a great deal of help. A young man in the house asked Giselle where our house was because he had heard clearly from God that he should take a team of young people and serve someone near Cambridge. However, he had no idea who that might be. The young man prayed and asked God if we were the ones He had meant him to serve, and thankfully, God said yes!

Thus he got a small team of youngsters together. Some of the people had come off the streets of London. Some had come off drugs and come away from crime. All of them had been saved through the YWAM outreach there. They came and stayed with us for a couple of weeks. We fed them, looked after them, and had times of worship with them, and in exchange they worked really hard for us.

One morning in December, the tears flowed from my eyes as I turned again at the front door. This time it was not a vision I saw but the fulfillment of the vision God had given me. Six people were cleaning and painting the giant hall, which had twenty large doors to be sanded down, undercoated, and glossed. Large expanses of wall and the very high ceilings also needed two coats of paint. They transformed our hall from dingy cream into two glorious tones of blue—into a house fit for a king. All we needed now was the wonderful red Axminster carpet someone else had "seen" on the stairs to complete it all.

Although we constantly had answers to prayer and miraculous provision, the Lord gave me another specific promise in the summer of 1983: "Someone will give you a thousand pounds." This money came from a most unexpected source in September 1984. It enabled us to pay some essential bills. We also purchased some beautiful new curtains and carpet for the drawing room, which Ginny and I had painted a glorious, vibrant pink.

Since we had moved in, we had done a massive amount of renovation. Outside the massive garden was now under control. To do this, we had bought a large ride-on mower to keep on top of the two acres of lawn. We had graveled the muddy drive. We had also hired a JCB to dig a large duck pond and help with the installation of two greenhouses. Inside, we had to replace the huge boiler. Peter had tried to mend the old one. Unfortunately, when he had just finished welding, somebody opened the kitchen door, allowing a wave of cold air to rush in and ruin his hard work. We insulated the roof, damp-proofed, and wood-wormed everywhere. We replaced floor joists in the study, installed new toilets, rewired all three floors, installed a lovely kitchen, and decorated throughout. Necessity dictated that we did much of this ourselves. It was a monumental task that was only made possible by God, who had from time to time sent supernatural provision. He sent the right people at the right time to help us, along with the money to do the job.

Our vision was to complete the practical work within two years so we could concentrate on the church. However, anyone who has bought an old home will tell you that it is never over! Egremont House was like the Forth Bridge; as soon as they finish at one end, they start again at the other end!

Later, in 1988, when the stairs and landing off the main hall needed painting again, we prayed afresh for new carpet, which we now needed desperately. When we had first moved into the house, the blue carpet, which was already on the stairs, had obviously been of such good quality that, after a thorough cleaning, it still had enough life in it to last until the Lord's provision came for a new one.

One Sunday God brought a young man and his family to the church from Harlow. Only God could have led someone to drive to church all the way from Harlow to Ely for several years with his whole family. He worked for a carpet firm. He was a carpet fitter, and his boss was a Christian. Between them, they let us have the prized carpet we wanted, which was worth four thousand pounds, for just half price, along with free fitting!

The carpet looked fit for the King. We searched diligently for the Axminster design with the traditional red, purple, and blue pattern. We were looking for the exact one that fit the picture that a church member had had years before. When we found it, it looked wonderful.

I prayed for a landscape gardener to join the church. He did, and with his men, he revamped some of the garden for us. The front doors needed replacing so it was such a blessing that there were some new front doors already in the garage. The doors were installed and painted for us by some dear friends we had met while leading a marriage retreat. They later moved to Ely to be part of the church and later ran our Christian bookshop. They also gave us the money to get an expert to repair the pillars at the front of the house, which were crumbling badly. I could go on and on telling of the blessings that were showered on us. The whole story is a tremendous catalogue of God's grace, which is put into action when we pray and trust Him for everything.

There were many incidents that happened that caused us great merriment. There was the night when Susie and I, for some reason, were alone in the house. I have never been a particularly quiet individual. As a girl I lived in an upstairs flat. It was a great source of irritation to me that we had to be quiet so as not to annoy the neighbours, even if they were not quiet for us! After all the children had gone to bed, there were occasional tensions about noise in Egremont House that irked me from time to time.

On this particular night, we came back from a meeting and for some reason all the children were away. Suddenly it dawned on me that there was no need to creep about to avoid waking them up. I said, "Hey, Susie, we are alone!"

Like silly children, we proceeded to go whooping joyfully up the stairs, shouting and singing raucous choruses at the tops of our voices. Suddenly I was aghast! I remembered we were not actually alone at all; there was a young man in the guest room who had come for a quiet, restful weekend. Instantly we were silent and mortified. As quickly as we could, we ran farther up the stairs to the top floor, stifling our laughter until we got into a room and shut the door. We were further mortified because in the morning, the young man had gone. We will never know whether our craziness frightened him away or whether he had already gone.

Another event also comes to mind when a man came to measure for a conservatory. It won't escape your notice that this tale also involves Susie! She had been cleaning the upstairs bathroom and had found a horse chestnut seed, stuck to the bottom of the rubbish bin, so she put some water in the bin and swished it around. Mindful of the fragile drains, she did not want to tip it all down the loo, so she opened the window and threw the contents of the bin out. Unfortunately, it was just the moment that the salesman stepped out of the back door and it all landed onto the head of the unsuspecting salesman below.

"Oy!" he shouted.

The first I knew about it was when he re-entered the house wet, coughing, and spluttering. Susie, having heard the loud protest, flew down the stairs and appeared in front of us, looking very apologetic. She explained that she had been washing out the bin in the bathroom and had thrown the contents out of the window because she did not want to block the drains.

"What was in the bin?" he said, looking wide-eyed and horrified, obviously imagining all sorts of horrible contents coming out of a bathroom. He was somewhat relieved when Susie was able to reassure him that it was only water. He then continued with his survey. Once again, she apologized profusely for what she had done, and I took his jacket and put it on the Aga to dry.

When he had finished measuring up, we both went into the study. "What is this place?" he asked.

"Well," I said reluctantly, "it's...um...er...a...Christian community."

"Christian! Is this how Christians treat people?" He was obviously not impressed that he had been baptised without personal consent! He never did send his estimate!

For a long while the house was the church centre, and when we needed to use the office as a bedroom for my husband's father, we installed a mobile home in the garden as an office. We rented buildings for Sunday services, but nobody wanted to rent a building to us on Christmas day, so the first Christmas we crammed fifty people into our sitting room for a Christmas-day service. When that became too small for us, we took our PA and a generator and went out into the market square to have our service there. These were really happy times when we had to jump about and clap our hands just to keep warm, never mind doing it to express worship! We also had midweek meetings in the house until we could not cram any more of us in.

Sunday lunch was tremendous fun. We regularly fed twenty-four people as we invited everyone who came to church for the first time to come to lunch with us. I would rise very early. I would pray and prepare my sermon and then prepare the lunch, which cooked while we were at church. Somehow by the grace of God I got there in time, feeling ready to meet the regular Sunday challenge. We spent the afternoon entertaining the guests, and then it was back to church for the evening meeting. It was all go!

The police and social services soon cottoned on to the fact that we had space for the needy, and we had a string of people arrive—unmarried mums and other people in various stages of distress. When people came, they always met Jesus, usually within days.

One of these unmarried mums was actually from Life for the Unborn Child in Cambridge, like one of our previous girls had been, when we were in Isleham. When I was asked to take her, we were told that she was an Iranian Muslim. I said they must warn her there was a lot of Christianity about in our house. When they told her, she said she did not mind that at all. And so, Minoo came to our house.

Minoo had come to England because she needed specialist medical treatment that could only be done at Addenbrooks. She was the daughter of a captain in the Shah's army. Her family was wealthy and somewhat westernized. Consequently she had not worn the traditional Muslim covering, and because of that some radical Muslim men had thrown acid over her, causing her to lose sight in one eye and disfiguring her face badly. Eventually the government gave her permission to leave Iran and come to Cambridge for plastic surgery. There she had met a man, fallen in love, and become pregnant. She refused an abortion, which resulted in her coming to us for support.

At that time, we had a young girl staying with us named Rosemary, who, although she was a lovely Christian, was mentally ill. She was staying with us because her family was hostile to her Christian commitment and she seemed to improve a lot whilst she was with us. She took Minoo under her wing and within days had given her the gospel, and got her to accept Jesus into her heart.

The genuineness of her conversion was obvious as straightaway, unbidden by any of us, Minoo threw away all of her Muslim artifacts and her Koran. She was soundly converted and a delight to have around. When she took a turn to cook, we would ask her what the dish was, and she would say, with a toss of the head, "It is kebab."

The next time she would be cooking something quite different. "What is it, Minoo?"

"It is kebab!"

She got a bit impatient with us asking her the same question all the time until we eventually realised that kebab simply meant meat!

I think of our boys, Ben and Giles, who seemed to be glad to share their home and their parents with everyone. There were so many people who passed through our house and received our love and care. Tony's father was also there with us for a few years. His distinctive personality added great flavor to the house. You might hear the jolly strains of, "Oh Jemima, look at your uncle Jim" or even "are you washed in the blood" floating though the house. He was rather outspoken, and you were never sure what he might say to anyone! He had only discovered the Holy Spirit late in his Christian life and at the drop of a hat would tell anyone that the Holy Spirit was the answer to every problem he or she had. He had an uncanny discernment of people's motives and character. Many times when we thought he was being a bit critical he turned out to be right.

Many of the people who stayed with us at the house for their own benefit ended up becoming part of the team that cared for the next wave.

Many became wonderfully committed members of the church. Chaste romance also blossomed in the house between two of the residents, helped a little by the rest of us!

One who deserves special mention was a Japanese man named Soichi. He had such a servant's heart. Despite working three jobs, he would unobtrusively do anything that he saw needed doing. We always knew when Soichi was about until we had the wit to buy him a new pair of slippers and got rid of his old, loose slippers that dragged along the floor—*clonk-clonk*... *clonk-clonk*!

One morning he was very excited when we all came down to breakfast because he had heroically rescued our dear little Russian hamster from the jaws of the cat! He had spotted that the cat had something moving in her mouth and thought she must have caught a mouse. On closer inspection, he saw that the creature had no tail and guessed it was the hamster. He made the cat release it and put it back in the cage. The hamster was very quiet and almost certainly dead. We took her out of the cage and prayed over her. She was soon running about as usual! Was she raised from the dead? I think so.

It was really all pull together to make life work in Egremont House. Everyone had an assigned task: cooking, cleaning, gardening, shopping, or helping to look after the animals. One day when I saw one of our young men crossing the lawn carrying a bucket on his way to milk the goats, God said to me, "Look at our Scripture." I knew He meant Isaiah 61. "Look at verse five." I ran to find my Bible, and it said, "Strangers shall stand and feed your flocks, and the sons of the foreigner shall be your ploughmen and your vinedressers."

There was never a shortage of young men willing to mow the lawn with the ride-on mower, but there was not the same enthusiasm for other tasks. We often had to chase people to do what they were supposed to do, but we had many very able and willing cooks who took turns to produce excellent meals. Some years I hardly ever cooked a meal!

We started with three children in the house: our boys and baby Zara, our co-owners little girl. But Zara was quickly followed by the family's second child, James. We loved them both as our own, and Giles was very relieved not to be the youngest in the house anymore! At one time, however, we had eight children who were mostly well behaved and got on brilliantly together. You could always tell if Tony was around the children because there would be some kind of riotous fun going on. He always claimed that he did not stir them up, but well. . .

We also had streams of people who came and stayed a weekend for prayer. Many precious visiting speakers stayed with us. We had lots of fun with them. Giselle schooled us in the art of hospitality, and I think our house was definitely five star for the visitors.

Over the years we proved that by the grace of God, it was possible for Christians to live together in love and harmony, but it did take a lot of effort and a strong desire to make it work by bearing with one another's faults. It could work if we allowed God to change us and permitted Him to use other people like sandpaper to smooth out the rough grain of our different characters.

The twelve years we lived there were a testimony to God's promises and His faithfulness in every way. Lives were changed including ours because everything challenged our selfish desires. In challenging moments, we had to keep our eyes firmly on *why* we were doing it.

We had not lived at Egremont House long before we needed yet another car. We looked to the Lord for guidance about which car we should have and where we would find it. Every car we have had since we became Christians has been obtained with God's guidance. On this occasion the men of the church agreed that we definitely needed a new car. We preached prosperity, and our old crock was not a good advertisement for a generous God! An elderly person in the church was willing to lend the money, so we started to look for a suitable car. One day after starting the old car on the handle yet again, Tony sent me to buy a new battery. I drove to the garage and stopped outside, but I just could not bring myself to go in and buy a battery. I felt strongly that it was wrong to patch up the old car yet again.

Just around the corner from us on Lynn Road was a Fiat garage, so I stopped the car outside on the forecourt with the engine running and rushed inside. I asked the sales representative if they had an automatic Mini Metro because this was the kind of car God had said to buy.

He showed me a beautiful little red, X-registration Metro, which he assured me had only had one previous, careful owner. People think this is what every salesman says, but it looked wonderful. I had a witness in my heart that it was the right car. I drove home really excited and told Tony, "I have found our new car."

"Oh," he said. "Is it red, and has it got an X-registration?"

"Yes," I said. "How do you know?"

"Well, I saw a red, X-registration Mini Metro on the drive one day, and God told me that we would have one just like it."

We were thrilled that between us we had heard from God and knew which car to buy. We both loved the little car, got it checked over, and bought it. The delighted car salesman said, "Oh . . . er . . . I've never sold a car to a commune before!"

The very day we got the car, a couple who lived in an outlying village had a baby. Their car had broken down, and the husband had no means to visit his wife, so straightaway we lent our car to them until his car was repaired. The first time another member of the church drove the car, this time carrying a load of our youth, he turned it over and crashed at a bend in Sutton. Praise the Lord nobody was hurt and the car was repaired and seemed none the worse for its misfortune

We were blessed to be a blessing like Abraham. It's the story of our life!

CHAPTER 26

We Enter into Our Calling with Trepidation

When we were grappling with all the initial difficulties with Egremont House, the dream, or should I say the drama, of a new church was also unfolding. Every step of the way was uncharted. At the time we knew nobody else who had started a church, and it all felt rather intimidating. Would the dream turn out to be a nightmare?

Officially we began the church on Palm Sunday, April 4, 1982, at ten thirty sharp!. We did not really know how many people would be there because we knew some people had decided to stay in their denominational churches and were continuing to pray and believe God would move there.

On that first morning there were thirteen of us: Tony and me, our boys, Ben and Giles, and nine others. Another lady, for family reasons, could only join us in the evening. She was an interesting addition because she had received a word from God as a child that she would be involved in the start of a church like ours.

Small numbers did not bother us, and neither did it matter that people chose not to join us. We only wanted people to be with us if they knew they were really called by God to be there. We knew it would not be an easy path to tread.

We few were all committed to the newborn church called Ely Christian Fellowship. We wrote a declaration of intent—a sort of church manifesto— and all stood and solemnly, made the declaration, and meant every word of it. We were determined to be a different kind of church from the ones we had experienced. We were determined to allow God to move in our meetings without knowingly frustrating Him or His purposes. We wanted to give God the reins.

One night our heartfelt praise and worship caused a dramatic reaction! In our customary enthusiastic manner, we had worshipped for about an hour when the visiting speaker, Rod Anderson, suggested that we should each take a chair to represent a problem we had in our lives and do a victory dance around it. He told us to praise God for His miraculous answers. It felt a somewhat silly thing to do but one man received a healing right there and then for a leg condition. Everyone participated except for a new couple, who sat at the back looking immensely puzzled and disapproving.

During the announcements, it was Tony's custom to ask, "Who is here for the first time?" We would then offer people an information pack and welcome them. That night the couple at the back raised their hands and received their pack. I don't know what made him do it, but with a chuckle, Tony followed the first question with a second: "And who is here for the last time?"

The woman at the back lifted her hand aggressively a second time, making it obvious she entirely disapproved of all she had seen. Afterwards they left quickly, and we were sure we would never see them again. The amazing thing is that although they came from a very traditional local church and appeared to dislike everything about us, they came back and stayed for many years. Our service was a shock to them, but they recognized the genuine love they were shown and appreciated the wholeheartedness of it all.

We always preached the Word of God in a way that gave practical answers. It is all very well to tell people that they *ought* to pray; every Christian knows that. We wanted to go much further and teach people from the Word how to do it. It is also one thing to know about God but quite another to know God. We wanted to create a radical group of believers who were eager to *do* the will of God, eager to preach the gospel and reach the lost, eager to lay hands on the sick and see them recover, eager to pray, eager to give sacrificially. . .

We wanted a church that would be full of life and power, a true expression of the greatness and goodness of God. We wanted people to know the righteousness and victory that are ours in Christ Jesus. We wanted them to know how to receive, by faith; all God has given us freely through His grace. We wanted them to understand new creation realities. We wanted them to know how to reign in life by the one man Christ Jesus. So much traditional church teaching seemed to centre on the idea that we were worthless sinners and that we had to grovel to God to get His blessing. How could this be when He has already given us "all things that pertain to life and godliness" (2 Peter 1:3) through the New Covenant Jesus made with the Father on our behalf?

We knew the ordinary believer could do the work of the ministry, not just the pastor or the vicar. That is how the church was until it became institutionalized and man took control. Then there became a separation between clergy and laity, with the clergy ministering in the service and the laity filling the pews.

Instead of the old way, we wanted to empower people to *do* the ministry by teaching them how to use the gifts of the Spirit, how to hear God's voice, and how to preach the gospel. I recently read this, written by Rick Renner[2], which he says is a literal translation of the Greek text for 1 Corinthians 3:6.

> Everything that you have heard and believed about Jesus Christ has been authenticated, proven beyond a shadow of doubt, verified and guaranteed to be true by the gifts of the Spirit.

It is the gifts of the Spirit that authenticate the message. They *are* the signs following or release the signs to follow. Sadly, in those days, there was very little work of the ministry happening in the true biblical sense in the majority of denominational churches. Ministers mostly seemed to be caretakers of buildings. Christianity had sunk to ritual and form without reality.

We sought God for the biblical standard that makes Christianity real to unbelievers; they were the very reason for our existence. As a foundational Scripture, God gave us Jeremiah 30:18-22:

> Behold, I will bring back the captivity of Jacob's tents, and have mercy on his dwelling places; the city shall be built upon its own mound, and the palace shall remain

according to its own plan. Then out of them shall proceed thanksgiving and the voice of those who make merry; I will multiply them, and they shall not diminish; I will also glorify them, and they shall not be small. Their children also shall be as before, and their congregation shall be established before Me. And I will punish all who oppress them. Their nobles shall be from among them, and their governor shall come from their midst; Then I will cause him to draw near, and he shall approach Me;" For who is this who pledged his heart to approach Me?" says the Lord. "You shall be My people, and I will be your God."

We must always interpret the Old Testament in the light of the New, and we understood that in the light of New Testament teaching, we are not fighting flesh and blood. Our enemies who would be punished would be the powers of darkness! But this Scripture was clear that our leader would be from the group, that we would rebuild the church in Ely, that the sound coming from us would be a happy one, that God was going to establish us, and that we would be a large church!

Awesome promises. . . and how funny that people insult us by calling us "happy clappies," and there it is plainly in that Scripture. At least God likes it when we make merry! We had no idea that literally hundreds of churches like ours were being started all over the world. We were just a small part of a large, worldwide move of God to bring the life of the Holy Spirit back to His world.

Being a large church seemed a little unreal at this stage because there were not many of us, but we only wanted people to join us to make that core who had strong guidance to do so. We had also had a word from God which said, "You are in the upper room. . . Go now into the highways and byways." Our aim was not to attract people who already knew God but to go out onto the streets and get unbelievers in.

We were up front with other churches that we were starting a church and sent a letter to all of them stating our intent. We did not want churches to feel that their membership was threatened, but of course they did. They all shunned us. We were unconventional. We were noisy. . . *but* we were free!

Much later, we applied to join the Ely Council of Churches and were invited to an interview with a group of people representing all the churches. The chaplain of the Kings School, John, had twisted their arms to allow us to explain ourselves. He had told them that if they did not let us in, he would resign from the group himself. What a brave man. What an ally!

The meeting was a stilted and solemn affair. They gave us time to talk about what we really believed, and then the Methodist minister launched in, "Is it true you live in adultery at Egremont House?"

The question took my breath away. "What?" I said. "What makes you think that?" I was rocked to the core! It was possibly the last question I was expecting.

"Well, you told a young man that you did."

The wheels of my mind turned over, considering any conversation I may have had with any living soul that could possibly have communicated such rubbish. Slowly, it dawned on me. "Ah, do you mean the conversation I had with a young man when I gave him a lift into Cambridge some while ago?"

I remembered him well. During the thirty minutes or so that it takes to get to Cambridge, I explained to him who we were and that we lived with another family as a Christian community. I talked a bit about our life together and said that despite the difficulty of living in this way, we loved each other more now than we had when we first moved in together. Oh dear! His idea of love was obviously quite different from mine! Having cleared up the misunderstanding, the Ely Council of Churches reluctantly invited us to join.

Tony had continued to teach physics at Ely College, but we lived expecting the day when he would be released from secular work to pastor full time. At the time much of the organization and pastoring fell upon my shoulders. The load was particularly heavy because the minute we began the church with our band of committed workers, each of the young couples involved had a baby and were too busy to be at meetings all the time. I can remember Sunday morning meetings when there would be a row of women with their backs turned, all busy feeding hungry babies.

Of course, everything works together for good to those who love the Lord. As a trained antenatal teacher with the National Childbirth Trust, it was easy for me to train all of our young women, and their husbands, on how to cope with pregnancy, labour, and breast-feeding. We had a great class!

A prime mover in beginning public meetings had been our Australian friend Barrie—the embodiment of the active church member. He was an eager evangelist, but his labours produced a few problems for us. In his spare moments, he was scouring the streets for what proved to be an interesting collection of unsaved rascals.

There was a young man whose nickname was Sheepie, a wild-eyed, strange-looking chap with long, straggly blond hair. He had a problem with setting fire to things and was caught trying to use the altar candles in the cathedral to set light to the altar cloth. He also was not too honest. One day after he had left the house, we discovered that all of the money in our telephone fund had gone. People were amazed that we wanted to reach out to these untouchables, but we did.

Then there was Terry. He had been living in a caravan with two dogs. He then came to live with us, bringing his dogs with him! Terry had spent time in a corrective youth institution. You could see this because of the perfect way he washed a floor. The finished result was like a work of art. He did a really perfect job because when he had been in the institution, he had to do it repeatedly if he did not do it properly the first time.

Terry was a tall shambling individual. He was not a very bright person neither was he a difficult person, and he fitted into our fledgling community quite well. Even his little black and white dogs, Spot and her brother Patch with their untrained ways, wormed their way into most of our hearts, but we could not keep both of them. Patch was the chosen one to go, and we found him a good home with very little difficulty.

It seemed unthinkable to get rid of dear little Spot, who was such a timid little creature. She, too, brought her own unique troubles. Because we had no experience of dogs, we failed to realise when she was in heat. A very large dog that was very persistent jumped the eight foot wall around our property and made her pregnant. In a very few weeks she had eight adorable puppies, which quickly grew to be massive and fed voraciously. For a few weeks she hardly left them and proved to be a great little mother but the day came when she was obviously frightened to go into the pen because she felt so overwhelmed with them and their insistent demands for food. She would sit outside the pen looking pathetic, pleading with her eyes not to be made to go into them. We started to wean them as soon as we could, watching enchanted at their bad manners as they elbowed each other out of the way and trod over each other and fell into the dish in their eagerness to get their share!. We had fun finding her handsome pups good homes for five pounds apiece.

Then there was dear Jack. He came along to the church whilst we were still living in Isleham. He gave us the greatest trouble out of all that little gang! Unknown to us, Jack had been doing the rounds of the fellowship families, asking for money in creative ways. We were a good catch for Jack because we knew that giving to the poor and needy was part of our calling in Christ, and we were all eagerly doing it. The left hand, of course, was also not telling the right hand what it was doing. Our giving was biblical; discreet and secret.

Unfortunately for Jack, the truth came out when his stories did not match up to reality. He asked one couple for money to visit his mother in hospital. Then we discovered he had previously asked someone else for money for a wreath for his mother's funeral. He had told another couple that he could not pay his rent because he had not received his pay. Each couple had a different story. Jack was coining it in, and just a chance remark from Peter and Ginny one day made me suspicious.

I decided to make some discreet inquiries. I rang the hospitals in the town he had named, asking if his mother was a patient or had been a patient. "No, we have never had anyone of that name." I rang the military base where he said he worked and discovered Jack had not worked there for months. The following Sunday, accompanied by two of the men, I confronted him with my discoveries. Jack was absolutely furious. He screamed at me, "You witch, you witch!"

He was not happy. We warned everyone about him, but because we had always been willing to give people a second chance, Jack continued to come to the church, having promised that he would behave. Jack was quite a simple soul. He had a girlfriend who lived in a local home for those with learning difficulties who came to church too. They had an acrimonious split just before Christmas, so we invited her to come to lunch on Christmas day and him on Boxing Day.

Christmas day arrived, and we took the girlfriend home with us. Driving home, we were dismayed to spot Jack walking along the road on his way to Isleham. Surely he was not coming? We had made it quite clear that he could come the next day. But just when we had all sat down at the dining table, and were just about to start dinner there was a knock at the door. It was Jack. We felt utterly heartless but we were determined Christmas Day or not we would not give in to him. Standing at the door we explained to him again, "Jack, this is just not right. We made it clear that you could not come to lunch today. We will not allow you to manipulate us. You must go home."

We shut the door and began to eat, watching him lingering outside. When he came and pressed his nose to the window pane, we closed the curtains. He continued to stand outside until the man across the road, who was a part-time police officer, rang us. "Do you know you have somebody loitering around outside your house?"

Very embarrassed we explained what was going on, but it sounded so horribly unchristian, and we agonized over whether we should relent and let him in. We decided to ask him once again to go away. Disconsolately, he walked off up the road. I did not feel much like eating anymore.

However, we had not heard the last of Jack. Half an hour later the phone rang. It was our friend Jean, who lived just up the road, sounding most displeased. In clipped tones she said "Jack is at my house and has fallen fast asleep. He says he has taken an overdose."

Jean had been at a loss to know what to do when Jack arrived. She was just serving lunch, and her tiny little cottage was chock full of family, with hardly a square inch to spare. She had reluctantly given him some food and sat him in her other room while she and her family ate.

Leaving our lunch, we found him with an empty bottle of pills and rushed him off to the hospital in Ely, where they pumped out his stomach, cast out the dinner, and kept him in. When we visited him the next day, he was cheerfully sporting a beautiful new dressing gown. He seemed to be enjoying his stay at the hospital immensely and appeared blissfully unaware that he had caused anyone any inconvenience at all!

In these early days, we often attracted people who were a mixture of the eager and the odd, and wondered how we were going to build the large church God had promised us.. I once read a book called *Building with Bananas*. It's difficult to build anything with bananas because of their odd shape, and that's just how the church felt in those days.

However, bit by bit our numbers grew, and steadily we became stable. We both grew stronger in our preaching and teaching and more confident in what we were doing. Slowly, more stable church members came along with their families, who began to build with us.

CHAPTER 27

A Church Growing into Maturity

I t would be far too difficult to chart the next twenty-five years, during which we laboured with all our hearts to bring the living Word, the living gospel, and the reality of God to Ely. I can only bring highlights and the patterns of where we went. The whole story belongs in another book.

Since God told us we would be a large church, we needed to put systems and structures in place to hold the growth. The foundations had to be right and legal, so immediately we created a trust to handle the money. We would not be directly involved with that.

God had told us in 1982, "Because you are here, prosperity will come to the city of Ely. The city will expand and be built right out to its boundaries. When it is fully built up, right out to the boundary, the multitudes will come in. People will be lining up to come into the church."

Ely was so small at that time, and there was very little development anywhere. It seemed almost impossible that what God had spoken to us could happen. We had no idea that it could take twenty years or more! I am glad we did not hold our breath but just got on and did whatever our hands found to do. It is now 2013, and only recently the council released plans for the next stage of development in the city.

The growth and development of the church came at a heavy price: much prayer and hard work and personal sacrifice. In hindsight, this also meant sacrifices for our children. We absolutely gave our entire lives to build His church and shepherd His people. Over the years, whenever we were tempted to be discouraged, we could always look at the developing city and check how the plan was going. If we knew what stage the development had reached, we had no reason to be discouraged. The time was obviously not yet ripe. Prayer was a significant feature of the church from the start because we knew Ely would not be won by human effort.

In one of our early meetings, I felt we should pray for a prominent member of the government I felt was in danger. We immediately prayed for his protection and found out from a newspaper report that he had been in a serious road accident at the very time we had been praying for him, but he had walked out of it unharmed. I wrote and explained how we had prayed for him. His reply was polite but unbelieving. I hope there will be a moment when he remembers that God touched his life that day.

Over the years, the patterns of prayer varied. We were eager to do anything! We did whole nights and half nights of prayer. We prayer walked the city street by street, and we prayed in the Spirit, praising God all the way around the city boundary, claiming the ground for Jesus. We prayed at historically significant sites in the city and went to the top of the cathedral to make declarations over all the land we could see. We were determined to leave no stone unturned in the spiritual battle for Ely. Our weeks of prayer were dynamic and successful. At one time we had three prayer meetings a day with sixty out of our hundred members attending each evening. They were always the most popular prayer projects we have done.

One memorable week of prayer was led by Robert Maasbach, a young Dutchman. Thirty or forty of us crammed into our sitting room each night. We did a lot of very (and I mean very) loud praying in the Spirit for an hour at a time. Our praying could be heard loud and clear right down the street.

These meetings were strong spiritual warfare, and about twenty people left the church in the following weeks, offended by what they deemed as wild extremism. I agreed; it certainly was extreme! But in the year following those wild meetings, over ninety people were converted, baptised, and added to the church.

During one of his meeting preparation times, Robert told us that the devil manifested outside Robert's bedroom window and challenged him. "What makes you think these people can keep the freedom you are winning?"

He said, "I am sure they will keep it."

At other times, we had all-age prayer meetings where we structured things so the children could play an active part in it all. I think some adults found this simple kind of prayer helpful too.

I knew that my walk with God was a key to stability in my life as well as the life of the church and that my own devotional life needed to be secure. In consistency lies power and good spiritual habits held me during times when my prayer life had lost its sparkle.

I usually used *The Workman's One Year Bible* by Charles Sibthorpe. With it I have read the entire Bible twenty times in twenty years. As I found a Scripture that spoke to me, I wrote it in a little book so it was ready for my prayer time. I had a section of Scripture promises for my children, for victory, for the church, for healing, or for God's supply.

I would also write down or journal what was on my heart and listen for God's reply, also looking with my spiritual eyes for what Jesus was doing in the situation. On the very first day I journalled, God said to me, "When you do not hear Me, you shut Me up in heaven. When you hear Me, My voice is released from heaven to earth, and I am able to have My divine hand in your life's business."

Every year I use a different daily devotional book, and it always amazes me that I can journal what I think the Lord is saying to me, and when I pick up my devotional book, it often says exactly the same thing. It happened this very morning. I also have a photograph album containing the photos of people I pray for. Just one look at their faces triggers the desire to pray for them.

A particular advance in my prayer life came when we met Fred Kropp at a meeting in Birmingham in the 1980s. The minute I saw him, God said, "This man has something special to impart to you that will meet your heart's deepest desires."

Fred was speaking in the first session after a leader's lunch that went on and on. All I wanted was to get back to hear what Fred had to say. I felt frustrated that we got back to the main meeting just as Fred was winding up his session. He said, "Does anyone want to receive an anointing for intercession?"

I was on my feet even before he had finished speaking. He prayed a short prayer for us all to receive a special, enabling anointing to pray. I did not feel anything, but I knew it was mine! The next day and for many years my eyes flew open at 5:00 a.m., and immediately I was ready to get up and pray. I had always struggled to get up in the mornings, so this was evidently supernatural.

Rain or shine, I put on a tracksuit, and sometimes wellingtons and a fur coat if it was cold, and I would walk and pray around the garden, sometimes sitting in the greenhouse to read my Bible if it was wet. I would worship in tongues and English. I would sing and praise Him. Maybe an hour went by or two or three hours. I would say to the Lord, "What do You want me to pray?"

He would say, "Just worship Me and wait on Me."

As I did this, the desire would come to confess a particular Scripture over certain situations or to take authority over the work of the enemy in a particular way. The energy of all that worship came behind the words, and I knew those prayers were full of power. Although I lost that *particular* anointing for early rising, thankfully, I never lost the desire to pray. It was just that some of the excitement of my prayer life declined a little.

The safety of others sometimes relies on our ability to be spiritually alert. One incident sticks out in my mind. One night I could not sleep; someone was in danger. I went downstairs and prayed in the Spirit until I felt peace in my heart. The next day I discovered that a couple in the church at the very time I was praying had had a serious collision with another vehicle on the A10, and although they had to write off the car, they had miraculously escaped injury.

God told us to pastor in the Spirit, not just the flesh, and because of that, I often knew exactly what was going on in the congregation. I knew when people were in trouble or backsliding or if there were people causing division because they were unhappy. It meant I could address issues from a position of inside knowledge and act and pray in a way that would make a difference.

As a church we did several forty-day fasts, with people of all ages fasting things like computer games and television and of course, food! People were encouraged to fast all meals or just one meal a day, whatever they knew would release time for prayer; whatever they thought was appropriate for them. We personally did a forty-day fast on a bowl of soup a day. It was a great personal blessing to our spiritual lives. It is amazing how fasting clears the mind and brings a sense of rest to the soul, making it easy to pray. I was actually sad when the time finished and we had to wean ourselves carefully back onto food.

When the passionate desire for prayer waned in the church, I was really sad. At that time a team of young people came to the church from South Africa who said the church was like a ship stuck in the mud. It was a Ginnyd and meaningful picture. They encouraged us to pray for the water of the Holy Spirit to come and help us to get afloat again.

We wanted a constant flow of fresh life coming into the church and felt people needed to experience different kinds of ministries, so we usually had a visiting speaker once a month. This fed us spiritually as well as feeding the rest of the hungry and growing church, and because of it, we made some long-lasting contacts with ministers of great integrity, like Rod and Julie Anderson, Robert and Virginia Maasbach, Dan and Nori Chesney, David Hathaway, and Mark Virkler.

In twenty-five years we had many inspiring people come to the church to preach and teach. These included: Hilton Sutton, Mark Meiners, David Cassidy, Eddie and Lori Hornback, Steve Ryder, Franz Estherhuizen, Benson Idahosa, Peter Youngren, Colin Urquhart, Clive Urquhart, Billy Smith, Ashley and Ruth Schmeirer, Carolyn Bounds, Freda White, Mary-Jean Pigeon, Mike and Rita McCann, Sharon Stone, Gordana Toplak, Francis Wale Oke, Michael Bassett, Peter Gammons, Rodd and Marco Palmer, Melvin Banks, Harmony Theissen, Chris Horwood, Emanuel Amoah, Francis Frangipane, Fred Kropp, Andy Elmes, Artie Gardella, Alan and Sherry Staggs, Roland Mwesigwa, Dennis and Melanie Morgan Dohner, Dr. Albert Odulele, Ruthie Dearman, Bob Barker, Larry Huggins, Wyatt Brown, Ash and Sharon Kotecha, Terry Law, Alex Afriye, Ron Williams, Roger King, Roger Price, and Ron and Barbara White.

There was only one man we regretted inviting. I cannot remember his name, but I would not even mention it if I could remember it!

We were so blessed by the singing groups and worship leaders who came. We hosted a singing group called Vinesong who were brand new to England. They were awesome and brought such a spiritual revitalization with their songs. They touched people's lives, and we were always grateful for their visits. They went on to become well known in the Christian world

Other wonderful visiting groups were Paul and Susan Hansen, Colour Blind, led by Eddie James, and Rick and Rosemary. It would also be impossible to forget our dear friend Lawson Spiller. He is a tremendous artist and ministers such inspiring songs. Three well-known British worship leaders came and made valuable input: Bryn Howarth, Dave BiIlborough, and Wynn Goss and his son Matt.

Because our first instruction from the Lord had been to get out of the upper room and find the lost, we obeyed, reaching out to Ely with every means possible. We went through the estates of Ely door to door, offering to pray for people and preaching the gospel wherever possible. It was on one of those very early calls that we saw a total skeptic instantly healed of a painful back condition. He was amazed! Ironically, his wife and children began to come to church, but he never did. After the couple was divorced, his ex-wife invited him to attend a service, and twenty years after our visit, he gave his life to Jesus.

On Saturday mornings, we sang and preached on the streets, doing puppet skits that delighted adults and children alike and giving away small gifts, tracts, and balloons. We had a dance and drama team performing on the streets. Tony developed a funny sketch called "My Secondhand Ideas." As a student, he had actually worked in a London greengrocer's, so he knew the patter, "Roll up, roll up, get your secondhand ideas here!" Holding up a card with the phrase on it, he would say, "now here's a good one; many of you will love this: 'Religion is just for children and old ladies.'" Then he would enlarge on the idea in a very funny way. Then "Here's another" and so on. It was priceless and proves that no experience in our former life need be wasted.

Often those who dared to stop and talk were tourists. We prayed with many of them, and some were saved. Our singles group was the backbone of this activity. Some of the men did sketch board presentations taking out prepared designs that, with just a few strokes of a brush, became a relevant message. We even did this in French on the streets of Belgium!

We were so grateful for the YWAM teams who came, including an enormous YWAM dance team, which one of our girls had joined. They provided wonderful and much-needed encouragement to us when we felt like a feeble few struggling on.

We booked the local school hall and held a meeting advertising that we would be giving away one hundred Bibles! There was not exactly a rush of people claiming their Bibles, but one small seed can lead to a great harvest.

Only a middle-aged lady and two youths came, but the lady became a most fruitful member of the church and one of the youths eventually became a most gifted church member as an adult. He married a wonderful young Christian woman, who was also in our church. She came to the fellowship as a teenager with her two sisters, who are also both now in ministry. He now ministers the gospel to youth and has a Christian band. Later on his parents came to the church. In their latter years, they began a very successful youth work called The Garage. This, through a link with the local council, enabled us to get a grant to refurbish the last building on our site. What an amazingly fruitful family they proved to be.

Years later we ran Alpha courses but we never had the wholehearted success that we had seen happen in Anglican churches. Our baptisms were exciting public affairs. Initially we baptised on the causeway of the River Ouse, next to the bridge near the Maltings. One Easter Sunday it was freezing cold, and there was even a little bit of snow falling, but it was no deterrent to us or any of the candidates. What a hardy lot we were! As the church grew and the weather was warmer, our band would set up by the river, and we would have a full-blown, noisy worship service with sermon and testimony before baptizing people. We always drew an interested crowd, and surprisingly, there was only one complaint about our volume in all the years we did it. They were such joyful occasions that I think the locals just went with the spirit of it.

We only stopped when the river became unpleasantly polluted. Then we moved to the Paradise Pool or a baptistery belonging to the church across the road. Most of our baptisms passed off uneventfully and with great joy, but we did have one baptism that nearly ended in disaster. A man who was a diabetic had decided of his own accord to fast before his baptism. He collapsed the moment he came out of the river. God had it in hand, though, because there was a passing doctor who rushed to help.

Another time we baptised Rowena, a wonderful young woman who was the matron at the local public school. Her uncle, a wonderful Spirit-filled bishop, came to her baptism service and joined in with great enthusiasm. There is a great testimony to her faith. One day a pupil came to her medical room with obviously broken fingers. They bundled into a taxi and she prayed over his fingers all the way to the hospital. When they got there, the child's fingers had been healed!

We were so thankful to have an extremely dedicated PA team and a band. Everything had to be hauled out of a trailer, painstakingly set up by the team, and packed away again afterwards. What a labour of love they performed week after week! Another popular outreach we did was a musical production with full choir, dance, and drama at Christmas or Easter.

We were passionate about bringing teaching of the kind that had set us free to the whole area, so as soon as we could we opened our own Christian bookshop selling Christian books and music that would get the message out. In 1983 we held our first East Anglian Faith Convention at the Maltings by the river. Several hundred people came, surprisingly from nearly everywhere in Britain except Ely! People were saved, healed, and filled with the Holy Spirit and sent away strengthened. It was a big step of faith for such a small church, but we felt that if God had commissioned us to do it, He would provide the money. On this occasion rescue came via Kenneth Copeland's video minister Kim Freeborn, who came with a bookstall and gave us a very generous donation.

Very few local Christians came—the hungry ones and sometimes just the curious. People were saved who came from far away, but only one elderly unsaved Ely woman came. It seemed that her attendance was more by accident than design, but she was soundly saved and added to the church. We sure treasured her salvation!

Some local ministers came to see what we were up to. Some of them sat cross-armed, glowering disapprovingly at what they deemed to be false doctrine. Nevertheless, these meetings were a great blessing. It was during one of these meetings that John Hughes prophesied to us, "You will go to Africa, where you will go before kings and governors, and you will preach the gospel to thousands, with signs following." We hid this in our hearts, puzzling over the impossible idea.

However glorious these meetings were, they were hard going because there was always great pressure on a very small number of us, and Satan always tried to create strife between us, sometimes succeeding. Nevertheless, we struggled with the pressure resolutely, having teams of people praying all the way through the meetings in a back room. We were determined not to surrender any of the blessings. The spiritual opposition certainly felt enormous and at times almost physically bruising, *but* . . . we were determined. We were going to bless Ely . . . *or else!* We were going to see a move of the Spirit in Ely!

We treasured the fact that we could worship freely in a way that brought the tangible presence of God. In our convention meetings, we had exhilarating times, praying vigorously in the Spirit and singing in the Spirit. This was extremely uncommon in those days in most churches and very controversial. Many of the people attending had never experienced anything like it. People's reactions were very mixed, but for many it was life changing—a taste of freedom they were unlikely to get in their own churches. I imagine we sowed divine seeds of discontent that eventually resulted in other churches being revitalized. It was a great joy to us that many were healed and saved at these lively meetings.

Some of our meetings were lively in quite a different way. Harmony Thiessen, a visiting speaker from Canada who obviously had a keen sense of fun, seemed to have a dramatic effect on the congregation. She announced that she was going to give away some cassette tapes to the most eager person. As she held up the cassettes, there was a pause, after which a young woman jumped up and ran forward to receive it.

"Well," she said, "next time you will have to show that you are a lot more eager than that!"

Unknown to us, in the break, a whole group of people made paper hats, and when she asked who was going to claim the free tapes, they all jumped up, put on the hats, and rushed to the front. It was hilarious. Someone had also given her a beautiful red rose, and in the midst of the hilarity, she was waving the microphone in the air and speaking into the rose!

The next night we could have had no idea what was going to happen. Nothing like it had happened before, and nothing like it has happened since. Several people prepared huge banners and waited at the gate of the school where we were holding the meetings for Harmony to arrive. They said, "Harmony, we are the most eager," "We deserve the tapes," and other such sentiments.

One young man made a massive banner, and it took three people to hold it up They waited for the car carrying Harmony to come through the gate and walked backward all the way down the drive in front of the car. The whole meeting became like a party. I have no doubt this strange phenomenon was a God thing. Joy and laughter relaxed the atmosphere; the Holy Spirit was released, and we had lots of healings as well as people coming to Christ.

The reality of God was revealed to people by the gifts of the Spirit in ways our hearts had longed for when we were Anglicans. Many churches will not risk allowing the gifts of the Holy Spirit in church meetings, but we were more concerned about grieving God than offending people and made room in our structure for the exercise of the gifts.

The weird or even the counterfeit will try to ruin the genuine, but we were prepared to risk it and allow God to move. We dreaded being like many of the established churches, a form of godliness without the power with the unscriptural divide between the clergy and laity.

CHAPTER 28

Starting as We Mean to Go On

Healing was very important to us, as I believe it is to Jesus. In His life, we are told in Acts 10.38 that He "went about doing good and healing all who were oppressed by the devil." Our understanding was that divine healing, as opposed to faith healing, which may not have Christian origins, is actually about wholeness. Vines dictionary of New Testament words says that the Greek word for salvation, *sozo*, actually means all kinds of salvation: body, soul, and spirit.

Isaiah 53:4 clearly tells us:

> Surely he hath borne our griefs, and carried our sorrows: yet we did esteem him stricken, smitten of God, and afflicted. But he was wounded for our transgressions; he was bruised for our iniquities: the chastisement of our peace was upon him; and with his stripes we are healed.

On the cross, His blood paid for our sin, and when we repent, we receive His forgiveness. Any record of our sin is utterly erased, and we become righteous in God's eyes. It was by the same sacrifice when He was cruelly flogged, His body being bruised and broken, that He paid the price for our physical healing. God is interested in the whole person, and the physical, spiritual, and the soul realms are inseparable. We knew Jesus wants to deal with all of them in people's lives.

When Jesus defeated Satan and took away his authority, He did not take away all of his power. After His resurrection, Jesus gave the body of

Christ the job of enforcing the reality of that authority. Because we knew we had been given authority over all the power of the enemy, wherever we found demons, as we sometimes did, we cast them out in the name of Jesus.

Deliverance always caused controversy, as does inner healing, but they were always part of our ministry, and we saw good results in people's lives. Soon we had people coming from everywhere. They usually came to stay for several days to receive prayer ministry, which we somehow fitted into our already-busy schedule. We continued this ministry for many years and trained others to do the same.

One of the most costly mistakes we can make is either to ignore the devil or to pay him too much attention so we tried to steer a careful middle course. We were passionate about healing of every kind, and we would lay hands on anything that moved! Several physical healings stick in my mind.

The first is Jeanie, who was knocked down by a car when she was riding home on her moped. Her leg was broken, which did not seem to be too complicated. However, complications arose due to something released from the bone marrow. Alarmingly, she was suddenly in intensive care with her life in danger. When my son Philip died and we failed to raise him up, I told the Lord that I would not be so passive in the future. I promised Him that if I had the opportunity, I would go into the intensive care ward, pray for the person I knew in there, and get him or her out. I would not stand by and let the person die.

As soon as the news came to us about Jeanie, we swung into action as a body. Backed by the fervent intercession of a group of our members, we went into the hospital ward and prayed over her. The result was that she was soon out of intensive care, and she did not have the threatened tracheotomy. It was a miracle. Today she is well and healthy and still in the church, ministering, bringing up her family, and firmly committed to the Lord.

Tilly received another remarkable healing. She came to one of our open meetings at the Maltings. She was an embittered old woman who was crippled with arthritis. She had almost been dragged to the meeting by her ex-daughter-in-law. At a word of command from the visiting minister, Mike McCann, her fingers instantly became straight and normal. They were mobile and without pain for the first time in years. She was utterly delighted. She invited Jesus into her life, forgave everybody she hated, became happy and content, and attended the church for as long as she was able.

We wrote a report for the local paper about the meeting, telling of the healings that had taken place. I was surprised when I read the published report that none of the healings were mentioned at all. They had edited out all references to them. When I rang the paper, a reporter told me they could not possibly print those testimonies because they were based on hearsay and opinion. The young man very seriously informed me that, as a newspaper, they could only print facts. I wanted to laugh aloud. And I said, "Since when did newspapers only print the facts!"

Tilly was very upset that her good news was left out of the newspaper report, so she wrote a letter of complaint telling them about her healing. This resulted in a second article in which her photo was published, and her testimony was given in full. Great! Then her daughter-in-law, Dora, had a terrible stroke.

We had just finished one of our large, successful conventions. We had gone home exhausted but happy to eat a meal and rest. While we were eating, a telephone call came from one of Dora's neighbours, telling us she had fallen over in her garden but a friend had helped her into the house. It did not sound too awful or too urgent, so I said we would be along when we had finished eating. She was a large woman, so just in case I needed someone else with me to help her, I asked a young man to come with me to investigate.

When we got to the house, I was absolutely horrified! She was unconscious, her breathing was laboured, and she looked ashen. If I had realised it was as serious as that, I would never have been so casual. Immediately I rang for an ambulance and a doctor. He came and dispatched her to the hospital, which fortunately was in Ely. I accompanied her, sending Nigel back to report the bad news and raise some prayer support for her.

She was put in a side room right next to the nurses' room. The medical opinion was that Dora was practically dead. The prognosis was that she would not recover and would die by the morning. The whole church began earnest prayer for her.

The next day we went with our elders to anoint her with oil. I stayed at the end of the corridor to stop any family members from coming to the room until they had finished praying. The racket that arose from that room as they prayed very loudly in tongues started to attract attention. The nurse came out of her room, which was next door. I watched her tiptoe gingerly into the corridor, peek quickly into the room, and then immediately beat a hasty retreat. I have to say, I was cringing and praying hard that nobody else would come along! We were determined not to let Dora die.

When we went into the hospital the next day, the nurse said, cheerfully, "I don't know what you did yesterday, but it worked! She is alive, and it looks like she might recover."

The previous night, one of our men had received a vision of Dora while he was praying and interceding. He saw Dora standing in a cornfield, waving from a great distance, so we believe she did actually die and go to heaven but God sent her back to be a witness to His glory. The hospital called her their miracle woman.

The improvement was slow but sure. Every day there was improvement, and she made a really good recovery, far beyond medical expectations and was sent for rehab. She is still alive today. While she was in the hospital, a whole group of us went into her home, which was in great need of a facelift, and gave it a complete makeover. With her permission, we sold some stuff to pay for some new furniture.

Then there was Michael, who God healed of throat cancer after just a short and simple prayer. We simply prayed, and he simply received. A wonderful healing happened at one of our early conventions, but the results were not quite what we might have expected. A man with a completely frozen shoulder received prayer. Immediately he received freedom of movement. He demonstrated his healing by picking up a chair and raising it above his head with the previously afflicted arm. His whole family was saved on the spot, both his wife and his grown-up children, and they all went home rejoicing. However, surprisingly, he declined to make a commitment himself, and as far as I know, he never has.

The whole family began to attend the church, but after a while, he forbade them to come to our church anymore. He told them he would disown them and cut them out of his will if they continued to do so. There was obviously strife going on in the home because of their church attendance, and so the family left and went to the local Methodist church, which he allowed. There is no accounting for folks!

One more instance of healing was remarkable. A man in the church named George had been kicked in the head by a carthorse when he was only about two. He nearly died. It was only the faithful prayer of his Methodist parents and church family in Sutton that brought him through. However, he was left with a somewhat flattened head and epilepsy. One day an amazing elderly woman named Mary, who I knew as an intercessor, suggested that we should set a time to pray for George's healing.

One day a few of us went to Mary's house and prayed with George. The Holy Spirit fell on him that day, and the effect of it continued for many days. Much to the alarm of his family, he quite dramatically kept going in and out of the presence of God. He was radically touched by this experience, but the best part is that it happened more than twenty years ago, and he has been completely free of epilepsy ever since. He is proud of his testimony and the God who gave it to him.

We also taught people that the power of the tongue, or more specifically the power of our words, was a factor in receiving and maintaining any healing. We encouraged them that they could receive healing simply by faith when they took communion. God has many means to touch people's lives. He is not a one-method God. We were also never the kind of Christians who told people doctors were wrong or that they should not seek medical help. We were determined to arm people with all the information they needed to maintain victory in their lives, so we taught them how to exercise the spiritual authority given to us and how to use the power of the name of Jesus over our enemy, the devil.

Initially at our conventions, we imported gifted people like Eddie and Lorrie Hornback to do children's ministry, but in our regular services at the Maltings we had no children's ministry. Nobody had the desire to do anything with the children. This was troubling because we had lots of babies who would soon need their own meetings, and we knew if we could make the children happy in church, then for the most part their parents would be happy too. As always, prayer was the answer, and soon a family came along who had a heart for the children. We began to develop very special children's meetings alongside the adult sessions, using dynamic material from a man named Willie George. This team eventually did the children's work at the conventions too.

Our own children had experienced Willie George meetings when we went to America. I am sure my children went through the whole three-year scheme at least twice, but they did end up knowing the Word! The children's ministry absorbed a lot of manpower, but it was always worth it. Our youth were very involved with this ministry too. They helped practically as well as spiritually, and they performed dramas. We never had any doubt children could be saved, be filled with the Spirit, and minister for God too, so we encouraged them in this.

We were small and apparently weak when we began, but God was with us in a marvelous way. We held the first of many holiday clubs in the back garden of Egremont House in a marquee. A couple named Eddie and Laurie Hornback came up from London to lead it. They roped as many of us as they could into the daily routine as well as the dramas.

About forty children attended. We had lots of fun, and we also saw many children invite Jesus into their lives and receive the baptism of the Holy Spirit. If any of the children attended another church in the city, as a courtesy we sent out letters to the minister of the church and told them what the child had experienced. One minister was not at all pleased. He wrote us a letter of complaint, asking, "How are they to appreciate confirmation now they have received all of this?" The joy of it seemed to escape him. Perhaps we should have said nothing, but we hoped the children would get encouragement and follow-up from their own churches.

As part of the fun, I played Faith Woman, a female version of Superman. For the first part of the sketch, I had to appear as an ordinary young woman talking to someone who was experiencing some difficulty or other. I then dashed behind a screen in lieu of a telephone box and stripped off my regular clothes to reveal my Faith Woman costume—tights, union jack boxer shorts, and a red and blue cape. Maybe the role was prophetic! I would then leap out with the Bible's answer to the problem! It was great fun.

Tony played Mr. Crabtree. He was a bad-tempered man with many problems. I hope that was not a prophetic role! Every day Ed the doctor performed a mock operation on him, and his personality was miraculously changed. This illustrated different spiritual truths. For instance, they took out his old heart and gave him a new one. This improved Mr. Crabtree no end, as indeed it does when Jesus does that wonderful spiritual operation on us, making us new creations in Him.

The finale was a party. To celebrate, we made an enormous banana split, attempting to make the biggest banana split ever made since records began. We made it in a long piece of plastic guttering. We had to do it very quickly because it was a very hot day, and we were worried it would melt. The moment it was finished, all sixty of us, armed with spoons, gleefully attacked it to eat it up before the sun could melt it. It was the easiest part of the week!

After our first experience with this kind of children's ministry, we were eager to do more holiday clubs with puppets, games, and Bible teaching. Therefore, after our first Children's holiday club, we started a midweek children's club called Seekers. This was never without drama. One week we gave a child a Bible, and the next week she came back upset because the dog had eaten the Bible!

Our youth, of course, were not to be ignored. We were concerned that Ben and Giles would find friends they could share their faith with and have fun with. We were relieved when a young man named Jack who had an interest in youth and a heart to minister to them started a youth group. Most of this group, including our sons, later chose to make a personal declaration of their own faith and were baptised. Jack was one of God's trophies, an ex-biker and a Hell's Angel who had been wonderfully saved and then attended Bible school at Capenwray.

Recently a friend who used to be the chaplain of Kings School reminded me of a lovely story about Jack. Somehow he had encountered a couple of girls from the school who were being rebellious and difficult because they felt dumped by their parents at boarding school. When Jack met with these girls, they gave their hearts to Jesus. Immediately everyone noticed the difference in them, and as a result, Jack was invited to go to the school twice a week to assist with Christian Union meetings, where he was much appreciated.

We started Bible school classes with material from the States by Mark Virkler. We taught the whole Bible through from start to finish so many times. We taught people how to hear God's voice by using a course, which was then called "Communion with God." We also used many other courses, such as "Naturally Supernatural" and "Abiding in Christ." We wanted to grow mature believers who could minister confidently to others. We wanted, just as Jesus told us, to make real disciples, not just converts. Our cry was always, "Every man [meaning every person] a minister." We wanted this for adults and children alike.

When we taught people how to hear God's voice, it brought greater maturity to people and gave people more confidence to step out and witness with words of knowledge and prophecy. It enabled them to know what God was calling them to do in the church or the nations. There are so many demands in a growing church, and people can feel guilty if they do not respond to the pastor's many requests for help, but if they knew what God had said they should do, they avoided that guilt and condemnation. Most precious of all, people heard God tell them how much He loved them. I have experienced so much love, peace, joy, and encouragement through being able to hear God speak to me and record my daily conversations with Him. His guidance is essential to our success as believers. He is more willing to speak than we are to listen. One word directly from God changes everything. Most people experienced marvelous spiritual breakthroughs because of this course. I remember one particular young woman who had suffered from depression for years. She had a massive breakthrough simply because, for the first time ever, she was able to hear the Lord assuring her personally of His deep love for her. When God whispers into your heart, "I love you," Bible truth becomes reality. Logos in the Greek means the written word but it then becomes rhema which means the spoken word!

Tony and I sometimes travel out to teach this course, with similar results. It is such a privilege to see people's faces and feel the effect it has upon them once they know they have established two-way dialogue with God. It's a dialogue they can have every day of their lives as they take time out to hear Him.

In our eagerness to train people to minister, we also got involved with a wonderful, resourceful lady named Judy Bauer. She had a great scheme called KAM (Kingdom Advancement Ministries). This course was basically a kind of boot camp for teaching people how to preach the gospel, how to pray with someone for healing, how to lead someone into the baptism of the Holy Spirit and speaking in tongues, and how to lead a simple Bible study in a home. With this material we launched out with home visiting to every family in the congregation.

This knowledge and training meant our people could go out confident in what they knew. Consequently, other ministers asked us to send people to help with their church outreach meetings. Other believers would often recognize that our people had spiritual stature. Some were impressed enough to move to Ely to find out how to become like this themselves.

CHAPTER 29

Not All Plain Sailing, but Breakthrough Comes

T he stories I have told you so far, I am sure, all sound very positive. Most of what happened in the church *was* positive. It was a great joy to be part of such a wonderful church. However, there were some difficult areas we grappled with, and it took us some time to settle on what we felt was right and workable for us. We were a bit unsure about how to organize our structure, and it seemed hard to get the mind of God on it. We were assailed by many opinions, sometimes very strong ones, all of which claimed to be scriptural. This led to us making some fundamental errors, which caused a lot of pain.

We were strongly advised by the minister of a large Pentecostal church in Norwich not to have elders, but Tony was determined we should not be a one-man ministry, so we gathered a group of men together and called them deacons. However, it led to misunderstanding because everyone had come from different denominations where the word deacon meant something different.

Then, at a later point, we did foolishly give in to people's pressure and appoint elders. Again, it proved to be a terrible mistake. I do not believe God has only one formula for church leadership. However, I am sure God is concerned that a church should have godly leadership. There was also the problem that I was an obvious leader. Standing beside Tony, I was bearing a lot of responsibility, but biblically, the big question in some people's minds was; could women be in leadership?

I was also preaching and teaching, which was and still is a big doctrinal hot potato. In my heart, I knew God had called me to preach and teach, but many sincere Christians hold the view that women can only preach to women and children and cannot address men. It did seem a bit hypocritical to me that over the years missionary women had been sent out to preach the gospel to men in foreign countries, but they could not do it in their own home churches!

We had settled our own hearts what the Word said about the issue. Over the years I have also done deep studies on the matter, but convincing certain men was sometimes a bit harder. I had a man called Terry say to me, "Margaret, I am so blessed by your preaching." Then he said the same thing to me that John Hughes had said many years previously: "Every time you teach, it's wonderful; the lights turn on, but," sadly Terry could not be convinced. He would always return and say "but what about Paul's teaching?"

In all other respects we were on good terms with Terry so Tony would sit with him, and explain to him repeatedly what we believed, but he like many others could never get past his literal understanding of the words he read in Scripture and was obviously more troubled about it than others. One day he came to me after the sermon and said earnestly, "Margaret, today I asked the Lord to tell me what you were going to preach about so I would know whether what you were saying came from the devil or from God. You preached exactly what God told me you would." I didn't know whether to laugh or cry!

Another time he came to me and said, "Will it ever be possible for me to rise higher than you in the church and to be in authority over you?"

I thought it was a very strange question. For a moment I was totally nonplussed. To me, being in ministry had never been about having a position. I had never thought of myself as being in authority over people in that way. I was simply exercising a spiritual ministry. Then I remembered that Jesus had been asked a similar question when, as recorded in Matthew 20, the mother of Zebedee's sons came to Jesus with her sons to ask a favor of Him:

> "What do you wish?" Jesus asked. She said to Him, "Grant that one of these two sons of mine may sit, one on Your right hand and the other on the left, in Your kingdom."

But Jesus answered and said, "You don't know what you ask. Are you able to drink the cup that I am about to drink, and be baptised with the baptism that I am baptised with?" They said to Him, "We are able." Jesus said "You will indeed drink My cup, and be baptised with the baptism that I am baptised with; but to sit on My right hand and on My left is not Mine to give, but it is for those for whom it is prepared by My Father."

I pointed this Scripture out to Terry and said, "Two things are clear. First, if God gives it to you, yes. Second, if you are prepared to lay down your life for the sheep as I have, maybe yes! The greatest among you, Jesus said, should be the servant of all!"

At one time, tongue-in-cheek and a bit naughtily, I told him I was sure God would forgive me for all the people who had been saved, healed, and encouraged through my ministry!

Many years later we renounced using all the titles like deacon and elder. Without changing what anyone was doing we decided that we were just going to call people *leaders*! It seemed that once given certain titles, wonderful people changed in a subtle way and not always for the better.

I often felt very sorry for the men we appointed as Elders because instead of coming directly to us people often went and complained to them about what they disliked. This sometimes threatened to bring division between us and the leaders. Perhaps people were relating to us like parents, trying to play us off each other. Some unpleasant emotional tangles developed because people asked them to keep what they had said in confidence and as they sat on this information they eventually began somehow to see what was wrong through the complainer's eyes. Of course, if it was a church matter rather than a personal matter they should have refused as they owed loyalty to us. One man, although he had been a dear friend for many years, because of this divisive behavior ended up leaving the church with his family. It was all very difficult.

There was an interesting follow-up story to our change of structure. We had a wonderful friend named Brian Myers who was with us in Isleham years before and who we knew prayed for us every day. One day, a little while after we had made the changes, we went to visit him and his wife, Marilyn. She said to him, "Well, are you going to give them the word you had for them a little while ago?"

"Oh yes," he said. "God told me that you should change your leadership structure. Since I know you are well able to hear God speak to you, I prayed that He would tell you exactly what He had told me."

He did tell us! We did hear! What a lovely confirmation that was for us, because not everyone had taken kindly to our decision.

However, we did believe firmly that there could only be one head. Although Tony would always seek others' counsel, we believed he should always be the one who made the final decision about a matter. We were also convinced we were as one in the ministry, and Tony tried to make it clear that I was his closest and most trusted assistant. Interestingly, when Tony made that clear people often brought me their grumbles, which was much safer for the church because divide and conquer did not work with us. Over the years we learned, at our cost, not to ignore people's opinions and grumbles but to listen with humility. Many times we benefitted greatly from others' wisdom, but sometimes we missed good counsel because we did not have sufficient respect for the messenger, or doubted their motives and we lived to rue the day.

As the numbers grew and the workload increased, we needed Tony to be released from teaching physics to work full time in the church. We reckoned that we needed the financial support of ten tithing men to provide a salary. They seemed a long time coming, but we knew we could not continue long term with Tony's attention divided between secular work, where he was carrying all the responsibilities of a head of department, and being a pastor to a busy church. Tony also came home to a large house full of people and all of their problems. Although it was not a house of disorder, neither was it a haven of peace!

As I have stated, on our first day in 1982, we started with fourteen people, two of whom were our young boys. In 1983, the second year, we had twenty-five. In the third year, 1985, we had thirty people. In the fourth year, 1986, there were seventy-eight people! We and other key people knew that it was time to seek the Lord seriously about Tony being employed by the church. So, supported by the body and other men and women of God we knew and trusted, Tony and I prayed and fasted for a week, asking God to speak to us clearly. One of the Scriptures God gave to Tony was Leviticus 19:25: "And in the fifth year you may eat its fruit, that it may yield to you its increase: I am the Lord your God." I had also heard from the Lord clearly that this was the right time for him to be full time, so we had the solidity of our agreement.

Thus in 1987, in the fifth year of the church, Tony handed his notice in to the school. Although it meant taking a pay cut, we trusted God for the provision of his salary, and God has never failed us. The growth we experienced that next year assured us that the word we had heard from God about Tony pastoring full-time was indeed accurate. Greater fruitfulness had come from Tony entering the ministry full-time. By the end of 1987, we had nearly doubled. We had 130 people.

Our numbers continued to grow until 1993, when we had approximately 260 people. We had no reason to believe we would do anything but continue to grow into the large church God had promised. God remained faithful to us as a family during all those years. We had very little money to spare, especially when Tony went full-time, but God always seemed to come up with the extras we needed.

We were very concerned about maintaining good relationship with our boys. We were very busy but I always made sure I spent some time with them every day, and Tony put aside one night every week so they could do something together. Often they voted to watch a movie together. However, I think we had trained our boys to share too well because they soon wanted to invite their friends to share this time, which was hard to refuse when that was what they wanted!

Practical, personal provision was always there for us in many ways. One year a member of the congregation offered us a holiday cottage to use for a family holiday. After that another member of the congregation gave us a wonderful mobile home at Snettisham, which was less than an hour's drive away on the Norfolk coast. We were tremendously grateful for such a wonderful gift that meant we could get away easily and rest on our day off. It offered more than just practical provision because I find it especially easy to pray and hear God walking by the sea. We spent many refreshing hours in conversation with the Lord on that often deserted beach. Tony sometimes put his wellingtons on and walked out onto the mud flats. He prayed loudly in tongues all the way, blissfully unaware of how much the sound could be heard as it carried easily across the quiet stillness of the shore. It was also wonderful double-edged provision because we were able to lend it to others who needed a holiday. To me, the greatest joy of possessing good things is that they can be shared.

We would head for our little hideout every week after the Sunday-evening service and get there at about eleven o'clock. We would have some supper and then crash into bed exhausted. If we did not wake up before ten o'clock, we knew we were too tired! We came back on Monday evening or even early on Tuesday refreshed.

God answered prayer for special things for our boys too in big and small ways. Two answered prayers for special provision for Ben stand out in my mind. One Christmas Ben wanted a guitar. I had a chat with him about it. He wanted a twelve-string guitar with a case. I realised we would not have the three hundred pounds or so that such an instrument would cost, so I said to him, "Let's pray and ask God to send it. God gave you a violin years ago, so why not a guitar?"

Ben and I prayed a simple prayer of agreement. Later a man in the church said, "Margaret, do you know anyone who wants a guitar?"

I said that I did indeed! He told me that a young man who had left the church to go to university had a guitar to give away. He had said to him, "Give it to Margaret because she will know exactly who to give it to."

The guitar came just in time for Christmas, and Ben was thrilled with it. It was just what he had asked for, a twelve-string guitar with a case. Another time Ben needed money for a course at the local college. We prayed, and within a week, somebody gave me the five hundred pounds he needed.

The boys had joined the local sailing club, and they desperately wanted their own boat. We prayed together for a boat, putting the vision before us by placing a picture of a boat on the fridge door and thanking God for it every day. We saw an advertisement for a Mirror dinghy in a newspaper that was exactly what they wanted, and we were just able to afford it. Then someone who knew nothing about our prayer called us out of the blue. "Would you like a boat?" So in the end, we had two boats!

God's provision was, of course, about far more than just things. In spite of the busyness of life and the stresses of church, home, and family, God helped us to preserve our marriage intact and happy. It was no easy task to keep track of our relationship and keep it fresh and alive. We had to contend for it constantly and work hard at it. The Lord spoke to me about quite another aspect of us staying in unity. He encouraged us greatly in our attempts by telling us that if we were in unity, we would never have a church split. Unity always trickles down from the top!

God also blessed me with faith for the safety of my children, who were growing up rapidly. Because of what had happened to Philip, for many years I felt unable to let them have bicycles, but I began feeding my heart with the Word. God gave me the Scripture from Ephesians 6, "Children, obey your parents in the Lord . . . that it may be well with you and you may live long on the earth."

I personalized this Scripture, meditated on it, and prayed it over my boys until my faith was solidly built and I felt secure enough in the truth of God's Word to let them have a bicycle. This faith was sorely tested by them both as teenagers having accidents while they were riding their bikes in the city.

One day a phone call came with the news that Giles had been knocked off his bike in Ely High Street, right outside Curry's shop. When I heard the news, the first thing I thought was, *He is fine. My children obey their parents, it is well with them, and they will live long on the earth.*

How miraculous it is that I did not have one single thought of fear. Similarly, when Ben was knocked off his bike in the city, I knew he was fine. God had removed all fear and dread from me. In later years, both boys have had quite serious road accidents that landed them in hospital. I thank God for the stability of heart He has given me, enabling me to trust God for their safety.

A few years ago, on his way home from a works trip, late at night, Giles hit a deer on the A10 and his car was flung into a roadside ditch narrowly missing a serious collision with two large trees. The car was not visible from the road and he was trapped in the car. Fortunately he had enough power left in his phone to make an emergency call but because the car was hidden in the ditch the only way they found him was when they saw the dead deer. He was badly bruised and shaken, and the emergency services had to cut the roof off the car to get him out. We had just opened our front door returning from a holiday when the phone call came to tell us of the accident. We sped off immediately to where he was. It was easy to spot the scene of the accident as there was a doctor's car, a fire engine and an ambulance parked at the side of the road. We watched and prayed as they cut the roof off the car and handed him out over their heads on a stretcher with their arms lifted high in the air. At the hospital they were planning to remove his spleen because it was bleeding. They said that once it was damaged like that removal was certain. We all went into a small room and prayed. We refused to allow the spleen to be removed commanded it to be healed. Giles was kept under observation for a few days, and every day they expected to have to remove the spleen; but it was healed and he still has it intact! Only God could have stopped his spleen from bleeding that night and prevented its removal!

Ben also came off his bike yet again a couple of years ago and ended up in hospital with a head injury. It was a fairly minor injury, but because Philip died of a head injury, it had more significance to me and to him than it might have done to others.

I am sure of one thing, though: God's hand is on their lives

CHAPTER 30

We Need a Permanent Home

In 1988, we were inspired when Mike McCann prophesied to us about a church building. Our small numbers made what he said look impossible, but it kept our faith bright. Many times this is just what these prophecies did. They kept our hope and faith strong when everything looked impossible. He prophesied, saying, "Your building will bring great glory to Ely and the Fens. It will stand like a beacon in a rough sea, leading souls to safe anchorage. It will be a light in the darkness—a guiding light, a light of love and life. It will shine with the radiance of the Holy Spirit, brighter than gold or precious stones. It will shine with the light of the Lord. It will be huge and impressive, with room for many worshippers, whose praises will rise through the roof, through their up stretched arms to ascend into the throne room of the Almighty. Have faith for this building, and make preparation for it. Be ready for the right time. Keep seeing it. Nothing is impossible with Me."

When we began to grow more rapidly, the need for a building became much greater. Where could such a large number of people meet together on a Sunday? Six years later, in 1994, we stretched our faith to the limit to buy a building.

Until we regularly had a hundred people we met at the Maltings by the river. Then we moved to the infant's school in Downham Road. When that building was no longer convenient, we moved to the adult training centre called Larkfield in High Barns, where we stayed until we had about two hundred people and had to have double services every Sunday.

Having to have double services was exhausting, but it proved to have its advantages. We developed a two-tier system. A person could come to Larkfield at 9:30 a.m. and go to a small group. After a coffee break, they could then attend their main service at 11:00 a.m. Conversely, people attended their main service at 9:30 a.m. and their small group at 11:00 a.m.! By structuring things in this way, we satisfied the needs of many. People loved the small groups. We had a couples' group, a choir, a basic Bible study group, and a group for more established believers.

The children's ministry also had a two-tier system. At 9:30 a.m., we had one meeting for all the children over five. It was a meeting where the children worshiped, had puppets skits, learned memory verses, and listened to Bible stories. Then there were small groups for different age groups at 11:00 a.m. Another advantage of the double services was that no children's worker ever had to miss a Sunday service.

When both services were full, the question was where was our promised building? For many years we had our eye on a building by the traffic lights on Lynn Road across from the police station, but the owner simply refused to sell it to us at a price we could afford. This was understandable from his point of view because he wanted to get planning permission and sell it for building land. It would be much more profitable for him to do that.

We were stumped until we heard about the Fiat Garage on Lynn Road as a possibility. Encouraged by our solicitor, we approached the owner and found him willing to sell for a price we could just about stretch our faith to afford. Because of the generous and sacrificial giving of church members over a period of years, we had saved £90,000. With a loan and further gifts, we were able to buy the garage, refurbish some of it, and then move into what is a now our wonderful church home in the centre of Ely.

There were two things apart from the witness of the Spirit that confirmed it was the right building. One of our intercessors, Rosemary, suddenly found an old notebook where she had written two prophecies that we had been given many years earlier. They said two distinct things. One prophecy said we would buy a building that had something to do with cars. The other indicated it would be in the very centre of the city. I did vaguely remember them, but they had both been puzzling words. Mistakenly, we thought the centre of the city must be the market square, and there were no buildings that had anything to do with cars in the market square. The only building that seemed large enough was a Tesco store!

When we were negotiating to buy the old Fiat Garage, we were shown an old plan of the building, which included a map of the immediate area around the building. We were astounded. There, right outside the garage on this map, was a cross in the middle of the road stating clearly, "The Centre of Ely." What a tremendous confirmation!

We were given a further confirmation through a prophetic word given to Tony and me at Santa Rosa Beach in Florida. We were in Florida because a member of our church had returned to the United States after being over here in the military. She had invited us to stay with her and her husband. We had a lovely time with them and took advantage of our close proximity to Bill Hamon's prophetic ministry to go to a meeting. I say close; this ministry was actually hundreds of miles away at the other end of Florida, but hey, it was closer than England! Distance is relative once you've crossed the Atlantic.

We arrived at the church building in good time for their Friday-night meeting. After the vibrant praise and worship, an elderly man stood up to preach. He opened the Scriptures and began to read. Suddenly he stopped, looked up, fixed his eyes on us, and walked slowly down the aisle to where we were sitting. Standing in front of us, he said, "God pointed you out to me in the congregation. I am preaching about Jesus using Peter's boat and Peter letting down his nets for a catch. I must tell you that it is going to be like that for you. You are not going to be providing Jesus with a vessel as Peter did, but He is providing you with a vessel. It will push you out into the deep so you can be seen and heard in a new way. You will let down your nets and bring in the multitudes, so there's change in the air. You are going to have a vessel, and you are going to have the multitudes. You will be speaking, and you will have an effect. You will have the vessel and the multitudes promised."

We were astounded on two counts. First, he could have had no idea that we were in the middle of delicate negotiations for a vessel or building. Neither, could this man have known that for many years, repeatedly, and through many ministers, God had promised us multitudes! This word was particularly significant to us because we had come away slightly troubled. The decision about buying this building had divided our trustees. Of the five, three were game to go with it, but two of them had huge doubts. One of them, our treasurer, had resigned but graciously because his professional advice as a well-known and respected accountant for the council was that we simply could not afford it. He understood our stance of faith, but he felt that because of his position, he could not support the project. Although we were sad he felt this way, we understood. Through love and respect for each other, we remained friends!

The other doubter behaved unacceptably. He was very disrespectful toward Tony and was determined to block the purchase. He refused to resign as a trustee until the others put great pressure upon him to do so but not before he tried to create trouble with our bank and our solicitor. The solicitor told us he had never known anyone to do what this man did and that he had certainly never expected a Christian to behave like this. How painful it was to be exposed to unbelievers in this way! However, he no doubt acted with the best motives, believing that he was right and that he was saving us from a terrible mistake.

When I heard the statement that we could not afford it, I said, "Of course we cannot afford it!" Naturally speaking it was impossible, but we serve the God of the impossible. We knew beyond all doubt that it was the will of God for us to buy this building and that we must press through all of these objections. Consequently, I said to our trustees, "We have taught prosperity. We have taught our congregation that God will meet all of our needs according to His riches in glory by Christ Jesus ever since we started this church. It has caused us to be much criticized, and we have paid a high price for this belief. Now is the time not just to believe it but to act on it. Either we believe the Word of God or we don't! If we draw back now, it makes nonsense of our faith. We will be a laughingstock. The only question we have to ask is, has God said this is our building?"

So with much prayer and heart searching, we purchased the Fiat Garage and set about making refurbishments. We tackled the front building first because it had been the car showroom and was in the best condition. We got it ready as quickly as we could so we could meet there on a Sunday. It was fun with so many of us working together as a team on the job. It reminded me of the time when we moved into Egremont House.

Almost as soon as we had moved into the Lighthouse Centre one Sunday morning, God simply turned up in a brand-new way. The presence of God swept across the congregation. His presence enveloped us. There was laughter as well as tears. When it was time to go home, people just sat, seemingly unable to move, reluctant to go home. The presence of God touched us all that day in different ways.

After this experience in our church service, which seemed to continue each week, we heard about some meetings in Toronto. A minister friend named Ash who had originally scoffed at it called us and urged us to go. Just as thousands of others were doing, we went to the Airport Vineyard Church in Toronto and received great gulps of this wonderful 'new' anointing.

When we came home, I wondered how we would fare with this new phenomenon, which people called the Toronto blessing. It felt like we were always involved in something controversial as far as the church in general was concerned, and we were aware of the opposition that it might cause. I am sorry to admit that my first reaction was to say, "Oh no, Lord, not something else people will criticize us for!"

However, this wave of anointing was such tremendous refreshment to the weary, and I could not be sorry for long that God had chosen to visit us. I am so thankful that I have known the moving of the Holy Spirit inside my being in a very real way ever since that time. I had always known the presence of God but it seemed that God made His presence real to me in a more constant and tangible way. At times when I feel the Holy Spirit stirring within my being, you might hear a groan escaping from my lips! Sometimes it is irrepressible, and it gets worse when I pray or worship. Sometimes it happens when I feel great compassion for someone. It is a sign that I must pray. Even the mention of Jesus or a passing thought about Jesus can sometimes set me off. At times this has been very inconvenient, especially in a secular setting, so I quickly learned to turn the groan discreetly into something that sounds like a cough. Then, of course, I have had caring people come to me in church and say, "Margaret, can I pray for your cough!"

Of course, there were the manifestations some people did not like. Sometimes the laughing, crying, shaking, roaring, groaning, and seeming drunkenness, accompanied by people falling down, disturbed people. We had always had some of these manifestations in our church meetings from time to time, so we were not fazed. On the day of Pentecost, people were not only speaking in tongues, but the onlookers also thought they were drunk. It seems the Holy Spirit does not mind showing off a bit! Despite some Christians despising the manifestations that came with this fresh anointing, it brought more unity between the churches in the area. Things have never been the same between the denominations since then. What could have brought division created unity.

We held receiving meetings on Sunday nights to enable people to receive more of the anointing. People came from so many of the churches in the area. We trained a team of people in how best to minister, and we would all pray over the people who came that night without any hurry for as long as we felt the Holy Spirit moving. They would often fall down in the Spirit, and they would then lie on the floor, continuing to receive all God wanted to give. It was a beautiful time, and we were sad when the season seemed to be over.

If we study church history, we will find that manifestations like these have always occurred in revivals in the past. This has been the case from early centuries to the present day. They were particularly evident in a fresh outpouring that occurred in Azusa Street, Los Angeles, at the beginning of the twentieth century. Those who stifle the manifestations today would probably hold up Azusa Street as a wonderful example of what God can do to revive His church! Everyone acknowledges that the Azusa Street revival ushered in the start of modern global Pentecostalism, which has filled the earth with new life from God and is still causing revival right across the earth. When something happened a long time ago, people do not realise that what happened was not comfortable for the people involved and how it always causes divisions. Somehow we romanticize it. We want the fruit, but we would not want the discomfort

The truth is that today, in places where God's Holy Spirit is honoured and allowed to move freely, the church is in revival and growing fast even in the UK. In fact, globally the church is growing at 8 percent a year. Projections say that if the growth remains constant, by 2030 there could be eight and a half billion Christians on the earth—more than the world's entire current population!

My belief is that although we need to be discerning, we should not squash or mock anything that is supernatural and of the Spirit of God. We grieve Him at our peril. We had struck out from the safe and dull Church of England into uncharted territory and were not about to turn back now because we were afraid of what people might think.

Who wants a boring church that it entirely predictable where nothing supernatural ever happens?

CHAPTER 31

What Do We Do with a Building?

We firmly believed that a building would be a waste if it were only used for just one a day a week, so we set about making plans for projects to fill the building with daily activity. We sought grants from various bodies to help with the costs.

While we had been waiting to take possession of the garage, which we called the Lighthouse Centre, we rented an old clinic in Chapel Street so we could make a start on our projects. The way we got the clinic was miraculous. One of our intercessors, Gina, had been praying earnestly about it. She said to me one day, "Have you thought about renting the clinic in Chapel Street?"

We hadn't, but it suddenly seemed like a great idea. We were beginning to feel a little desperate, wondering where God's provision could be. We had projects planned, which we had already started to advertise in faith that we would have our building in time, so it was an absolute godsend to find a suitable empty building we could use as a stopgap. Immediately after Gina spoke to me, I called the council and spoke to the man responsible. He said, "Funnily enough, I am just going into a meeting where we are going to decide what to do with the clinic. I will put your proposal to them immediately." I was left marveling at the promptings of the Holy Spirit to bring about His will in the earth!

He immediately rang me back. They had gladly agreed that we could rent it from them. It seemed that they were just grateful to have someone in there to minimize the risk of vandalism. Our inquiry was their godsend too! They let us have it for the peppercorn rent of £1 a month. In addition, though, we had to pay for the contract costs, which cost a lot more.

In the clinic, we set up our offices. Tony and I each had an office, and so did our administrator, which felt like sheer luxury. We then began the projects, which included preschool and after-school care, a playgroup, Bible study groups, and classes for life skills.

The aim of the projects was to show the unconditional love of God with no strings attached, quite the opposite approach to our rather more confrontational preaching of the gospel. It is not that we had ditched the former, but we added another string to our bow, enabling us to reach our community in a different way.

One interesting project we began twenty years ago and are actually still running is now called EPIC; Ely Pregnancy Information Centre. It has now expanded to give away free baby clothes and equipment to people in need. This runs alongside the food bank, which, like pregnancy crisis, is a church-wide initiative. Our heart is to help the growing number of women with unplanned pregnancies who choose abortions without thinking through the possible consequences. We help them to make an informed decision—one they know they can live with. Other people come because they have already had abortions. It is a tremendous blessing when we see women come to a place of peace, having resolved the issues of their hearts. Salvation is not the primary aim of the project, but some do want to receive Jesus.

Our playgroup was another happy venture. It was a lovely, friendly group that was a joy and ran for a long time until the leaders were called to do other things. We also had a great project called Home from Home for the children of working parents. As the parents were setting out for work, they dropped their children off at the centre. We took the children to school, collected them after school, gave them a snack, and kept them until the parents were on their way home. We wanted it genuinely be a home away from home experience for the children. John and Jack, who ran it, were immensely creative. At one time they constructed a huge grotto for adventure play which filled one of the rooms. They made it such fun for the children to be at the club that many were reluctant to go home when their parents came to collect them.

Another powerful project was life skills, based on godly principles and devised by Paul Hengstrom a strong Christian man who had been an abuser himself. It dealt with domestic violence and other kinds of abuse in relationships. This project was wonderful and changed many of the marriages in our church. Our marriage was not abusive, but we were grateful for the effect the teaching had on our relationship. However, we gave it up because the lady responsible for it left and went back to the US and it was so time consuming that it was distracting us from our main calling.

Our parent and toddler group is still expanding and going strong after more than fifteen years and is the most popular group in the city. We have around seventy parents on the books. Our centre also provides a facility where estranged parents can meet with their children in a safe but homely environment for supervised visits.

In 1994 we transferred all of these projects from the old clinic to our new venue, the Lighthouse Centre. All the projects were supposed to be self-funding, so there was always a small charge for the service, but they almost never paid for themselves, especially when people failed to pay for the service. The people running them were not hard-nosed business people and failed to press for the fees because they allowed themselves to be swayed by hard luck stories!

Each project had been started by a visionary, and we only started a project if someone truly had a vision to do it. Tony followed the principle of the three Ps: project, person, and provision. However, we found that when people moved on because of new employment opportunities, the next generation of people did not take it on as a vision but as a job. It didn't matter how good these people were at the job, somehow the project never had the same impact as when run by a visionary.

Just as we were moving into the centre, we had an enormous disappointment. The local council had generously offered us a grant of £103,000 to refurbish the Dansk building on Lynn Road for church and community use but refused when we applied to have the grant transferred to the Lighthouse Centre. Vocal opposition came from one particular councilor, who used an extraordinary mixture of mockery and lies to oppose the plan so that even those council members who had agreed to support us caved in and agreed with her. I could hardly believe my ears when I attended the council meeting. I tried valiantly to counter such outrageous statements like all our money came from America. It seemed that people were afraid to vote against this scornful woman. I left the meeting with £10,000 toward equipment for our children's work.

What a blow it was to be so badly treated, but from the natural point of view, I imagine it was hard for the council to see how much the community needed us and how much we were prepared to give. They did not know we would keep our promises.

Many years later, having managed the centre successfully, we are much respected for the work we do and have more than proved that we were worthy of the grant. Ironically, the council has only recently given us a grant for £160,000 to refurbish the last building on the site. There is no doubt that the community missed out. I sometimes think, rather wistfully, that many of our projects would perhaps still be running today if we had received that grant.

However, we were used to believing God for financial provision. We had used our faith to obtain two houses we could not afford, so we applied our faith to the supply of things at the Lighthouse Centre. There almost never seemed to be a surplus of money. Tony would say to me things like, "We need a thousand pounds by Tuesday," or "We need ten thousand pounds by the end of the month." God supplied in many different ways, but He often kept us waiting for it until the very last minute, stretching our faith to the limit

On one occasion, when Tony informed me that we needed two thousand pounds by Friday, God provided it in a most memorable way. By the close of office on Friday, no money had arrived, but at our late-night prayer meeting, a young man asked for personal prayer. He had just lost his job and needed another one urgently. As I laid my hand on him, I said, "You will have a job within two weeks, and it will be a better job than you had before."

"That would be very nice," he said, not really sure whether to believe me.

"Truly," I said, "this is the word of the Lord. Will you agree with me?"

After the meeting, he sought Tony privately and pulled a check for £2,000 out of his breast pocket—from the very pocket I laid my hand upon when I prayed for him. It was a tithe on his redundancy money. What an amazing coincidence! What is more, he had a better job within the two-week period!

It was wonderful having a building, but the outworking of it was tough. This reminds me of another word John Hughes gave us around that time: "A work is going to happen here; a sudden explosion, not a progression. There will be a dark hour first and then a phenomenal revolution, accomplishing the deepest desires of hearts that are praying. It will be something to shake the whole countryside—not any minute, but it is definitely coming because this church is open to the Holy Spirit, and He can move freely. Get up, praise Me, and rejoice, for I am in your midst. I am walking forth in your shoes upon this land."

I did not like the sound of "a dark hour," but the second part of it sounded good and held us strong in the dark time, which came very soon.

CHAPTER 32

Victory Comes but Greater Challenge

I n ten years, we had seen many hundreds come in and out of the church. People come, but not everyone stays and builds. However, for one reason or another, our numbers began to fall dramatically. By the end of that year, we had lost about a hundred people in all. I found the loss devastating.

I cannot overstate the pain the loss of so many people caused us because we are not just talking about numbers. These were people we had loved and cherished. We had relationship with them, and some of them had even lived with us. They were family. We had been through life's traumas with them. We had seen them grow and develop in their gifting and ministries. I know they belonged to Jesus and not to us, but it tore my heart to shreds when they left. This was especially true when people left because they were offended with us!

Realistically, in a church, everything changes constantly. People come and go; they marry and move away. They go to college, get new jobs elsewhere, or backslide, and sadly, some fall out with you and leave. Whatever the reason people left, we blessed them and were as gracious as possible, ensuring that the door was open for them to come back at any time without shame. Our job is not to control people. I believe our open-handedness actually allowed many people to return when they were ready to do so.

When we lost people through death, we had glorious funerals. Some were for the elderly; some were not. The loss was painful, but a joy too because funerals are such a powerful outreach at a time when people's minds are focused on their eternal destiny. God made Himself real to many of the relatives and friends who came because of the love of God they felt in our midst. I remember at one particular cremation of a small baby the presence of God was so strong that as we prayed even the funeral director broke down and sobbed as he held the tiny casket.

Of course, on a more cheerful note, we also had many wonderful weddings, which as a church we provided for our members. They were great community affairs and again, very positive outreach. Our people's generosity often touched the hearts of friends and family members who had previously been resistant to the gospel. Everyone in the fellowship provided the food at no charge to the couple even when it involved two hundred people. We asked people in the congregation to sign up to bring a particular food or drink item from the menu, which we had agreed upon with the couple. People worked so hard. They arranged the room, made beautiful flower arrangements, laid the tables, served at tables, and then cleared up afterwards. We tried to make everything elegant and first class. I can recall many weddings when we had to hire a building and only had it for a limited time that I had to rush home after everything was set up and only had about ten minutes to wash and change before hurrying back for the start of the service

Before we had our own building, we had to ask everyone to leave the room once the service was finished so that we could set up for the meal. Fortunately most people wanted to participate in photographs which we all know can be interminable. We fervently prayed it would not rain and I do not remember one time when it did! We cleared away all the chairs and set out the tables usually for the sit-down meal. The entire amount of cutlery, crockery, and glasses would have been counted out and ready and were usually hidden behind a screen. Teams of people, each with their own designated job, would then swing into action each working in strict order and lay the tables. We arranged the food artistically on the buffet table, and when we were satisfied it was perfect, we would let the guests back in.

We got this whole procedure down to a fine art and learned to do it in about half an hour. It was a mammoth task and not for the fainthearted, but it was tremendous fun. A team of people were often cleaning up well into the evening, but at the end of it, we were weary but satisfied. All had been executed correctly, like a military operation! What a joy to give people a wedding for maybe a hundred to two hundred guests that they would never have been able to afford themselves.

We rejoiced when people left the church to go to Bible college, to YWAM, or overseas to become missionaries. People have left and established worldwide ministries. Some are now Anglican or Pentecostal ministries. These people left with our blessing to pursue the callings God had placed upon them, but when we entered a very alarming period in the '90s, we seemed to be losing people all the time; and not for the right reasons.

I had always enjoyed our ministry and knew we had a wonderful church. When we heard other pastors talk of their problems and recount how their congregation behaved, we were shocked. All we could say was that our people were wonderful, and they loved us and respected us. I especially enjoyed our life at Egremont House, but even that seemed to lose its sparkle, and eventually, with great reluctance, we decided it was time to end our season there. When the Kings School made an offer on the house out of the blue, we felt that this was the right time to sell. We knew we needed to have a quieter lifestyle, and so in 1995 we moved into our own home, accompanied by just one woman, her two children, and Tony's ninety year old father.

What had gone wrong? Numbers are not everything, but the losses were a tremendous blow that strained our church finances badly, adding stress into our lives. At that time I believe our losses were a clear indication of sickness in the body and the lack of health of our leadership. In a nutshell, we had become spiritually and naturally weary, which led to us being less able to hear what God was saying and caused us to make some very poor decisions. These decisions had these unfortunate consequences.

Part of the reason for our exhaustion was that in the '90s we took into our home a gifted woman with her two young children, and through no fault of her own, she took up a lot of our time and energy. She had suffered a great deal of abuse in her life, and after a traumatic attack, she needed a lot of care and attention. Some people thought we should not be dealing with her at all; another called it compassion gone mad. All I could ask them was, "What else can I do when somebody is obviously in such need? Will you help me?"

Some people struggled to be loyal with our decision to give this level of help; others believed Satan had sent this person as a distraction. Worse still, some thought this person was just fooling us and taking advantage. In the midst of these various opinions, we had to settle our own hearts and just get on with it! For whatever reason, although some did help, most people found helping too difficult.

However, despite the cost, I am certainly not sorry we helped her because today she has a wonderful international ministry, and her two children are fine adults also in the ministry. Whatever the rights and wrongs of what we did out of love and compassion, the fact remains that over a period of time, this and many other factors caused our vision to become clouded. In our weariness, we allowed others to take control and also took some costly wrong directions that created an unhappy church.

There were, of course, other more general factors. First, church growth experts reckon that you will naturally lose 10 percent of the congregation each year. This means a church has to grow at a greater rate than this to make any headway. We were certainly not growing at all. We saw many people visit the church, sense the atmosphere, and not come back.

Second, when we moved into the Lynn Road building, it had been a cozy squash, as it had been at High Barnes. When we moved into the refurbished auditorium, suddenly, despite the joy of our space, psychologically we felt like a small group. It was also really hard to get the sound right, with a small group in a large space, and many older people found the sound too loud and left us to go to a new church that had just started in the city. It provided an ideal place for them.

The fascinating thing about this church was that the pastor, a friend whom we loved, had been born again through us and had once been a member of our church! It would have been easy to fall out with Patrick and feel as if he was stealing our people but we weren't about to be ensnared by that trick of the enemy! Patrick acknowledged that it was easy for him to start this church because we had spearheaded the work of the Spirit in Ely and borne the weight of the spiritual change that had happened there.

The third factor was transitioning to cell groups using the big-bang method. The effect was like a bomb dropping into the congregation. Many people did not like the people we had asked them to meet with, were discouraged, and did not survive the discouragement. They say cells go through stages: forming, storming, norming, and performing. Many groups folded at the storming stage! Others did not like the rigid cell pattern and the strong system of accountability we set in place.

As the congregation shrank, our income shrank too. We both felt very stressed by this despite praying and seeking to cast the care onto the Lord. We tried hard not to communicate it, but there were times when we were so concerned about our inability to pay the bills that we may have pressured people to give. We had lost our unity, and an unhappy, divided church will not grow. We have only to look at the book of Acts to see that unity among the believers causes great growth.

For a while, even *I* did not want to be in the church. The pain was so great that I would gladly have left! For the first time in all our years of pastoring, I began to dread Sunday services. I felt spiritually paralyzed, and there were times when I could only worship or sit quietly in His presence and soak up His strength. I had also developed asthma. It was almost as if my body was reacting to my feelings of being slowly suffocated.

If we had not had visits from our friend Carolyn Bounds, we would have fared a lot worse. She always encouraged the church and was an invaluable light in an otherwise dark tunnel. We were also extraordinarily grateful for other church leaders and friends who prayed and sent us encouraging words from the Lord.

But to cap it all, it looked like Tony was about to have a nervous breakdown. The stress of his father's death probably played a part in it, but it was mainly because of what was going on in the church. When he was unable to make even the smallest decision, he took six months off to rest. He went away for a time alone, walked, prayed, and rested. People rallied to take responsibility so Tony could go off with peace of mind. I also found some wonderful vitamins and minerals that seemed to have a powerful effect on him and that I believe speeded his recovery a great deal. Later on I was also healed of asthma which I am sure was due to a mixture of prayer and these powerful vitamins and minerals.

Tony made an amazingly rapid recovery and came back recharged and ready to take the reins with new energy and a fresh spiritual edge. We realised we were not simply tired, but there were spiritual forces that had taken advantage of our mental and physical state. We sensed an evil wind blowing across the church. We knew we needed spiritual wisdom and insight to engage in some serious warfare prayer to combat it. As the Bible says in Ephesians 6, "We do not wrestle against flesh and blood, but against principalities, against powers, against the rulers of the darkness of this age, against spiritual hosts of wickedness in the heavenly places."

We were somewhat reluctant to acknowledge this, but it was confirmed to us again and again through different sources that a Jezebel spirit had somehow got a grip on the church. It was as if whichever way I turned, unsought new revelation flooded in about what was happening to us. We were unwilling to engage in the kind of spiritual warfare we had done before where we challenged the powers of darkness aggressively head on because it had seemed to attract more trouble from the enemy than it stopped. [2]John Paul Jackson in his book called *Needless Casualties of War* states; "to attack principalities and powers over a geographic area can be as useless as throwing hatchets at the moon. And it can leave you open to unforeseen and unperceived attacks" To us this appeared to be just what had happened.

As we sought God, He showed us exactly how to deal with this spirit. Over a period of six months, with the help of some of our bold intercessors and leaders, we read about it and prayed about it until we all knew we really understood its workings. Then God told us to repent of cooperating with it either by being like Jezebel or Ahab. When we were satisfied that we really had identified and understood exactly what we were dealing with and were confident we were standing in total agreement, Tony stood up in his authority as pastor and quietly told it, "In Jesus's name, go and never come back." It went.

We knew it had gone because the next Sunday, the atmosphere in the church meeting was completely different. It was somehow clean! We also had to make some bold decisions and refocus determinedly on the essentials. Miraculously, God pulled us out of the doldrums and set us on our feet once again. Once more we were happy serving Him. Most importantly, we could hear God speaking to us clearly again, which made everything feel different. The lesson is, when we do things God's way, it is always much better than our own efforts. God had clearly taught us to pastor in the Spirit, especially when all looked lost, but sometimes in the busyness and the rush of life, we forgot to take time to be spiritually aware, with disastrous results.

When things began to resolve themselves, it was wonderful to see God's faithful guiding hand bringing us through into victory by humility, prayer and discernment, instead of fleshly effort alone. I can Ginnydly remember the first time when God first spoke to us about pastoring by the spirit and not by what we could see and I am convinced that any success we have had is due to diligently seeking Him in this way. We first did this when we were a very small church; we had two people who seemed to be in disagreement with us in a way that might split the fragile little church apart before it could be established. We knew if we said anything to either of these men, other people might take sides and make things far worse. So we appealed to God for His wisdom and God showed us clearly how to deal with it. We were to take bread and wine, kneel down, check that we were in unity and forgiveness, and humble ourselves before Him, taking responsibility for anything we had done to create the situation. Then we should solemnly take communion together. We took the bread and wine and called on our covenant with God, asking Him to act on our behalf and resolve the situation supernaturally.

It was hard not to be amazed at the result. One of the men left the church, but the other man became united with us in a new way. If we had acted clumsily, we could have made such a mess of the situation. We saw how important it was to be tough on the devil and gentle with precious and sometimes very fragile people.

While we were in this painful time where we seemed to have taken one wrong turn after another and alienated people, Mark Virkler came to speak at the church. We shared with him our distress and as much of the situation as we understood. Thoughtfully, he gave us some invaluable advice: "It sounds to me like more people are ready to leave. You need to take steps to close the distance between you by encouraging them to share their hearts with you."

So to follow up on the spiritual warfare, we met with a number of our key people and spent a lot of time mending the breach. We encouraged people to open their hearts and speak honestly about what they were feeling, and we were able to open up in return and share how unhappy we had been with some of our decisions. How sweet reconciliation is!

Our rigid organization of cell church, which we had mistakenly started with the big bang method, had ruined what had been the free spirit of the church. Many of our established members, although they were keen for small groups, had disliked our approach, feeling that the meetings were too structured and too prescriptive. They were used to much more freedom. It felt to them as if we did not trust them anymore. They hated the paperwork. We grew to dislike it too because the whole system felt like a straightjacket. We simply stopped using those systems without losing the small groups, which prevent a large church from becoming impersonal.

We had also embraced the idea of creating a more inter-generational church, which meant doing things in a way that sought to integrate the children much more into the fabric of the whole church. We knew that it was a biblical concept and felt it could prevent the children from falling away from God in their teenage years because they did not really feel part of the body. This inclusiveness was a wonderful idea, and there was some good fruit. We had always encouraged our children to be an active part of the church. We believed children could be born again and filled with the Spirit, as well as being able to minister to others. Our son Giles at four years old had laid hands on me, and a headache had completely gone. In line with this thinking, we had taken steps to create church services where the children could stay in all the time. We also developed creative prayer meetings that accommodated the children. Many parents were pleased that their children were more a part of things. However, managing meetings in this way seemed to take a very special gifting, which not many of us possessed. We really wanted it to work, but sadly, the outworking of it seemed to weaken the church further and divert us from our original mandate.

Having taken some clear steps to bring back the freedom of the Spirit in 2002, we began to grow again, and by the time we retired from the main leadership in 2007, the church had once again reached 220 in Sunday attendance. Happily, it has continued to grow and has now reached well over 250 regular attendees.

CHAPTER 33

The Wider Circle of God's Love

Tony and I have taken some wonderful journeys and had amazing, life-changing, and mind-bending experiences. Some of the greatest excitements of our pastoring life were our trips abroad, sometimes to observe and sometimes to preach. These trips strengthened us and kept our vision of a large, vibrant church alight.

We visited Bogota, Colombia, to see a vast church of ninety-five thousand people. We witnessed the excitement of three church services each Sunday with thirty-five thousand people attending at a time, held in a huge stadium. They had a tremendous supporting structure that seemed to work magnificently. Everyone was in a group of twelve people, and anyone who got saved was encouraged to start their own group of twelve.

This amazing church was right in the firing line and very unpopular with the drug barons. As people were converted, they were delivered from drug dealing or drug taking, and the gangs had lost key people. The pastor narrowly missed death when he was shot at as his car stopped at a set of traffic lights. I actually met this pastor in America while he was recuperating.

This was a church full of young people on fire for God. The worship was modern and dynamic. The preaching was passionate. The whole experience was wonderful, and it was interesting to see an alternative cell system at work to the one we were familiar with, which is used in Korea, America, and most of England.

Then we went to Korea to see a church with seven hundred and fifty thousand members, where prayer goes on all night, six nights a week and people take their holidays in order to pray at Prayer Mountain. We went to America to conferences, and I did several preaching tours in Holland, Sweden, and Scotland. We both went to Siberia at different times. Tony went for three weeks with David Hathaway, and I went with Daphne Kirk, preaching about the inter-generational cell church. Russia was a wonderful experience and involved full preaching schedules.

At another time, both Tony and I went to Russia and preached at a huge pastors' and students' conference in Novomoskovsk with Francis Wale Oke. What a privilege it was to meet old-time believers, persecuted in the past for their faith during the communist era. In addition, many young, vibrant Africans were there, some of whom were our interpreters. The Russians had invited many Africans to study in Russia, who they expected to indoctrinate with communism. However, these wonderful, Christian men and women were in fact turning the tables. Instead of communism affecting them, they were getting Russians saved.

Of course, most of the people at the conference were already Christians, but I had my eye on the couple who had been appointed to videotape the meeting. The lady, a really beautiful girl, exchanged shy smiles with me for a few days. On about the fourth day, knowing she had been hearing the Word of God for all that time, I thought she must surely be ready to meet Jesus personally by now. I spoke to her through an interpreter and gave her the gospel. She cried and agreed that she would love to give her life to Jesus. The next day I gave her a Bible, and she brought me a beautiful book about Russia, which I treasure. We hugged and continued our relationship of smiles.

Then Tony and I went to Turkey to support Rachel and Abraham Shin and to do some teaching with their American, English, and Korean friends. Later an invitation came from Turkey again to teach a post-abortion counseling course to a group of women.

To my amazement, the *University of Izmir* invited me to talk about the implications of abortion to a group of 350 young Muslim medical students and the whole medical faculty! What a privilege! I gave a comprehensive PowerPoint presentation about the effects of abortion and a woman's needs, and they asked many questions. It was perhaps the second-most-exciting occasion of my preaching life. The first I have yet to tell you which happened during our Nigerian adventure.

In 1992, Tony and I took a group of our church members including our son Giles, who was only eighteen at the time, to Nigeria, principally to preach in a huge crusade in Calabar. It was a most colourful experience.

Marie, our church administrator, had gone there with another church in 1991, and Francis invited us to go the following year, asking us to take a small party of people. We struggled to get visas for Nigeria and only got them on the morning of our departure. Marie had to go to London by train and line up to collect them and only just made it to the airport in time with them.

We had booked our flight with Bulgarian Airlines because they were the cheapest stopping at Sofia, the dingiest and bleakest airport I have ever been to. The building had definitely seen better days; lethargic, miserable staff dragged themselves mournfully around, working as slowly as possible. There was almost nothing in the shops, and everywhere was rundown and dirty, especially the toilets, which apart from being broken and flooded, were obviously communist because they had bright red toilet seats! We were not sad to say good-bye to Sophia.

We arrived at the Lagos airport. Sights, sounds, and smells hit us such as we had never experienced in our lives before. There was a tumult of fierce customs people, men asking for money or offering us taxis, and the roar of traffic flooding in from outside the airport doors. The customs people asked us fiercely, "Where is your food?" What food?

We were very relieved to meet our two escorts, Yemesi and Kyode, who were lovely. Six of us struggled through the crowd with our seventeen pieces of luggage and piled into aged Peugeots, which swung out onto the incredibly bad roads. All the vehicles we could see were rusty and dented, and we began to see why. Cars are supposed to drive on the right, which they do most of the time. I say most of the time because we constantly had to swing across the road from one side to the other to avoid potholes as well as all the other cars, who were avoiding other potholes on the other side of the road. We wove in and out of each other! It was complete chaos!

There seemed to be no respect for any traffic laws. I wondered if there were any. There was a lot of aggressive hooting when the heavy traffic ground to a standstill. Pedestrians wove in and out of the cars. Street sellers and ragged beggars with missing limbs accosted drivers and knocked on the car windows, trying to attract our attention. People carrying tall stacks of goods on their heads crossed in front of us, seemingly heedless of danger. We passed buses without any doors with people hanging all over them. Obviously there were no health and safety laws here.

There seemed to be a lot of anger in the air but also many smiles. Despite all the depressing aspects of what we could see, it was very exciting. The people, whom we had now met, were lovely. . . and funny. On the journey, I had developed a cold, and every time I sneezed, Yemesi said, "Sorry!" We all felt a bit desperate and very hot and longed for the awful, bouncing journey to stop. We were extremely relieved to get to the hotel, have a meal, and sleep.

The next day at 7:30 a.m., we were supposed to be going on to Calabar for the big crusade, but actually we spent all day in the airport until eleven o'clock at night, when we at last got onto a plane. Apparently the holdup was the president's fault. His plane was scheduled to land at the airport, and so, for security reasons, other planes had been forbidden to land. However, one of the air-traffic controllers had allowed a Red Cross plane to land. He was sacked by the authorities and immediately, all the other controllers went on strike in sympathy with him. Thus no planes took off all day until the issue was resolved.

When we landed in Calabar, it was well after midnight, so we had missed the first night of the crusade, which had carried on without us. We felt weary and discouraged until we saw the welcoming committee waiting on the tarmac. They had been waiting there *all day*! Their dedication and good humour were a testimony to their ability to overcome in this difficult environment.

As we got off the plane, they surrounded us and thanked God for our arrival, and we soon felt immensely cheered by their warmth and love, and every bit of weariness melted away. With great jubilation, they bundled us into a fleet of waiting cars that were covered with stickers advertising the crusade and drove us to the hotel.

Calabar is a leafy and beautiful coastal city, quite unlike dusty Lagos. It is where the intrepid missionary Mary Slessor took the gospel many years ago and we were excited when we passed her statue on the main road into the city.

Tradition decreed that we make several courtesy calls. Our first was to *government house* to meet the governor. As we went into this glorious residence on top of a hill at the side of a lagoon, we felt overawed by the sumptuous surroundings. The governor's wife, a stunning beauty, resplendently dressed in a green robe, received us graciously. Francis proceeded to give a speech about why we were there. "First," he said, "it says in the Bible to give honour to whom honour is due. Second, it says to preach the gospel to every creature. Third, the Bible says to pray for kings and all who are in authority."

As Francis continued to preach the gospel, she did not bat an eyelid. When all was done, she spoke very formally to us, saying, in effect, that she was thrilled to bits to see us. She proceeded to offer us a small feast, which was served formally with much bowing by houseboys in smart white coats.

Our second courtesy call to meet the Obong was quite different. Nothing could have prepared us for the shocking contrast to the day before. We stopped outside peeling wrought iron gates, which opened to reveal an incredible sight—something like Steptoe's yard. There were chickens, turkeys, monkeys, a dog, and a crocodile in a pond, which was thankfully in an enclosure. Outside the front door, there was a huge statue of a colourful man brandishing a cutlass. The house, designed like a Swiss chalet, looked crumbling and unstable.

A servant ushered us into a room filled with Christian objects, but there were other things that looked suspiciously like juju objects. A man in a white robe carrying an axe processed in with the aged king. Francis gave the rehearsed speech as before, and we all prayed with many fervent amens. At one point, the old man nodded off, and I had to dig my nails into the palms of my hands to prevent unseemly laughter. When we left, I was exhausted from the effort!

Despite the demonic feel of the place, the Obong turned out to be a committed Christian! However, when he was made a king he probably had to go through some strange rites, like eating the flesh of his predecessor. Before we left, His Excellency graciously posed for a photograph with us on the steps of his house.

The third courtesy call was to the Edem Oso of Qua, who is a chief among chiefs. We were escorted solemnly into a long, low house where a dear old man of eighty-nine with a kindly, wrinkled, smiling face joined us. He was dressed in long velvet robes. His servant read his interesting life story to us. He was in fact an elder in the Presbyterian Church, and there was quite a different atmosphere there. After the preaching and praying, we all signed the visitors' book, posed for a photo, and left.

It was an awesome moment when we realised that the prophetic word John Hughes had given us in 1984 was being fulfilled: "You will go to Africa, where you will go before kings and governors, and you will preach the gospel to thousands, with signs following." I had spoken at a women's meeting that afternoon, but what I was looking forward to most of all was the big crusade meeting still to come that evening.

In the field, a large stage had been set up with blinding, bright lights. Massive loudspeakers towered over us and blasted out songs sung by the choirs. It would later carry our voices across this vast field. They all swayed in time to the music, smiling. I loved it! Thousands came to the field, which looked impressive to us, but Francis was glum because he sometimes saw as many as one hundred thousand. The next day there was a bit of a palaver about it. This was a special meeting where everyone had their say, very politely, about the reasons why so few had come.

Tony spoke to the crowd about the prodigal son, and I was so proud of him. Then Francis spoke a gospel message with such power and strength that thrilled my heart. He talked of Jesus—of changed hearts and changed lives, of hope for the sick and the downtrodden. In a country where there seemed so little security and help for anyone, I longed for them *all* to respond.

Hundreds did. As they came forward, I felt overcome by the beauty of their faces and their wide-eyed sincerity. It was so moving that when Tony was asked to pray over them, he did so while weeping copiously. I could not have done differently. I was not ready for what happened when we were all involved in prayer for healing. When we prayed for people, we saw dramatic results; people's faces and bodies registered change as they were healed. Some fell down screaming and writhed on the ground. I could see demons moving about inside people's bodies before they eventually came out, leaving the people limp until they finally got up, full of joy and obviously delivered.

It was an experience straight out of the pages of the Bible. People were so grateful and happy to be free from the things that had been tormenting them. It all felt like a wonderful dream, and it was thrilling to be doing the works of Jesus. We returned to our hotel exhausted and deliriously happy, where we tumbled into bed and slept like babies.

Every day was full of meetings of different kinds followed by evening repeats of this wondrous crusade. One day I crept into the back of a meeting where Giles was preaching on healing and witnessed the signs that followed him, just as Jesus promised. I was amazed that at eighteen, and with no previous experience, he could preach so well. I was so happy and so proud of him, remembering the prophecy on his life that he would one day be a pastor.

Two more experiences were particularly significant for me. One Sunday I was to preach in a small church and had waited for ages for the driver to come, so one of the pastors took us to the church instead. As we set off, the roads got progressively smaller and bumpier, and the surroundings became more and more decayed. I had a rising sense that this was going to be a full-blooded adventure—a day to remember!

At last we pulled up outside a small shack that was emitting a lot of loud noise. Inside there were about thirty people sitting on wooden benches or praising, worshipping, and dancing. The service lasted well over two hours, with special songs and choruses, some of which I knew, followed by my preaching, which I delivered to the best of my ability. I wanted so much to be a blessing to these people. The pastor was a nice, young man who told me that he had applied to go to Bible college in California. Despite the squalor, the small numbers, the poor-quality musical instruments, and the decrepit building, an unmistakable touch of heaven was there.

I was thrilled to preach for those people. Africa really captured my heart. I could quite understand how missionaries had come out and stayed for the rest of their lives. What we had thought of as sacrifice must have been a joy to them. After the service, the young pastor invited me to go to his house for refreshment. We walked down a side road to a small shack and went in. Even though it was not dirty it did not look terribly wholesome, so I sat down very gingerly on one of the chairs. Suddenly, I had a picture of myself sitting in the plush governor's house. The realization hit me that if I did not let the surroundings put me off, I could relax and be comfortable here too. Suddenly I was ashamed of my attitude and instead felt grateful to be in this little home with its scarce amenities.

As we talked, he handed me an envelope with a gift of money for coming to preach. *Help,* I thought. *I cannot possibly take money from those who have so little.* I demurred and told him I could not possibly take it. I had already had a crisis over him offering me an expensive Coke to drink.

"Please take it," he said. "He who gives to the prophet receives a prophet's reward."

I realised that if I really believed what I had preached for years about giving, I could not stop him from giving and receiving his harvest.

My second life-changing experience happened on our second Sunday. Francis discovered that he had double-booked himself and asked Tony to preach instead of him. Tony, ever generous and quick to promote me, suggested that he ask me instead. He was a little bit surprised but readily agreed. I was a little scared but also thrilled beyond measure. Tony was to accompany me to preach my first true gospel message at my very own mini-crusade in a field, in the jungle, in a Muslim village!

I rushed back to the hotel to shower and change, praying urgently that God would tell me what to preach. As I was in the shower, I was given three Scriptures. I shouted to Tony to scribble them down so I did not forget them. I just had time to look up the Scriptures, iron my beautiful new white Nigerian outfit, which they had lovingly made for me, and hurry to the car.

We drove for more than an hour, and the roads gradually got worse until they were simply cart tracks, worse than the fen droves I had been down at home. As we approached the village it was a sea of flickering lights. There was no electricity, just kerosene lamps. It looked eerie, to say the least, as we saw glowing faces and shadowy forms moving in and out of the darkness.

The pastor met us at the edge of the village and guided us into the centre through a maze of densely populated streets with the usual mêlée of goats, chickens, and people wandering all over the place. We arrived at a clearing where at least five hundred people were paying rapt attention to a speaker. People stared at us; we were an enormous attraction because they had never seen a white person before. I would have liked to have made an elegant approach, but in the dark, I stumbled along, hopping onto the platform with difficulty because my skirt was a bit tight.

The only lighting was one strip light at the side of the platform and another right at the back of the crowd, powered by a generator. I was not exactly nervous, but I was wondering how I would manage the logistics. I was speaking with an interpreter, which I was not really accustomed to, and there was no comforting pulpit on which to rest my Bible. Fortunately, my notes were minimal, but I had my Bible in one hand and a microphone in the other. Turning the pages of my Bible was virtually impossible without losing my flow. I obviously looked uncomfortable, so mercifully, they went to find me a pulpit.

I found it hard to think clearly and to keep the thread of my message going because I could feel insects crawling all over me, obviously attracted by the light. My white dress seemed to be a particular source of attraction to all winged and creeping things. They were flying into my face and onto my Bible, crawling up my legs and down my back. They were getting stuck in the sweat that was pouring off me, but I dared not swat them or scratch the itch. It was only the wonderful responsiveness of the congregation that kept me going.

Tony said that as he saw insects busily crawling to their hidden destinations, he knew they were probably freaking me out. When we got back to the hotel, exhausted but happy, and I undressed, I could feel something like a soft ball of cotton wool in my bra. As I took it off, a huge moth-like creature flew out. I lost all presence of mind and screamed loudly!

It was all worth every bit of discomfort. I had spoken about five choices people in the Bible had made. The first was when Adam and Eve chose to be independent from God and go their own way, which cut them off from God's life and God's wisdom. My next example was in the book of Joshua, where the people were encouraged to follow God and choose life rather than death. The third choice was from the story of Elijah and the prophets of Baal. Elijah challenged the people to abandon idol worship and choose to seek the one true, living God.

I then told them about Jesus and the woman of Samaria who, as she talked with Him, realised Jesus was a very special man God had sent. I told them that the woman was so impressed with Jesus that she made the choice to bring her whole village out to see Him. I told them that the Bible said Jesus was not just a good man but God's own Son, whom God had chosen to send to die for them to pay the price for their sin so that no matter what they had done, if they accepted Him, they would be forgiven of every sin.

When I finished, I asked people to raise their hands if they were like the Samaritan woman who had recognized who Jesus really was. I invited them to raise their hands if they wanted to accept Jesus as their Lord and Saviour and to have all their sins forgiven. About 150 people of all ages raised their hands. There were so many that I thought they had maybe misunderstood what I had said. Consequently, I asked them to put their hands down.

I then explained it all again. I said that I only wanted those people to respond who had never, ever made a commitment to Jesus before. Just to be sure, I asked the pastor if he thought they had understood properly. He said he thought they had understood perfectly, so I repeated the request for them to raise their hands. There was exactly the same number of hands, so I invited the people to come forward and pray. I led them in a prayer of commitment. As they laid their hands on their hearts and prayed with a seriousness and fervency that I had rarely seen in England I was deeply moved. What a moment!

As we left, we were very aware that we needed to continue to pray for those converts because they would almost certainly face persecution from their families. Sometimes Muslim families are very hard on their own people when they are born again. They think of it as a betrayal of the family. When Muslims are baptised, they fare even worse.

As we drove back, I sprawled in the back of the big car, quite exhausted but feeling such a deep contentment and amazement that I had been used by God to bring so many to Him. I knew there would be a party in heaven that night and Jesus would be pleased.

The full story of our trip to Nigeria contains far more than I have written here. We attended many more great meetings, where we preached and ministered to people. We met so many lovely people and came home with so many gifts. We also saw answers to prayer in our personal contact with people, like the waiters in our hotels who came to Christ. We also had many more harum-scarum adventures, which caused great merriment. So many more wonderful things happened.

The second time we went to Nigeria Francis Wale Oke had invited us to preach at his Holy Spirit Conference which was a wonderful experience especially the morning I preached to a smaller congregation than in the evening meetings; a congregation of a mere eleven thousand people. As I could not see the people at the back of the room I assumed that they probably could not see me very well and I quickly realised that people would not get the message from my facial expressions as they would in a small auditorium but that I needed to use my body and my voice more to communicate. We had a great time and some unforgettable moments, but that night in the Muslim village on our previous trip was the most wonderful moment of my life with God . . . ever.

CHAPTER 34

An Envisioning Trip to Korea

For a long time we had longed to go to Korea to see the largest church in the world, which at the time had six hundred thousand people in attendance. It now has about seven hundred and fifty thousand. It was not just the size that interested us; we were fascinated with their extraordinary prayer life, and we wanted the same! However, we got there in rather a novel way.

A large advertisement appeared in *The Times*. British Airways was offering free seats to about a dozen destinations on April 23. Cara, who lived in our house, spotted the opportunity first, but when it said there was only one offer available per household, she graciously gave it to us. We filled in the coupon and put forward our three preferences; Israel, America and Korea, although Korea was the only place we really wanted to visit at that time.

As we drove home to Ely a few weeks later after being away on our day off, I told Tony that I knew in my spirit that our tickets would be there when we got back. Sure enough they were. We were excited and tore open the envelope only to be devastated to find that they had offered us a trip . . . to Brussels! I could not believe it! This was definitely not what we had expected. Immediately I telephoned the airline office and explained that we did not want to go to Brussels. The operator said, "I am very sorry, but this is your only option; everything else is spoken for."

I told the operator why this could not be so. I explained that we were Christians and that we had prayed and believed for tickets for Korea to see the biggest Christian church in the world. I told her that the minute we had seen the advertisement in *The Times*, we had known British Airways would give us tickets for Korea. "Well," she said uncertainly, "I will just have another look for you."

After a short pause and the clicking of the computer keys, she exclaimed in surprise, "Well, would you believe it! I have just this minute had two returns for Korea pop up on the screen! Shall I book them for you? The only thing is that you will have to travel club class."

"Hmm. . ." I said. "I am sure we can endure that!"

So we got the seats and travelled in luxury. The food was lovely and the cabin service attentive. There was much more room for our legs so we did not feel like sardines squashed into a tin as you do in what people call cattle class! It was very comfortable indeed, and we arrived at our destination feeling fresh and ready to go. This was only the beginning of God's amazing and perfect supernatural provision for our needs when we were there.

We hurtled, and I mean hurtled, in a terrifying way from the airport by taxi into Seoul. We arrived at the impressive church building, *Sum Bog Um*, in Yoido, where we had been given a room in the church's large accommodation block. Originally I was told a room in the church would be impossible, but after many frustrating phone calls, eventually I spoke to an American missionary's wife named Lydia Swain, secretary to Yongi Cho. She confirmed that there was unlikely to be any accommodation available on the church site but she would book us something somewhere as cheaply as she could. However, prayer obviously opens doors because she called later to say that somehow a room had become available. The difference in cost was quite significant as at the church building we paid five pounds a night but in a small hotel we would have had to have paid about thirty pounds a night. But again it was not the cost that was the issue but the fact that we wanted to be on site and be involved in the daily action of this remarkable church

Lydia took us under her wing while we were there. She sent us a meal, and she arranged for us to go to a cell group. She organized a meeting for us with a district pastor and gave us lots of useful advice, like how to get to the briefings they put on for visitors, where to find food we would be able to eat, and most important in my mind, where to catch the bus to get to Prayer Mountain.

Our room was very simple but pleasant, and we unpacked as quickly as we could because we could not wait to explore. We went downstairs and walked into the church sanctuary and immediately met a young man who spoke English very well. I guess it was not difficult for him to spot that we were strangers as we were the only westerners in sight! He took us to the 7:00 p.m. service and helped us to understand what was being said. Many of the hymns were old-fashioned ones we knew well, so we fared well with the worship.

On our way back to our room, we bumped into an English pastor named James. He filled us in a bit about what we could expect during our stay, which whetted our appetites even more. I could hardly wait to get to the services, and then later in the week Prayer Mountain.

We fell into bed and slept like logs until 5:00 a.m., when we were aroused from sleep by a great deal of shouting, hooting, and the revving of engines in the street below. It was just not possible to sleep any more, not simply because of the noise but because of what we could see. In an instant we were out of bed, dressed, and ready to explore.

Everyone there was dark-haired and small, we by contrast felt enormous and we really stood out. Adults stared at us, and groups of children passing in buses waved, pointed at us, and laughed. Every day we saw many schoolchildren walking in orderly crocodiles all beautifully dressed in identically coloured uniforms; they were an impressive sight.

The Korean food not only looked unpalatable, but it was also either very bland or so hot we could barely eat it. Lydia advised us that we could eat comfortably and cheaply at the Uke Ship Psalm, which at that time was the tallest building in Asia. However it was fast food, which under normal circumstances I would have avoided at all costs! I have never been so glad to eat Kentucky Fried Chicken!

We were thrilled to find that there was to be a baptism service on the next day in the Jerusalem Chapel. As we walked into the building, we tried to ask someone the way to the baptismal service, but the usher spoke to us very sternly. It seemed that he was telling us that we were not allowed to go in. However, when another man who spoke English well overheard what was being said to us, he intervened on our behalf. Apparently the man had misunderstood. He had thought we wanted to be baptised! When we explained that we only wanted to watch, he waved us in with a smile.

In the chapel, people were rocking backward and forward, praying fervently. We assumed they were praying in tongues, but we had no way of telling! A pastor stood up and started a hymn. The singing then went on, practically nonstop for hours, right until the end of the marathon service. A thousand people were baptised every single week. We did not stay and see all of them

As we sat in the auditorium, in front of us on the stage were two large picture windows which we could see were two large water tanks with water lapping halfway up the window. Steps at each side of the tank came down one side and up the other side. Suddenly two white-robed figures appeared in the window, and a constant stream of baptismal candidates then began coming in one side of the tank; bobbed down into the water, received prayer, and went up the steps other side rejoicing and disappeared from sight. It went on and on and we probably sat there fascinated for at least an hour

Every now and then the room where we were sitting cleared, and a new lot of people came in to watch their friends or family go through the waters of baptism. When we left the chapel, hundreds of people who had just been baptised were lining up in the foyer to receive their certificates, which were being churned out in a constant stream by a whole row of computers.

That night we were thrilled we were going to attend the Friday all-night prayer meeting. We arrived an hour early to ensure we would get a seat in the upstairs section where there was translation given through earphones for foreigners for the first two hours. Obviously they don't expect us westerners to want to pray any longer than that! The band, consisting of a piano, drums, saxophone, trumpet, and guitar, was already playing, and several hundred people were there already praying fervently. In the West, we would probably have been chatting to each other before the meeting, but here they do not waste a minute!

Soon people started pouring into the auditorium by the thousands, and at ten o'clock, what looked like a choir, resplendent in flowing white robes and blood red sashes, came in. We soon discovered that they were not a choir at all; they were hand-bell ringers!

We sang another verse of "Amazing Grace," this time with a hymnbook. Next a man preached from Ephesians 5:8-11. He exhorted us to walk in the light and to look into the Word, which is light. He said that if our lives were full of sin, things would not go right. He talked about how, twenty years ago, he was diagnosed with cancer, so he went to seek God and pray. It seemed to him that God was far away, which he realised was not true because he said Jesus had always been his Saviour. He prayed for peace for himself and that he would know the presence of God. When he went to the hospital, they gave him up to die. However, church leaders came and anointed him according to James 5. At that moment, he said God met him and he was healed.

Another pastor spoke who was obviously starting the prayer. The leader gave the details of a prayer request for the nation. Then we nearly jumped out of our skins because he suddenly without any warning he roared passionately three times, "Oh God! Oh God! Oh God!"

Then, like a fantastic explosion, everyone began praying full on all together at the same time. They had such fervour, passion, and intensity, almost like greyhounds or horses when given the signal to go at the start of a race. It was stunning. It sounded like I imagined the sound of many waters as described in Revelation.

We prayed for the nation for half an hour without stopping for breath. We sang again and then had another burst of prayer for half an hour, asking the Holy Spirit to come and change the world. I don't know about the world, but I felt changed! After that we prayed for ten minutes to receive healing for ourselves.

An usher then arrived to move us downstairs, where we could stay for the service but would be on our own without translation. We were tired, but the last thing we wanted to do was leave. It was such a wonderful atmosphere. We wanted to stay and pray whether we understood what it was all about or not because the presence of God was so real.

Most of the twenty thousand people left at midnight, leaving just a few thousand people. Some had their children with them, who were bedded down on the floor on little duvets. Ushers patrolled the congregation, waking anyone up who dared to fall sleep. A girl sat down next to us and introduced herself to us as Cho Sang Ni. She was a nurse. Her English was limited, but she was glad to translate for us and practise her English. She was studying ICI courses in English at their Bible school, as they all do.

Each hour the leadership of the meeting changed, and there were testimonies, exhortations, hymns, and songs. Some of these were action songs to help people keep awake. There were alternate bouts of fervent prayer. What a joy that I could pray in tongues or English, and they could pray in tongues or Korean, and God heard and understood us all!

We stayed until about 3:00 a.m. We had sent in two prayer requests: one for a sick man in our congregation and the other for £250,000 for our building, but we could not tell if they prayed our requests! Unlike most of the people at the meeting, we had the privilege of being able to sleep in the next day. Most of those who stayed until four in the morning went straight to work! Because our room was near the exit from the auditorium most nights we were woken up by the noise as they all left!

We heard a wonderful story about a baby who was brought into one of these prayer meetings by his parents because he had just been run over and crushed by a car. He was miraculously healed and is now six years old, perfect, and making good grades at school. Prayer requests have come into these prayer meetings from 108 different nations.

However the following morning we did not sleep in for long because outside our window on the Saturday, we could hear a lot of activity. As soon as I could bear to rouse myself to look out, I could see a wonderful sight of several beautiful brides and bridal parties having their photos taken. What beautiful dresses they we wearing! How smart the grooms looked. I soon threw my clothes on, I couldn't wait to get down there with my camera to record what was going on.

One of the parties was very pleased when they saw that I wanted to take photos of them, and with much sign language they pressed me to have my photo taken with them. I saw more than a dozen wedding parties spill out of the buildings at fairly regular intervals because there was a wedding every half an hour in each of the chapels. When the service is over they are encouraged to leave the chapel as quickly as possible because they have just ten minutes between the ceremonies, just long enough time to get one lot out with their guests and flowers and the next lot in.

Tony wanted to rest and pray that morning, so because it felt a very safe place, I walked up the road on my own and found the Plaza where there was a lovely carnival atmosphere. Crowds of people were enjoying themselves in various ways; children with balloons, cyclists and roller skaters milling about, and other people just walking and sitting around. There was a fast food stand which seemed to be selling the Korean equivalent of pot noodles. After a while when my stomach began to tell me that it was lunch time I walked back to the church, a young woman introduced herself to me. Yang Soon Choi was on her way to the Saturday-afternoon service, and not being one to miss an opportunity, I forgot all about lunch and I asked if I could go with her.

I tried to put my finger on what was so special about these services. They are very formal, but the atmosphere is electric, and it made me want to cry. The prayer was so moving that somehow you were simply pulled into it, and it made me want to go to greater heights in my spiritual life.

In this particular service, the choir members were wearing white robes, and the conductor was wearing a black, formal evening suit. After this formal service, everyone streamed out, and then the next crowd, who were all young people, streamed in and filled the chapel. This time a young band played consisting of three youths with guitars that sang modern choruses. It was just like home except they were wearing long robes which seemed incongruous. When I eventually dragged myself away and left the service to find Tony and share the excitement of what I had seen, the young ushers bowed me out, shouting, "We always have the victory in Jesus!"

We both went out and ate noodles in the plaza. We then found another shop, where we bought strawberries, grapes, juice, and scrumptious-looking plaited doughnuts. They would be supper and breakfast. So much had happened I could hardly believe this was only our third day. We had used up three rolls of film, and we had already spent twelve hours in four church services. I had prayed so much and so loudly that I was in danger of developing what you might call Korean croak. I felt great excitement. It was Sunday the next day!

At six o'clock in the morning, again a tremendous din under our window—revving engines, whistles, shouts, and hooting—awakened us. We could even hear a band playing. We rushed to look out of the window. Down in front of the building, we could see the band and a group of women were dancing sedately to the music, wearing their voluminous traditional Korean silk clothing. It was so colourful and so beautiful. A steady flow of buses and taxis were continually drawing up outside the church building, disgorging dozens of people. These people all were congregating outside the building, waiting, we presumed, for their opportunity to go into a service. It was the ushers with colourful sashes who were blowing whistles, waving their arms, directing people, and keeping them moving. It was godly crowd control!

It was an unfolding pantomime that we watched for a long time, utterly amazed. We were so caught up in it that we missed the first service! As we continued to watch, more buses drew up and parked in a row, and we could see people lining up to get into them! It was very puzzling until we realised they were blood donor stations. Apparently these buses come every single week to take blood from the crowds of people coming to church.

We made our way to the second service. Inside the church building, the sight was amazing. It is impossible to describe the scene adequately. Wall-to-wall people were crammed into a vast number of pews. The ushers were going from row to row, making people move up and squash together to get the maximum number of people in. They told us they would never be able to seat as many Westerners as they do Koreans. They are tiny, and in comparison we are like giants.

We had a wonderful bird's-eye view of everything from up in the huge balcony. We were fascinated to see a large orchestra assemble and tune up. A hundred-strong choir came in this time dressed in green, and at nine o'clock sharp, the hundred-piece orchestra began to play, the choir swept to its feet and sang the most glorious anthem. It was a heavenly, penetrating sound that sent shivers down my spine. A psalm was read out, a doxology was sung, and then, led by this wonderful choir, we all sang the Apostles' Creed. I was glad that I knew it by heart. The choir sang another anthem and sat down. It seemed very odd to us that it was all so formal but did not feel in the least like dead formalism.

A huge screen lit up behind the pulpit, and we saw a report of Pastor Cho's visit to New York. The choir then appeared on the screen and sang again. There was such a sense of occasion, and it was just such a marvelous celebration. We prayed for the nation with a roaring of voices enough to shake the building, and then Pastor Cho brought it all together as he stood and preached about Jairus's daughter.

After the sermon there was an altar call for people to accept Jesus as their Lord and Saviour. Hundreds stood up to respond, and all who had responded were quickly ushered into side rooms by ushers waving flags to indicate where they should go to be counseled and prayed with. Good organization was a big key to the success of this spiritual operation.

Pastor Cho prayed for the sick. He then told us all to lay our hands on any afflicted part of our bodies and agree with him for healing. After this, he urged us to offer thanks to the Lord with a grateful heart and to give our offering. I counted thirty-eight ushers involved in the collection of the offering. As the choir sang, they collected it in gigantic bags, far bigger than I have ever seen in any church, and took them to the front of the auditorium. Suddenly giant doors in the front wall opened, the bags were loaded onto huge trolleys, and the trolleys were safely locked away. Apparently it takes them a whole week to count the offerings from the seven services.

They told us that immediately Pastor Cho had finished preaching in the first service, the video recording of his message was rushed across town by nine pastors who had their cars revved up and ready to go to nine other churches that Cho has started with members of his own congregation.

Suddenly the benediction was given and the service ended abruptly. Of course we all had to leave quickly to make room for the thousands of people who were waiting to come in for the next service. The ushers were very polite, but they were also very firm and made sure we moved out quickly. As we were moving out, an usher with a flag signaled for us to follow him because we were going to a briefing about the church in Cho's conference room. We had already met the lovely woman named Lydia Swain who gave the interesting briefing. She was the prayer coordinator and Cho's personal assistant.

We were shown an awesome moving video about the church, its philosophy and works, and how it started. It made me cry to see the scope of what they had done when they had come from such humble beginnings. It was a wonderful story.

The church began in 1958 when Cho bought a tent for fifty dollars from the American military just five years after the end of the Korean War. He had just graduated from a seminary that had less than thirty students. At the time the church began the whole nation of Korea was in a terrible state. Eighty percent of the people had tuberculosis, eighty percent of the city had been destroyed, and many people were homeless, discouraged, and sick. Some of them had lost their minds because they had lost their homes, their families, and everything. Russia, China, and Japan had tried to drive the Koreans to the south and drown them in the sea, so thousands of families had been separated. Money, food, and medicines were scarce. People lived under bridges and in the streets. When Cho told them that they must pray, they said, "We don't want to pray. We haven't time to pray. We pay you to do the praying."

Cho insisted that *they* must pray to break through. God said to him, "I can see the needs of these people, but they will never know it until they break through for themselves."

Cho and his mother-in-law began to pray day and night. Mostly she prayed in the daytime, and he prayed all night. They did this persistently for three and a half years. The tent was freezing cold at night, and Cho said that often his clothes froze to the ground in winter. However, as the people began to pray for themselves, they began to see miracles. Spontaneous healings began to happen. They told us that there were so many miracles that they became commonplace. This was to the point where people didn't get excited when the deaf could hear and the blind could see. Nobody was particularly interested because they had seen and heard it all so many times before. The people said, "Now we have an open heaven."

In 1964, they were growing at a rate of one thousand a year. In 1987, they were growing by eleven thousand a month! The church was organized into sixty-three thousand cell groups, which were the backbone of the church. The church had a cell group within walking distance of every single home. Everyone belonged to a cell, where they received twenty of minutes of teaching written by Cho himself, followed by forty minutes of prayer, praise, and ministry to each other. The cell aimed to train the believer to be able to minister to others and to get them saved.

Cho taught his people to win the lost by finding a need and meeting it, finding a problem and solving it, and finding the sick and healing them. One woman apparently spent all day going up and down in the lift of her apartment block, helping people with their bags, praying for them, and loving them in any way she could. She then invited these people to come and share their religious views with her. Naturally this gave her a reason to share hers and tell people how wonderful Jesus was. Soon all these people were saved, so she invited them to the church, and started her own cell group. This in turn led to the start of another cell, and another. By these simple means, this one woman won almost her whole apartment block for Christ.

We asked for a copy of this video as it was full of more information than I felt able to retain. We staggered out after this impacting experience struggling to digest all that we had seen and heard

Arrangements had been made for us to visit a cell group meeting. The cell meeting we visited was very prescriptive, but by organizing it like this, was how Pastor Cho got the men to accept women leaders. Most of his men had refused to run a cell group, saying they had not the time to do it, but when Cho said God had told him to ask the women to do it, there was an outcry from the men. They said, "Women preachers? No! It is unthinkable! What if women are deceived as Eve was?"

Cho was very wise and settled the argument by saying that no woman (or man) would be teaching his or her own ideas because he would write it down and provide the whole thing for them. It was not an easy task to convince the men, but he persisted until eventually he silenced all their objections.

A whole team of district pastors monitor sixty-three thousand cells and one of these women pastors was detailed to look after us to show us around the church and take us to a cell group. The cell group received us so graciously, and we all sat on the floor around a low table. We sang, prayed, and studied a passage of the Bible. The meeting was formal, just like the services, but it was a great experience. Then they asked us to pray for them all, which we did, asking God for a special word for each of them which the district pastor translated. We were then served a beautiful lunch. They treated us with such honour, which we did not feel we quite deserved. What a lovely meal. What a beautiful time! Day after day, we were subject to the overwhelming sights and sounds of revival.

The cell leader showed us that she had to keep detailed records of everything they did and everything that happened in the cell. The cell was not allowed to get larger than twenty people, so because of the constant stream of new people coming in they had to rapidly train up assistants to begin their own cells. She told us that if someone went to the cell three times, they would certainly be born-again.

Their evangelism was such simple and effective evangelism because it was actually their changed lives not just their words that drew others in. So exemplary were the newly saved Christian workers that bosses even allowed their workers an hour off to go the cell group. The bosses were curious as to why their employees had changed so much, and as soon as they heard their testimony and heard the gospel, they wanted to know Jesus themselves. This, they said, was why the church had so many millionaires.

The pastor also took us to her home and gave us sweet hospitality. We drank tea, and then prayed together kneeling on cushions on the beautiful shiny wooden floor. It was a strangely moving experience. The spiritual quality of this humble woman was so evident and I mused on the fact that her attitude and behavior was multiplied over and over in this church causing a complete revolution in the society

Now, about Prayer Mountain; for us this was the pinnacle of our visit. We stood in line just round the corner from the main building and caught the crowded bus to Prayer Mountain. We were surprised it was so far away from the church and it is in the mountains near the demilitarized zone between North and South Korea. It is near enough to the border for the North Koreans to play their propaganda over loudspeakers and be heard by South Koreans. Frequently people go to the border and pray fervently for their brother Koreans in that horrendously repressive regime, which actually is just like one big prison camp.

The whole of Prayer Mountain is an amazing complex of chapel buildings, a canteen, and accommodations for visitors. We were shown to the second-class accommodations, which we chose because we wanted to do what the ordinary people would do rather than experience a more western style accommodation which we could experience anywhere in the world. There were two prayer mats in our room which we could take out with us to use in the little prayer boxes. We discovered that many people did not use the hospitality rooms but actually brought their own mats and blankets and simply bedded down on the chapel floor, which had under-floor heating. They spent days and nights praying, sleeping, and joining in with the organized services. From time to time pastors went around praying for people. It was common for people to take a couple of weeks of holiday and go to pray, especially if they were sick. At the end of two weeks, even if they came with a terminal illness, they went home healed. We sat in one of the big auditoriums and watched this in action

As we eagerly explored the grounds of Prayer Mountain, we were fascinated to hear loud praying coming from dozens of little boxes cut into the mountainside, each with a little door. Outside each of the occupied ones was a pair of shoes, but of course it was not just the shoes outside of the booth that told you it was occupied! We took our turn in the boxes, where without any worldly distractions; it was surprisingly easy to pray. We simply sat in the services and imbibed the atmosphere, sometimes understanding what was happening and sometimes not. It was the easiest place I have ever found to pray. It was as if I was taken by a spirit of prayer into a deeper place of prayer than I was normally accustomed to.

Although people largely go to fast at Prayer Mountain, one day we were offered a special breakfast. When asked what we would like, I asked for a fried egg. Little did I realise that it would be a lovely fried egg but accompanied by rice and spinach and eaten with chopsticks! It was lovely but it wasn't quite what my taste buds were expecting, and it's also very hard to eat a slippery fried egg with metal chopsticks!

We fasted part of the time we were there, but when we wanted to eat, we went into the canteen and stared at the picture advertisements for the food unsure what to choose. It was mostly noodles and rice with something. One of the dishes was called *muk*! This, surprisingly, did not appeal to us at all. However, we did eat some noodles, which were very tasty. Our efforts with the chopsticks did cause some behind-the-hand sniggering from other diners as we struggled to keep the slippery noodles wound around slippery metal chopsticks.

For a number of days, we had a wonderful time. We walked about praying or knelt in the little boxes with our special little mats, praying. We joined in with the awesome services and found, repeatedly, that many people spoke English and were happy to try and help us understand what was happening. The whole atmosphere there was one of revival. We had previously been to large, impressive churches in Africa, America, and Columbia, but nothing matched what we saw and felt in Korea. The Spirit of God was a more tangible presence there than anywhere we have ever been. How privileged we were to have this experience. Thank you, *British Airways*!

The time to return home to England came all too fast, but our hearts were marked forever. The desire to pray and get other people praying was stronger in us than ever. When we got back, we had to be careful not to scare people with our fervour. We began asking people to sign up as prayer warriors to join us praying an hour a day and many responded.

I wonder, can we ever see something like this Korean revival happen in England? I sincerely hope so! In my own prayer-life experience, my heart's desire has always been to have a meeting with God, and to a large degree I have succeeded, but I could never simply decide what to do and then keep it up consistently. God has always had to breathe His power into it. I do not believe people in general can be motivated to pray as often or as fervently as these people in Korea do without a special move of God. Roll on a move of God!

CHAPTER 35

Beyond our dreams

A s I think about our work in the last forty years, I am amazed. Just writing this book has been a revelation to me. Everything that we have done has been through *His* person, *His* power, *His* love, and *His* grace and the steadfast love, support, and loyalty of *His* people.

When I consider the lives God had used us to change, I am full of wonder. When I consider how God led us to do things we never dreamed we would do, I can hardly take it in.

During the last five years of our pastorate, we knew we should prepare to hand over the running of the church to someone else. For many years we had known it was right for our son Giles and his wife, Rosilyn, to eventually take our place when we retired. They, however, were very settled where they were and did not seem to want to move back to Ely. Sometimes it was hard not to put pressure on them to come back, especially when we were tired and discouraged and feeling an increasing need to retire. But eventually, to our joy, God spoke to Roz and Giles and showed them that their place of future ministry was destined to be in Ely.

When at last they told us they had heard from God, we knew they could take the church to a greater level of growth, just as we have seen happen in some of the other churches where pastors have handed over to their sons.

We took great care with the process of handover because we had seen one church disintegrate when the changeover happened suddenly and unwisely, without the agreement of the congregation and the leadership. There was no way we wanted to see twenty-five years of hard work go down the drain!

Most of all, we wanted Giles and Roz to be known by the congregation for who they were, and we did not want people just to accept them because we told them to, so initially we invited Giles and Roz simply to come to Ely and work alongside us

The congregation got to know them and took them to their hearts. Over a period of at least a year, we worked at getting our close leadership on board. To begin with, there were some mixed reactions, but because people need time to adjust to new ideas, we worked at it patiently. When we knew our main leadership group was in agreement with us, we spoke to our wider leadership of about sixty people during our annual leadership day. We shared the step-by-step guidance God had given us, and I believe that is what ultimately won people's hearts. It speaks well of our people that they were won over more by what God had said than what they felt.

Once sixty people knew about the handover, we realised it would be damaging if the rest of the congregation found out on the grapevine, so the following day we shared everything with the whole church. We were so happy that our intentions were for the most part well received and that people were excited. Many people had already guessed what was going to happen anyway, and many already knew it was the will of God for Giles and Roz to take over from us. I believe God gave Roz and Giles favour with the people and that people, in the main, trusted our judgment. For those who were less sure, we felt it was a testimony to their spiritual maturity that they were able to take it to the Lord and trust Him for the outcome.

It has not been an easy journey for us or Giles and Roz. Since our ministry in Ely had not been a job but an all-consuming way of life, it might have been natural for us to wonder what on earth could be beyond retirement from our main position in Lighthouse. However, since our ministry did not start when we were called to be pastors, we could see that although we would not function in the same calling anymore, God still had much more work for us to do. Could we ever retire from the ministry?

I received a wonderful prophetic word from Jane Hamon in 2006, which encouraged me to believe our church would go from strength to strength and we would still have a key role to play in it as well as in the wider world beyond. Just as we were preparing strategically to hand over the church to Giles and Roz, at a Deborah Day in London where Jane Hamon was speaking, I had just said to the Lord, "I can hear You for myself, Jesus. If someone else needs a word, please give it to them."

At that moment, she touched my arm and said, "Margaret, the Spirit of the Lord says, 'Daughter, I want you to know that this has been a season of positioning for you. I have been positioning you in the city. I have been positioning you in the Spirit, not so you can simply watch but so you can watch and pray and begin to decree change. Daughter, there is even an alignment that is coming, and I am causing you to speak a word of vision that is going to cause people to begin to line up and mobilize. This is going to be a season of mobilization and a season of visitation, for in the midst of visitation, I will bring mobilizations for change. I will bring an anointing for revolution to come through you, and I want you to know that the glory of your latter years is going to be greater than your former. That which you have prayed for all your life, you are going to see in your latter days.

"'You are going to see a church of glory begin to rise up. You are going to see a church of power begin to be released. You are going to see signs and wonders begin to come forth out of the church, and you are going to see the harvest of souls manifested. Don't listen to those voices the enemy has been sending, which have been trying to get you to give up on your vision and say, "Well maybe it won't happen in my lifetime, but maybe in my children's or my children's children's lifetime."

"'No, daughter I am telling you, in the glory of your latter years, you are going to see it. Don't lose your focus. Hang on to the dream, for I put it in your heart years ago, and you are going to carry it through, all the way to the end. I'm giving you that finishing anointing to see it carried through,' says the Spirit of the Living God."

So I have made my decision: I will not lose my focus; I will not lose my vision; I will press on with that finishing anointing to see the task of filling Ely, and anywhere else God calls me to go, with the life of God. I believe for revival right here!

Another word of encouragement for our future came from a friend who had prayed for us faithfully for years. She gave us both this word at the handing over ceremony: "My beloved faithful ones, this is not the end but a beginning. The best is yet to come. Like the wine that was brought forth at the end of the wedding feast, so are you this matured wine, which tastes delightful. I have a plan and purpose for you in these latter years. You will bear more fruit than the former years. Seek my face diligently, for I have much to share with you and to show you."

God reminded me recently of my first call, which He gave me way back in the '80s, from Isaiah 61: "The Spirit of the Lord God is upon me, because the Lord has anointed me to preach good tidings to the poor; He has sent me to heal the broken-hearted, to proclaim liberty to the captives, and the opening of the prison to those who are bound; to proclaim the acceptable year of the Lord" the jubilee. In the midst of a broken world there can never be an end to this ministry!

We also have a desire to go wherever God wants us to go to teach people how to hear God's voice because our ministry and all successful fruit-bearing ministry springs from hearing God.

The day we handed the church over was glorious. It was a tremendous celebration of the past and an anticipation of the future. It was a moment of great joy. I was not sure how I would feel when it came to the crunch. It was a bit like the moment when your children leave home; you can have very mixed emotions. A little while before the handover I panicked and lost a few nights of sleep. Could I really let the church go? I talked to Giles about it, and he sent me this e-mail:

> When we have the handover, things are going up and up, and we will see what God has promised come to pass. Let's be filled with faith and totally relaxed in Him, like Jesus asleep in the storm. And when the challenge comes like a storm, we have the authority to rebuke it, and people will be amazed at who we are in the Spirit. We know that it is the Holy Spirit who has set us in this place—that in the Bible pattern, God's promise is fulfilled through the son. We see this when Moses passed to Joshua and David to Solomon. Things went from good to great. Let's be positive and confident that God knows what He is doing here— that it is not man's idea but God's idea. The transition time will be glorious. This, we believe, will be the crowning glory for our church. You know God has given it to us and that you will say the things that will fill our leaders with faith.

It was a wonderful service. Over 350 people came—people from far and wide. They came from Folkestone because they knew Giles and Roz from their time there; most of the local ministers attended, as well as many past and present members of the congregation.

We felt it was important to make the handover clear—a spiritual as well as a natural transition. On the day, I had complete peace because I knew we were in the centre of God's will, it was God's perfect timing, and Giles and Roz were God's chosen people. Best of all, as far as I am aware, we lost nobody directly through the change.

I was so exhausted after we handed over that it took me at least a year to feel able to be completely back in the swing of things. Over a longer period, I have regained both energy and strength and a desire to take on new things.

Looking back, do I think we ever did the wrong thing when we pastored? Oh yes! Do I have regrets? Oh yes! However, I have had to let them go. Do I know that I sometimes caused people pain? Oh, yes. . . and that is truly regrettable. However, it was never deliberate, and I can only pray that people have forgiven me. Have I learned a lot? Almost certainly yes! We have plenty of wisdom to pass on to others. Maybe my next book will be about pastoring!

Many times over the years we were under enormous pressure and experienced a good deal of pain. Pressure comes from many sources. Sometimes it is natural, and sometimes it is spiritual. Wherever it has come from, I do know that in times of extreme pressure, as long as we turned to Him, God stretched our faith and deepened our trust in Him. Without that strong, abiding faith, I know how easy it is to yield to temptation, fear, and discouragement, especially when the trial is intense or prolonged. At all costs, we must nip discouragement in the bud because it is the root out of which much bitterness can develop. Many ministries flounder and ministers fall into sin because of it. In 2 Corinthians 4.17 St. Paul called all his many troubles "a momentarily light affliction." His afflictions were beatings, shipwrecks, hunger, imprisonment, and much rejection and opposition. Nothing we experienced even came close to that, but St. Paul is keen for us to know that whatever the affliction we experience, it is working in us "an eternal weight of glory"!

We have to trust the one who has called us. God can develop our trust until it becomes unshakeable. He is still developing mine! Whatever trial I have faced, I have been able to return in my heart to the secure knowledge and understanding that God loves me unconditionally and is entirely for me. Even if things do not always go just how I think they should, if I keep this in mind, then God is always glorified. Faith turns our mountains into molehills!

I have found that we can help ourselves greatly in these difficult times if we keep in mind some very simple truths:

- Always look behind what is going on in the natural realm to perceive what is happening in the spiritual realm; learn to see beyond what we can see to what God sees.
- Keep yourself encouraged by remembering your past victories and answers to prayer.
- Cast the care of everything onto Him—the one who can truly fight the battle and win! It is His strength, wisdom, energy, and power that will bring the victory.
- Keep a thankful, forgiving heart.
- Always believe the best of people, and always love.
- Don't try to make things work by your own efforts but rely on the truth and the power of His Word alone.
- Rely on His faithfulness to keep His covenant
- Take time to seek His face and listen to His voice.
- Know that we have an enemy, and never give in to him.

I believe our longevity of service has come through keeping our vision strong that God can do far above all we can ask or think with our lives. As we allow ourselves to be encouraged by the little things we can do, He will do the rest. As with the Bible story of the water turning into wine, we do the natural thing of filling the pots with water and He does the miraculous, the part that we cannot do.

I am really looking forward to the day when I can do more overseas missions. I should have gone to preach in Nigeria again in 2012, at a big ladies' conference, but sadly, the government of Nigeria would not grant me a visa to visit for religious purposes.

I also want to do more creative things. I have had phases of appliqué or tapestry and decorated boxes, and lately I have made many pressed flower designs on trays. . . and of course there is always the garden and the allotment, which make their own demands.

We sold Egremont House long ago in 1994, but of course we are still showing hospitality to others and having people live with us. We are still sharing our lives and still loving people. My mother is ninety-one and lives with us now. She is the sixty-fifth person to share our home, and I do not suppose she will be the last.

Since our retirement, Tony has also been involved in local government as a conservative councillor and is now the chairman of the East Cambridgeshire District Council. It is position of honour that I believe recognizes his wisdom and many abilities. We are hoping that it will result in an invitation to a Buckingham Palace garden party to meet the Queen!

We have felt it is such a privilege to go to places where in the past we had a different kind of influence. Through Tony's new position, we still have godly influence. The main difference is that now we go wearing a gold chain and dressed in our finery! God always arranges divine appointments, and everywhere we find people who are hungry for God.

The honour for everything we have done goes to Jesus Himself and the wonderful ongoing work of the Holy Spirit. However, a personal thank you is always wonderful. Over the years we have received a great deal of gratitude. This is a letter from Jeremy, a young man who lived with us:

> I look forward to reading your book. I owe you and Tony so much—so much—and I have not appreciated that enough over the years. I understand more now about how much than I did when life was so hectic, way back. I feel like the chap in the commercial of whom the little dog says: "But he can't say that—he's just a bloke really." I have never really known how to say the thank you to you and Tony that I should, but in this small way, thank you for everything, which is so much kindness and thoughtfulness, and so many meals and such tolerance of me too! Thank you, thank you.

I am stopping now, but it is not the real end of the story.

CHAPTER 36

What Do You Want to Do Now?

Some of you may want to make a response to what you have read in my story. If you have read this book and you do not personally know Jesus yet; this is what you can do. It only takes a simple prayer to invite Jesus into your life if you genuinely want Him. Don't invite Him to come just as a visitor, as I did for many years; put Him into the very centre of your life.

As you believe in Jesus and call on Him, His blood is waiting to pay for your sin and to wash it all away. Through His death and His resurrection, He made it possible for you to be forgiven and have the Holy Spirit live in you, giving you a wonderful new life with Him.

Right now if you want to, you can yield all you are and all you have to Him. Simply repent of running your own life, of living independently of Him, and choose to trust Him to do for you the same as He did for me. He never, ever turns anyone away, and He will be faithful to you for the rest of your life. His promise in Hebrews 14.5 is that He will never leave you nor forsake you

You will never regret it.

In one moment, in the twinkling of an eye, you will experience the divine exchange. He takes away your sin, and He gives you His righteousness.

Ask Him to fill you or baptise you with the fullness of His Holy Spirit. He takes you just as you are and then gently begins a wonderful transformation of your life from the inside. All you need to do then is keep listening for what He wants you to do. You have become a child of God and it is a delight for our father to lead you. Get into relationships with other

Christians in a good church that really believes the Bible and honours the Holy Spirit. Begin to read about Jesus in the New Testament, and expect God to speak to you through its pages.

Just come to Him right now with sincerty and say:

> Dear God, I come to You in the name of Jesus. I now realise that I have a choice to make about my life. I believe and accept that Jesus died for me, shed His blood to wash away my sin, and rose from the dead. I know His act of love paid the price for me to have fellowship with You and live eternally with You. Heavenly Father, I repent by turning my back on the life I have lived without You. I choose to follow Jesus from this moment on. I ask You, Jesus, to be the Lord of my life and to live within me. I will tell others about Your love. I believe that right now I am born again. My spirit is a new creation. I stand before You, heavenly Father, forgiven because Jesus paid the price for my sin. Thank You for loving me so much. I gladly give my life to You. Amen.

If you wish to contact me, please see the contact information below:

My church address: Rev. Margaret Cornell, Lighthouse,

11a-13 Lynn Road, Ely, Cambridgeshire, CB7 4EG

My e-mail: Margaret@lighthouse-ely.org

Book web site with blog www.alifeshared.net

You can also find out more about our ministry that teaches people how to hear the voice of God by going to www.hearinggodsvoiceuk.net .